roast

recipe collection

by **Sainsbury's**

100 recipes including sides, trimmings, desserts and ideas for leftovers

Welcome...

It's a great British tradition and still one of our favourite family meals. But these days, a roast is so much more than just a basic joint of meat, served with potatoes and two veg. In this collection of recipes, you'll discover not just how to cook the perfect classic roast meal, but how to take it to the next level by adding new flavours, trying different ways of roasting, and serving up unusual side dishes and accompaniments. Whether your roast of choice is poultry or beef, pork or lamb, you'll find plenty of classic recipes in this book as well as some with a twist! And it's not all about meat – there are also great ideas for fish and vegetarian roasts, delicious sides and trimmings, plus a selection of mouthwatering desserts to round off your roast perfectly. What's more, there are lots of clever, money-saving recipes that use up the leftovers, enabling you to get maximum value and enjoyment from your roast. As always, every recipe has been tried and tested to ensure perfect results. Happy roasting!

We've added icons to make everything as clear as possible:

 Suitable for vegetarians

 Recipes containing 1 or more of your 5-a-day, to help you plan for healthier eating. Aim to eat at least 5 different portions of fruit and veg a day. Fresh, frozen, dried, canned and juice all count.

contents

Roasting essentials...

When it comes to roasting, getting perfect results depends as much on your kitchen kit as it does on the quality of your ingredients. Whether you're prepping, roasting, serving or storing leftovers, you can find all you need instore and online at sainsburys.co.uk

PREPPING

Kitchen string
For a roast that keeps its shape and cooks evenly, you'll need to truss it with kitchen string.

Mixing bowl
Whether you're mixing stuffing or batter for a pudding, a deep mixing bowl is a kitchen staple.

Pestle and mortar
Essential for grinding up herbs and spices for flavour-enhancing rubs and marinades.

Oven thermometer
Roasting at the right temp is crucial – get accurate readings with this clever in-oven thermometer.

Apron and oven gloves
Scorching tins and hot oil splatters go hand in hand with roasting. Use these to protect clothes and yourself.

Mandoline
A fuss-free way to slice fruit and veg with ease. Choose one with adjustable thickness settings for more versatility.

Chopping board set
Prepare ingredients and food safely with a set of colour-coded, flexible plastic chopping boards.

Colander
An indispensable piece of kit for washing and prepping veg, and straining and draining food after cooking.

ROASTING & CARVING

Steamer
Steaming veg helps to lock in nutrients and retain moisture for healthier, easy-cook side dishes.

Pans
No kitchen is complete without a set of sturdy pans. Copper bottoms are great at conducting heat evenly.

Roasting tins
Heavy-based metal tins that can also be used on the hob are key for browning roasts and getting perfect gravy.

Pot roaster
Ideal for slow cooking. Buy one with a lid to help lock in flavour and avoid splashing in your oven.

Baking dish
Usually ceramic or heatproof glass, they're essential for savoury sides as well as desserts, and can go straight from oven to table.

Baster
This simple tool will help you get those roasts nice and crisp on the outside while maintaining a moist, succulent flavour.

Meat thermometer
There's no easier or more accurate way to ensure your roast is cooked to perfection. Choose a digital version for the most accurate results.

Yorkshire pudding tin and measuring jug
Measuring your batter and using a purpose-built tray will help you get just the right amount for perfect puds.

Gravy separator
Pour pan juices into this jug – the fat will rise to the top as the liquid cools, leaving the dark flavourful drippings at the bottom.

Carving board
A solid wooden board with a groove to catch the juices while you carve is a must. This one has prongs to hold the meat in place.

Carving set
A sharp carving knife and fork will make slicing up your roast much easier. You'll get lovely thin slices as a carving knife is longer than a regular one.

Tea towels
Keep a few nearby and use them for everything from blotting excess water from prepared veg to protecting hands when serving.

SERVING & STORING

Gravy boat
Don't let a beautiful roast down by serving up gravy in a measuring jug. Warm a gravy boat before filling and serving.

Platter
Present whole roasts in style with a porcelain platter. This one is wide enough to allow easy carving at the table.

Airtight containers
A hassle-free way to store your leftovers. Look for containers that are both freezer- and microwave-safe.

Freezer bags
When freezing leftovers in plastic bags, choose ones with a zip seal to make squeezing out air easier.

'Bring your roasted joint or bird to the table on a rustic board and carve neat slices with a professional carving set'

poultry

Choosing and roasting
poultry...

Roasted birds are a firm favourite for Sunday roasts and special celebrations. Get the best from your bird with this handy guide

Chicken

A great choice for a regular family roast, chicken has quite a mild flavour, so it goes well with lots of different ingredients. It's juicy yet lower in saturated fats than most meats, especially if the skin is removed before eating. If there's just the two of you, roast whole leg portions, or breast portions with the wing still attached. And if you buy a chicken with giblets inside, you can use them to make a lovely stock for soups and stews.

Perfect partners
Garlic and lemon; bay leaves, parsley, rosemary and tarragon.

Turkey

It's the number one choice at Christmas and, as such, is seen as a special-occasion roast. But with less expensive cuts, such as drumsticks and thighs available, it's becoming a popular roast year round. It does have a reputation for drying out during roasting, but you can easily prevent this by basting regularly and sticking exactly to the roasting time - don't be tempted to give it an extra 10 minutes for good measure!

Perfect partners
Oranges, cranberries and cherries; thyme; ginger.

Duck

Rich and flavoursome, duck has a higher fat content and less meat than other poultry, but a little goes a long way. Roasting a whole duck is a great idea for special occasions or dinner parties as it requires little attention, but gives amazing and impressive results. Best of all, you'll be left with lots of duck fat in the tray at the end of roasting - spoon it off and keep it for roasting potatoes in.

Perfect partners...
Chinese 5 spice and hoisin sauce; oranges, pomegranates, apricots, plums and figs.

Cook's tip
Sitting your bird on a roasting rack within a roasting tin will stop it becoming greasy and soggy on the bottom, and help it to cook more evenly. If you don't have a rack, pop it on a bed of roughly chopped veg.

Roasting tips and tricks...

Q How do I get a crisp golden skin on my roast?

The skin of the bird should be as dry as possible to get a crisp result. Leave it uncovered in the fridge overnight so the skin dries out, or pat all over with kitchen paper.

Q Can I do anything with the giblets?

Giblets are the bird's organs - the heart, liver, stomach and kidneys - as well as the neck. If you buy a bird with them included (usually in a bag inside the cavity) don't discard them! Livers can be used to make pâté, while the rest are perfect for making a stock.

Q How do I safely defrost poultry before roasting?

The best way to defrost poultry is to let it gradually thaw in its packaging on the bottom shelf of the fridge, but for larger birds, this can take up to 3 days - in general, allow 10 hours per kilogram. Put the bird in a tray to catch any juices, and make sure other foods don't come into contact with the juices. Before cooking, check the inside of the bird to make sure it is defrosted and the giblets have been removed.

Q How long can I keep leftover meat in the fridge and freezer for?

Let the roasted meat cool completely before transferring to airtight containers or freezer bags, sealing and putting in the fridge or freezer. Don't forget to label with the date and contents. Roasted poultry meat keeps in the fridge for 48 hours, and in the freezer for up to 3 months. If chilling or freezing stuffing, first remove it from the cavity so it cools completely and then transfer to containers or bags.

Nice to slice

Carving a chicken, turkey or duck is as easy as one, two, three...

1 Insert a knife between the leg and body; remove the thigh and drumstick in one piece.
2 Use a carving fork to steady the bird, then divide the drumstick and thigh, cutting through the joint so you have two leg portions.
3 Cut off the wing, then slice the breast. Repeat on the other side of the bird.

All about stuffing

A traditional stuffing for poultry adds flavour and makes a fab accompaniment for roast meat. However, there are some food safety issues you should be aware of if you want to stuff your bird. Stuffing a chicken or turkey can affect the cooking of the meat - if the bird is overstuffed, it may result in it being undercooked. Always follow these guidelines, or cook your stuffing in a separate dish.

- Don't use raw ingredients. In particular, if a stuffing recipe includes meat or eggs, it should be cooked and cooled before stuffing the bird.
- Loosely fill both the neck and body cavities with stuffing - don't overfill or tightly pack the bird with the stuffing.
- Allow a bit of extra cooking time than normal. In general, cook a stuffed bird for an extra half an hour.

Classic roast chicken

A simple recipe that allows the flavour of the meat to shine through

**Serves 4,
with leftovers**
Prep time: 10 mins
Cook time: 1 hour
40 mins
Rest time: 15 mins

Large (about 2kg) Taste the Difference
whole British chicken
1/2 unwaxed lemon

1 bulb garlic, halved horizontally
and left unpeeled
Small bunch fresh flat-leaf parsley
50g butter

1 Preheat the oven to 200°C, fan 180°C, gas 6. Put the chicken,
breast-side up, in a large flameproof roasting tin and rub all over
with the cut side of the lemon half. Pop the lemon into the cavity
of the chicken, along with the garlic bulb halves and parsley. Tie
the legs together with a length of kitchen string. Smear the butter
thickly all over the skin, then season with a little salt and freshly
ground black pepper.

2 Roast for 1 hour 40 mins, basting with the pan juices every so often,
until the chicken is cooked through: the juices should run
clear when a skewer is inserted into the thickest part of the thigh.

3 Remove from the oven, cover with foil and let rest for 15 mins before
carving. You can make the gravy, below, while the chicken is resting.

● **Per serving (150g chicken): 354 cals, 20.7g fat, 8.4g saturates,
0.5g sugars, 0.19g salt**

Chicken gravy

Spoon the excess fat out of the roasting tin, put the tin
on the hob and squeeze in the garlic pulp from the bulb
that was in cavity of the chicken. Sprinkle over 1 tbsp
plain flour, stir and let sizzle until you have a light brown
paste – about 1 min. Gradually pour in 400ml chicken
stock and bring to the boil, stirring all the time and
scraping all the meaty residues left at the bottom of the
tin. When the gravy has thickened, strain into a small pan,
then simmer and season to taste. When you carve the
chicken, add any extra juices to the gravy.

Serves 4 Prep time: 5 mins Cook time: 15 mins

Per serving: 73 cals, 5.6g fat, 0.7g saturates, 0.5g total sugars, 0.1g salt

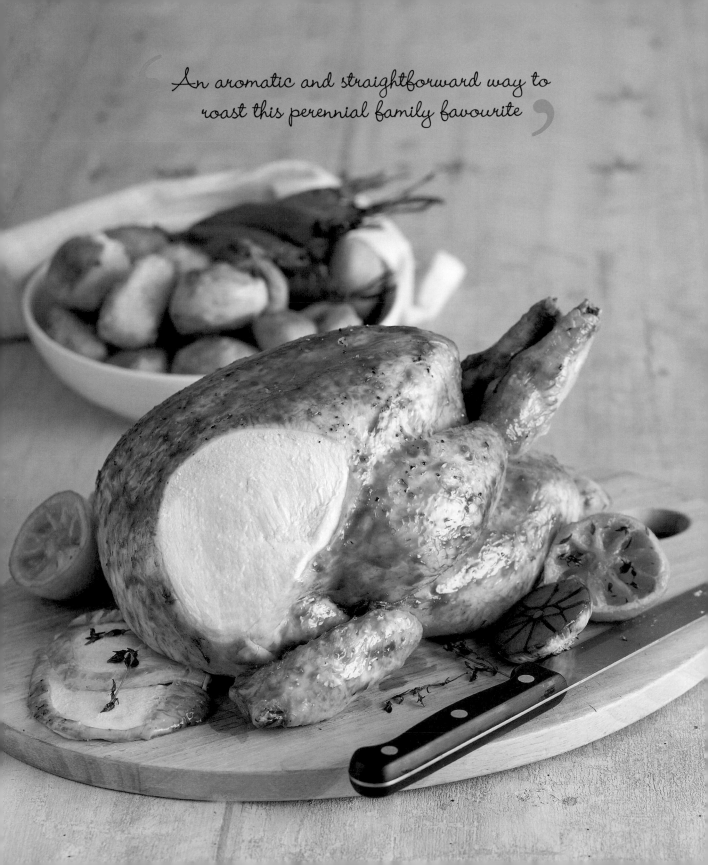

An aromatic and straightforward way to roast this perennial family favourite

Tandoori roast chicken

**Serves 4,
with leftovers**
Prep time: 20 mins
Cook time: 1 hour
40 mins
Rest time: 15 mins

Inspired by classic tandoori cooking, this richly flavoured bird is rubbed with a fragrant, spicy paste and served with a cooling cucumber raita

5 cardamom pods
5 cloves garlic
1cm piece fresh root ginger, peeled
and finely sliced
$1/2$ tbsp vegetable oil
2 tbsp garam masala
300ml natural yogurt
1 lime, halved, plus extra wedges to serve

2kg whole large British chicken
by Sainsbury's
1 tbsp chopped fresh mint
1 tbsp chopped fresh coriander
1 cucumber, trimmed and cut into ribbons,
or batons, to serve
Roasted sweet potato wedges,
to serve (see recipe, p152)

1 Crush the cardamom pods with the back of a spoon to release the seeds. Discard the husks. Put the seeds into a food processor with the garlic, ginger, oil, garam masala and half of the yogurt. Blend until smooth.

2 Put the lime halves in the chicken cavity. Rub the yogurt marinade all over the chicken. Cover and chill in the fridge for at least 1 hour.

3 Preheat the oven to 200°C, fan 180°C, gas 6. Remove the chicken from the fridge and transfer to a roasting tin. Roast in the oven for 1 hour 40 mins or until cooked through: the juices should run clear when a skewer is inserted into the thickest part of the thigh. Check the chicken after 1 hour and cover with foil if it's browning too quickly.

4 Remove from the oven, cover with foil and rest for 15 mins before carving. Meanwhile, make a raita by mixing the remaining yogurt with the mint and coriander, then season lightly. Serve the chicken with the cucumber, lime wedges, raita and sweet potato wedges.

● Per serving (150g chicken, plus raita) : 308 cals, 13.2g fat, 3.7g saturates, 3.8g sugars, 0.43g salt

**Serves 4,
with leftovers**
Prep time: 15 mins
Cook time: 1 hour
20 mins
Rest time: 15 mins

Spatchcock chicken

A different method of roasting chicken that's easy, versatile and gives a succulent result. The peppery rub adds lots of savoury flavour, too

2 tsp freshly ground black pepper
Pinch of sea salt
4 tsp fresh thyme leaves, chopped
3 cloves garlic, crushed

Zest of 2 unwaxed lemons, grated
2kg whole large British chicken
by Sainsbury's

1 In a small bowl, mix together the pepper, sea salt, thyme, garlic and lemon zest.

2 Place the chicken on a chopping board, breast-side down. Using kitchen scissors, cut along one side of the backbone up to the neck cavity. Now do the same along the other side of the backbone. Using your hands, carefully remove the backbone and neck skin.

3 Pull apart and open out the sides of the chicken to flatten it. Clean out any remaining giblets or fragments of bone from the cavity. Use gentle but firm pressure to press the chicken down on the chopping board to flatten it out. The legs will easily fan out to the sides.

4 Turn the chicken over and rub the lemon and pepper mixture all over the skin.

5 Preheat the oven to 200°C, fan 180°C, gas 6. Place the chicken, skin-side up, in a large roasting tin and roast for 1 hour 20 mins until cooked through: the juices should run clear when a skewer is inserted into the thickest part of the thigh. Let rest for 15 mins before carving.

● Per serving (150g chicken): 289 cals, 13.9g fat, 3.9g saturates, 0.5g sugars, 0.52g salt

Olive & tomato tapenade chicken

A homemade tapenade gives this roast a strong Mediterranean flavour

Serves 4,
with leftovers
Prep time: 20 mins
Cook time: 1 hour
40 mins
Rest time: 15 mins

200g pitted black olives, drained
60g sundried tomato paste
Zest and juice of 1 unwaxed lemon
1 tbsp chilli-infused extra virgin olive oil
Handful fresh flat-leaf parsley leaves
2kg whole British chicken by Sainsbury's

200g baby leeks, washed, trimmed
and halved lengthways
2 whole garlic bulbs, halved horizontally
1 large red onion, cut into wedges
200ml white wine
1 tbsp olive oil

1 Preheat oven to 190°C, fan 170°C, gas 5. In a food processor, whiz together the olives, sundried tomato paste, lemon zest and juice, chilli oil and parsley until you have a chunky tapenade. Set aside.

2 To prepare the chicken, use your fingertips to gently loosen the skin covering the chicken breasts. Carefully push the tapenade under the skin and spread all over the breasts, being careful not to tear the skin when doing so. Set aside while you prepare the vegetables.

3 Gather 3 leek halves together in a bundle and tie tightly with a piece of kitchen string. Repeat with the remaining leeks and put in a large roasting tin, along with the halved garlic bulbs and onion wedges.

4 Arrange the chicken on top of the vegetables, and pour over the wine and the oil. Tightly cover the chicken breast with a piece of foil and roast in the oven for 1 hour 40 mins until cooked through: the juices should run clear when a skewer is inserted into the thickest part of the thigh.

5 Allow the chicken to rest for 15 mins before carving. Serve with the roasted vegetables.

● Per serving (150g chicken, plus vegetables): 433 cals, 25.4g fat, 5.6g saturates, 4.5g sugars, 1.03g salt

Pot roast chicken with vegetable rice

Serves 4,
with leftovers
Prep time: 15 mins
Cook time: 1 hour
50 mins
Rest time: 15 mins

This one-pot meal is so simple – and it saves on the washing up!
The chicken is meltingly tender and falls right off the bone

2 large leeks, trimmed, halved
lengthways and finely chopped
1 fresh bay leaf
1 red onion, chopped
1 red pepper, deseeded and chopped
2 cloves garlic, chopped
4 sprigs fresh thyme
600ml chicken stock, made with

1 stock cube
390g carton Italian chopped tomatoes
in tomato juice
2kg whole large British chicken
by Sainsbury's
150g basmati rice
100g frozen peas
1 tbsp olive oil

1 Preheat the oven to 180°C, fan 160°C, gas 4. Place the leeks,
   bay leaf, onion, pepper, garlic, thyme, stock and tomatoes in the
   base of a large casserole and mix together well.

2 Tie the chicken legs together with kitchen string and place on top
   of the leeks. Season with salt and freshly ground black pepper.
   Cover the casserole with a tight-fitting lid and put in the oven to
   roast for 1 hour 30 mins.

3 Remove from the oven, carefully lift the chicken out of the pot
   and put to one side. Add the basmati rice and peas to the casserole.
   Stir well, then return the chicken to the pot. Drizzle the olive oil
   over the top of the chicken and return, uncovered, to the oven.
   Roast for a further 20 mins until the rice is tender and has absorbed
   most of the liquid, and the chicken has turned golden brown on the
   breast and tops of the legs. The juices should run clear when a skewer
   is inserted into the thickest part of the breast.

4 Remove from the oven and allow the chicken to rest for 15 mins
   before carving and serving with the vegetable rice.

● Per serving (150g chicken, plus vegetable rice): 326 cals, 6g fat,
  1.6g saturates, 6.5g sugars, 0.37g salt

A simple, one-pot roast with juicy, succulent meat

Ready in 5 mins
Chicken & green lentil salad

A speedy salad that uses leftover roast chicken and tinned lentils, so you can have it on the table in mere minutes. Sliced radishes add colour and peppery flavour

Serves 4

Prep time: 5 mins

2 x 410g tins green lentils in water by Sainsbury's, drained and rinsed

100g young leaf spinach

4 spring onions, trimmed and finely sliced

100g radishes, trimmed and finely sliced

4 tbsp be good to yourself honey & mustard dressing

300g leftover roast chicken, skin removed, thinly sliced

1 Put the lentils, spinach, spring onions and radishes into a large bowl. Drizzle over the dressing and toss together to combine.

2 Add the sliced roast chicken and gently fold through. Season with salt and freshly ground black pepper to taste.

3 Divide between serving bowls and serve immediately.

● Per serving: 283 cals, 7g fat, 2.2g saturates, 3.6g sugars, 0.3g salt

Cook's tip
This works with lots of grains and pulses. Try using Puy lentils, giant couscous, bulgur wheat or quinoa instead of green lentils.

Ready in 50 mins
Chicken & broad bean risotto

Goats' cheese gives this easy dish a lovely creaminess and earthy flavour – perfect for a summery lunch. Use frozen broad beans if fresh are out of season

Serves 4

Prep time: 15 mins

Cook time: 35 mins

400g fresh podded broad beans

1 tbsp olive oil

1 onion, finely chopped

2 cloves garlic, finely chopped

350g arborio risotto rice

1.75 litres hot chicken stock, made with 1 stock cube

300g leftover roast chicken, skin removed, torn into strips

70g goats' cheese, crumbled

1 tbsp snipped fresh chives

1 Bring a pan of water to the boil, add the broad beans and blanch for 3 mins. Cool slightly, then pop out of their skins. Set aside.

2 Heat the oil in a large pan over a medium heat. Add the onion and garlic, and sauté for about 5 mins until soft and translucent. Stir in the rice until it's coated all over with the oil.

3 Add a ladleful of stock, stirring continuously until it's absorbed. Repeat until all but 2 ladles of stock remain – this should take about 25 mins.

4 Add the last 2 ladles of stock, the cooked broad beans and roast chicken, and stir to heat through until piping hot. Scatter over the cheese and chives, season with freshly ground black pepper and serve.

● Per serving: 614 cals, 15.3g fat, 5.7g saturates, 3.8g sugars, 0.44g salt

Cook's tip
Taste the risotto as you go – you may not need to use all the stock to get the rice tender but al dente, and the risotto itself creamy and smooth.

Ready in 40 mins

Baked chicken wraps

These tasty wraps are a great all-in-one family meal – kids love them! Serve them with a simple green salad and a dollop of soured cream, if you like

Serves 4

Prep time: 20 mins

Cook time: 20 mins

1 tbsp olive oil

2 cloves garlic, finely chopped

100g mange tout, trimmed

200g Taste the Difference caramelised red onion chutney

400g leftover roast chicken, skin removed, cut into chunky strips

200g couscous, cooked to pack instructions

Small handful fresh flat-leaf parsley, leaves picked and roughly chopped

4 plain tortilla wraps

60g Cheddar, grated

1 Preheat the oven to 180°C, fan 160°C, gas 4.

2 Heat a large frying pan over a medium-high heat, add the oil and garlic, then add the mange tout. Stir-fry until they start to soften. Stir in the chutney and the cooked chicken and cook for 2-3 mins until piping hot. Transfer the mixture to a large bowl and stir in the couscous and most of the parsley.

3 Divide the filling between the wraps. Fold the sides over the filling and roll, enclosing everything like a burrito. Arrange the wraps in a baking dish and sprinkle over the grated cheese.

4 Bake for 15 mins, until the cheese is melted and golden, then serve with the remaining parsley sprinkled over the top.

● Per serving: 779 cals, 18.3g fat, 7g saturates, 31.8g sugars, 1.20g salt

Cook's tip
If you don't have couscous to hand, use rice instead. Just cook to pack instructions before adding to the mixture.

Chicken & vegetable casserole

Packed with colour and flavour, this one-pot dish is so easy to make, and tender asparagus and punchy tarragon go especially well with chicken

Serves 4

Prep time: 10 mins

Cook time: 15-20 mins

Knob of unsalted butter

Drizzle of olive oil

2 leeks, trimmed and sliced

1 1/2 tbsp plain flour

450ml hot chicken stock, made with 1 stock cube

500g leftover roast chicken, skin removed, cut into chunks

2 sprigs fresh thyme

200g sugar snap peas

150g asparagus tips, halved

4 tbsp single cream

1 tbsp chopped fresh tarragon or parsley

1 Heat the butter and olive oil in a heavy-based flameproof casserole or deep lidded frying pan over a high heat. Add the leeks, season with salt and freshly ground black pepper and sauté for 3-4 mins until softened. Stir in the flour and cook for a further 1 min.

2 Gradually pour in the hot stock, bring to the boil, then reduce the heat and simmer for 2 mins. Add the chicken, thyme, sugar snap peas and asparagus tips and simmer for 3-4 mins until the vegetables are just tender and the chicken is piping hot. Stir in the cream and tarragon or parsley and simmer for 1-2 mins.

3 Serve with mini jacket potatoes or steamed rice.

● **Per serving: 355 cals, 15.7g fat, 5.7g saturates, 5g sugars, 0.38g salt**

Cook's tip
Turn this into a pie by topping with a sheet of ready rolled puff pastry, trimmed, or scrunched up sheets of filo, brushed with melted butter, before baking in the oven.

Ready in 20 mins

Japanese-style udon noodle soup

This quick, aromatic soup is full of authentic flavours – sesame, pak choi and chilli.
Using leftover chicken and adding udon noodles makes it substantial enough for a meal

Serves 4

Prep time: 10 mins

Cook time: 10 mins

1 litre chicken stock

3 tbsp light soy sauce, plus
extra to serve

1 tbsp toasted sesame oil

1 tbsp sesame seeds

2 tsp chilli sauce

300g pack straight-to-wok
udon noodles

240g leftover roast chicken,
skin removed, shredded

2 large pak choi, cut in
half lengthways

1 red chilli, chopped, to garnish

2 spring onions, trimmed and
sliced, to garnish

1 Put the stock, soy sauce, sesame oil, sesame seeds and
chilli sauce into a large pan and bring to the boil.

2 Add the udon noodles, roast chicken and pak choi to the
soup. Bring back to the boil and let simmer for 3-4 mins,
or until the pak choi is tender.

3 Spoon into 4 bowls, garnishing each with a few slices of fresh
chilli and the spring onions. Season with extra soy sauce to taste.

● Per serving: 298 cals, 11.9g fat, 2.6g saturates, 3.3g sugars, 1.67g salt

Cook's tip
If you can't get hold
of pak choi, shredded
green cabbage is a
good substitute.

Ready in 25 mins

Chicken & sweetcorn soup

A Chinese restaurant favourite that makes a delicious starter or warming supper for those nights when a bowl of soup is just what you need

Serves 4

Prep time: 15 mins

Cook time: 10 mins

---

1 tsp sunflower oil

2 cloves garlic, crushed

2cm piece fresh root ginger, peeled and grated

1.2 litres hot chicken stock, made with 1 stock cube

1 tbsp cornflour, mixed with 2 tsp cold water to form a paste

240g leftover roast chicken, skin removed, shredded

325g tin sweetcorn by Sainsbury's, drained

2 medium eggs, whites only

2 spring onions, trimmed and finely chopped

2 tsp toasted sesame seeds

1 Heat the oil in a large pan, add the garlic and ginger and cook for 1 min. Pour over the stock and stir in the cornflour mixture. Simmer gently for 2-3 mins until the liquid has slightly thickened.

2 Add the chicken and the sweetcorn and bring to a simmer.

3 Beat the egg whites in a jug and slowly pour into the soup – stirring the soup as you go – to create white strands.

4 When the chicken is piping hot, ladle into 4 bowls and serve garnished with the spring onions and sesame seeds.

● Per serving: 195 cals, 7.3g fat, 1.9g saturates, 5.5g sugars, 0.31g salt

Cook's tip
For an authentic flavour boost, you can season this soup with toasted sesame oil and some ground white pepper.

Classic roast turkey

A roast turkey at Christmas is an absolute must. You can't go wrong with this easy recipe for perfectly moist roasted Norfolk Black turkey

**Serves 6,
with leftovers**
Prep time: 30 mins
Cook time: 3 hours
Rest time: 30 mins

125g unsalted butter, softened, plus extra for greasing
Handful fresh rosemary leaves, chopped
4.8kg Taste the Difference free-range Norfolk Black turkey, giblets removed
1 onion, halved

1 fresh bay leaf
125ml chicken stock, made with 1 stock cube
400g shallots, peeled and kept whole
2 tbsp redcurrant jelly
1 tbsp mint sauce

1 Preheat the oven to 190°C, fan 170°C, gas 5. In a bowl, mix together the butter and half the rosemary leaves.

2 Use your fingertips to separate the skin from the turkey breast meat. Push the herb butter into this 'pocket' and spread over the breast in an even layer by pressing down on the skin with your hand to smear.

3 Put the onion and bay leaf into the cavity of the turkey then tie the legs together with kitchen string. Put the turkey on a rack inside a large roasting tin, breast-side up. Roast, uncovered, for 30 mins.

4 Remove from the oven and add the stock to the tin. Loosely cover with a piece of buttered foil, return to the oven and roast for a further 2½ hours, basting every 30-45 mins. About 1 hour before the end of the cooking time, add the shallots to the tin and continue to roast.

5 Meanwhile, put the redcurrant jelly and mint sauce in a pan and heat gently until the jelly has melted. Stir in the remaining rosemary and set aside. About 30 mins before the end of the cooking time, remove the turkey and brush all over with the redcurrant glaze. Return to the oven, uncovered, for the final 30 mins until cooked: the juices should run clear when a skewer is inserted into the thickest part of the thigh.

6 Transfer to a warmed serving plate to rest for 30 mins, covered loosely with foil. Serve with the roasted whole shallots.

● Per serving (150g turkey): 451 cals, 24.5g fat, 13.6g saturates, 4.1g sugars, 0.45g salt

Serves 4
Prep time: 10 mins
Cook time: 1 hour
45 mins

Sticky roasted turkey drumsticks

Turkey drumsticks make for an inexpensive, flavoursome family roast

2 x 650g Sainsbury's basics
turkey drumsticks
1 bulb garlic, broken into unpeeled cloves
250ml white wine
2 tbsp olive oil
2 tsp dried oregano

Zest and juice of 1 unwaxed lemon, plus
2 extra unwaxed lemons, cut into wedges
750g new potatoes, halved
2 tbsp clear honey
2 tbsp chopped fresh parsley

1 Preheat the oven to 180°C, fan 160°C, gas 4. Cut 3 slashes in each drumstick and put in a large roasting tin with the garlic and half the wine.

2 In a small bowl, mix together the oil, oregano and lemon zest and juice. Spoon over the turkey and use your hands to rub the mixture into the skin and cuts. Cover with foil and roast for 1 hour.

3 Increase the oven temperature to 200°C, fan 180°C, gas 6. Take the tin out of the oven and scatter the lemon and potatoes around the turkey. Pour the remaining wine into the roasting tin and brush the drumsticks with the honey. Return to the oven, uncovered, and roast for 45 mins until the turkey is cooked and the potatoes tender. Serve with the parsley.

● Per serving: 390 cals, 8.4g fat, 1.6g saturates, 11.6g sugars, 0.29g salt

Orange & thyme turkey crown

Preheat the oven to 200°C, fan 180°C, gas 6. In a pestle and mortar, crush the zest of 1 orange with a small handful of fresh thyme leaves, 1 large clove garlic and 2 tbsp olive oil to make a marinade. Rub all over a 2kg Taste the Difference free-range Norfolk Black turkey crown and put in a roasting tin. Season and cover with foil. Roast for 1 hour. Remove the foil, drizzle over the juice of 1 orange and roast for a further 1 hour. Rest for 20 mins before carving.

Serves 6, with leftovers Prep time: 20 mins Cook time: 2 hours

Per serving: 252 cals, 13.7g fat, 3.8g saturates, 0.7g total sugars, 0.18g salt

Ready in 25 mins

Spaghetti with turkey & pesto

Quick pasta dishes make great midweek family dinners. This tasty recipe combines the Mediterranean flavours of olives, peppers, pesto and pine nuts

Serves 4

Prep time: 5 mins

Cook time: 15-20 mins

50g pitted black olives, drained and roughly chopped

225g roasted red peppers in olive oil, drained and roughly chopped

1 tbsp pine nuts, toasted

400g roast turkey, skin removed, torn into bite-size pieces

4 tbsp Taste the Difference pesto alla Genovese

400g spaghetti

Handful fresh basil leaves, torn

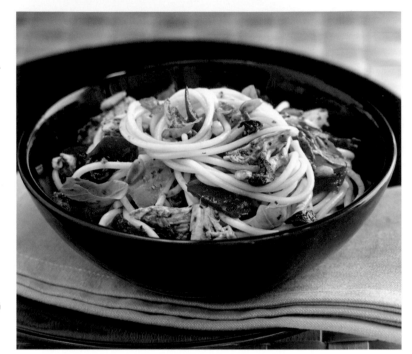

1 In a mixing bowl, toss together the olives, peppers, pine nuts, turkey and pesto until well combined. Set aside.

2 Cook the spaghetti in a large pan of lightly salted boiling water for 10-12 mins, or according to pack instructions, until al dente. Drain the spaghetti, reserving a ladleful of the cooking liquid.

3 Put the turkey mixture and the reserved cooking liquid into the pan over a medium heat and cook gently for 5 mins, stirring, until the turkey is piping hot throughout. Return the spaghetti to the pan and stir to combine. Serve in bowls and scatter over the basil.

● Per serving: 646 cals, 16.8g fat, 3.8g saturates, 3.8g sugars, 1.02g salt

Cook's tip

Toasting pine nuts brings out more flavour. Scatter them on a baking tray and roast at 180°C, fan 160°C, gas 4, shaking occasionally, or toss in a small frying pan until golden.

Ready in 40 mins
Turkey chilli tacos with salsa

Spice up mealtimes with this simple version of chilli con carne that uses leftover turkey instead of beef. The dark chocolate adds a rich flavour to the sauce

Serves 4

Prep time: 15 mins

Cook time: 25 mins

1 tsp olive oil

500g roast turkey, skin removed, cut into small pieces

500g jar medium chilli con carne cooking sauce by Sainsbury's

215g tin red kidney beans, drained and rinsed

1 small red onion, finely diced

4 ripe tomatoes, deseeded and chopped

Large handful fresh coriander, leaves picked and roughly chopped

Juice of ½ lime

15g dark chocolate, broken into pieces

1 Heat the oil gently in a large pan, add the turkey and stir-fry for 1–2 mins. Add the sauce and the kidney beans. Bring to the boil and simmer for 20 mins.

2 Meanwhile, make the tomato salsa. Put the red onion, tomatoes, coriander and lime juice in a bowl, and mix to combine. Season with salt and freshly ground black pepper, and set aside.

3 Stir the chocolate through the chilli until melted, then serve with the taco shells and tomato salsa on the side.

● Per serving: 560 cals, 18.5g fat, 5.9g saturates, 15.7g sugars, 2.05g salt

Cook's tip
This chilli mix is also great as a topping for jacket potatoes or a filling for burritos.

Ready in 20 mins

Turkey & bacon club sandwich

Create the ultimate turkey sandwich with this delicious double decker that combines crispy bacon, melting cheese, and leftover roast turkey

Serves 4

Prep time: 10 mins

Cook time: 10 mins

8 rashers smoked back bacon

12 thin slices white bread

2 cloves garlic, halved

100g Brie, sliced

A few lettuce leaves

300g leftover roast turkey, skin removed, cut into thick slices

4 tbsp cranberry sauce

1 Preheat the grill to medium. Put the bacon on a grill rack and cook for 5 mins, turning, until cooked and crispy. Set aside.

2 Put the slices of bread under the grill and toast one side until golden. Remove from the grill and rub the cut side of the garlic clove halves over the untoasted sides of the bread.

3 Divide the Brie between 2 pieces of toast, placing them on the garlic side. Put both slices of toast under the grill for a few mins until the Brie has melted.

4 Top each with lettuce and another slice of toast. Add turkey and two slices of bacon, and spoon over cranberry sauce. Top with more lettuce and the remaining toast. Cut into halves to serve.

● **Per serving: 602 cals, 21g fat, 9g saturates, 11.4g sugars, 2.44g salt**

Cook's tip
Brie, cranberry and turkey is a popular Christmas combo, but you can use any cheese and sauce in this – try it with blue cheese and onion chutney.

Ready in 30 mins
Turkey tikka masala

If you love a Friday night takeaway, why not whip up our healthier version instead? This speedy tikka masala, uses leftover turkey as a leaner, cheaper alternative to chicken

Serves 4

Prep time: 5 mins

Cook time: 25 mins

1 tbsp vegetable oil

1 onion, chopped

2 red peppers, deseeded and sliced

2 tbsp tikka masala curry paste

390g carton Italian chopped tomatoes in tomato juice

200ml chicken stock, made with 1 stock cube

Handful of fresh coriander leaves

250g Greek-style yogurt

500g leftover turkey, skin removed, cut into chunks

1 Heat the oil in a large pan, add the onion and cook for 5 mins until softened. Add the peppers and cook for a further 5 mins, until they start to soften.

2 Stir in the curry paste and cook for 2 mins, then pour in the tomatoes and stock. Bring to a simmer and cook for 5 mins. Stir through half of the coriander, then add the yogurt. Stir until well combined, then add the cooked turkey and simmer for 5 mins until it is piping hot throughout.

3 Meanwhile, cook the rice in a pan of boiling water for 10 mins until tender. Drain, divide between bowls and serve with the curry and the remaining coriander.

● Per serving: 627 cals, 17.5g fat, 6.7g saturates, 15.8g sugars, 1.02g salt

Cook's tip

If you like your curry hot and spicy, add in some chopped fresh green and red chillies along with the red peppers in step 1.

Classic roast duck

Try this sensational roast – and save the duck fat to make your roasties

**Serves 4,
with leftovers**
Prep time: 20 mins
Cook time:
2 hours 10 mins
Rest time: 15 mins

2kg whole oven-ready duck
2 large oranges
1 bay leaf
2 onions, 1 cut into wedges and 1 sliced

4 tbsp fine-cut orange marmalade
250ml full-bodied red wine
250ml chicken stock

1 Preheat the oven to 220°C, fan 200°C, gas 7. Put the duck on a rack in a roasting tin. Pat the skin dry with kitchen paper and prick all over and rub with sea salt. Cut 1 of the oranges into quarters and squeeze the juice inside the duck cavity. Put the orange quarters inside the cavity, and put the bay leaf and onion wedges inside the cavity, too.

2 Roast in the oven for 20 mins, then reduce the temperature to 180°C, fan 160°C, gas 4 and roast for a further 1 hour 15 mins. You will need to spoon off fat from the roasting tin at intervals during the roasting time. Reserve this for roasting potatoes instead of goose fat, if liked.

3 Meanwhile, grate the zest of the remaining orange and mix in a bowl with the marmalade. Remove the duck from the oven and brush the glaze over the skin. Return to the oven and roast for 15 mins or until the glaze is starting to caramelise. Transfer to a platter, cover with foil and leave to rest for 15 mins.

4 While the duck is resting, make the sauce. Skim off nearly all the fat from the roasting tin. Transfer the remaining cooking juices and any caramelised meat residue from the base of the tin to a medium pan. Add the sliced onion and fry for 5 mins. Increase the heat, squeeze in the juice from the remaining orange and add the wine. Pour in the stock, bring to the boil and simmer for 10-15 mins until reduced by half. Add any meat juices from the rested duck and simmer for 1-2 mins. Season to taste then strain into a warmed serving jug.

5 Carve the duck and serve with the sauce. If you like, serve with the pomegranate and fig couscous on p168.

● Per serving (150g duck): 386 cals, 16.1g fat, 5.2g saturates, 18g sugars, 0.45g salt

Roast duck legs with plums & figs

These fruity, sticky duck legs are an easy way to roast duck

Serves 4, with leftovers
Prep time: 10 mins
Cook time:
1 hour 15 mins –
1 hour 30 mins
Rest time: 10 mins

4 duck legs by Sainsbury's
1 tbsp fresh thyme leaves
8 shallots, halved

3 fresh plums, destoned and quartered
4 fresh figs, quartered
2 tbsp clear honey

1 Preheat the oven to 200°C, fan 180°C, gas 6. Prick the skin of the duck legs all over with a fork and put in a large shallow roasting tin. Scatter over the thyme and season with salt and freshly ground black pepper. Put the shallots around the duck and roast in the oven for 30 mins, turning the shallots after 20 mins to coat in any duck fat.

2 Reduce the oven temperature to 160°C, fan 140°C, gas 3 and roast for a further 45 mins to 1 hour, adding the plums and figs and drizzling with the honey for the final 30 mins of cooking time. The duck skin should be crisp and golden and the plums and figs softened and just golden around the edges.

3 Cover and let rest in a warm place for 10 mins before serving.

● Per serving: 371 cals, 16.8g fat, 4.9g saturates, 18.7g sugars, 0.55g salt

Roast whole duck with pomegranate & mint

Rich meat, crispy skin and a sticky sauce make this roast duck irresistible

Serves 4,
with leftovers
Prep time: 20 mins
Cook time:
1 hour 35 mins –
1 hour 50 mins
Rest time: 15 mins

2kg oven-ready whole duck
Large handful fresh mint sprigs
3 red onions, thickly sliced
500ml no added sugar pomegranate

juice drink by Sainsbury's
2-3 tbsp clear honey
Seeds of 1 pomegranate

1   Preheat the oven to 190°C, fan 170°C, gas 5. Pat the skin of the duck dry with kitchen paper and prick all over with a fork. Season with salt and freshly ground pepper and put half the mint sprigs inside the cavity of the duck.

2   Put the onions, pomegranate juice drink and a couple of the remaining sprigs of mint in a roasting tin and sit the duck on top of the onions. Roast in the oven for 1 hour 30 mins – 1 hour 45 mins, brushing the duck all over with the honey for the final 10 mins of roasting time. To test if the duck is done, pierce a thigh with a skewer – if the juices run out light pink, the duck is done; if they are dark pink, the duck needs further cooking.

3   Transfer the duck and onions to a warmed platter, loosely cover with foil and leave to rest for 15 mins. Strain the liquid from the roasting tin through a sieve into a small pan. Bring to the boil and boil rapidly for 5 mins until it becomes thick and syrupy. Season to taste.

3   To serve, carve the duck and arrange on warmed serving plates with the red onions, pomegranate seeds and sauce. Garnish with mint leaves pulled from the remaining sprigs.

●   Per serving (150g duck): 356 cals, 12.5g fat, 3.8g saturates, 19.3g sugars, 0.56g salt

Ready in 1 hour 10 mins

Mini duck pies

These delicious mini baked pies are perfect finger food when you're on the go. Pack them in a lunchbox - they're just as nice served cold as they are warm

Serves 4

Prep time: 15 mins, plus
30 mins' chilling

Cook time: 20-25 mins

1 tsp Chinese five spice

1 tbsp clear honey

1 tbsp dark soy sauce

1cm piece of fresh root ginger, peeled and grated

200g leftover roast duck, shredded

375g pack ready rolled shortcrust pastry by Sainsbury's

1 medium egg, beaten

Hoisin dipping sauce, shredded cucumber and shredded spring onions, to serve

1 Put the five spice, honey, soy sauce and ginger in a bowl and whisk together to combine. Add the duck and mix thoroughly.

2 Line a baking tray with baking paper. Unroll the pastry on a clean work surface and stamp out 4 x 9cm discs and 4 x 12cm discs - re-roll the pastry trimmings to get the last disc.

3 Divide the shredded duck mixture between the 9cm discs, leaving a 1cm border all round. Brush the borders with egg and top with the larger discs. Press around the edges with a fork to firmly seal. Put the pies on the baking tray and chill in the fridge for 30 mins.

4 Preheat the oven to 200°C, fan 180°C, gas 6. Glaze the pies with egg and bake for 20-25 mins, until the pastry is crisp and golden. Serve warm or cold with the hoisin, cucumber and spring onions.

● **Per serving: 630 cals, 36g fat, 16g saturates, 11.4g sugars, 1.46g salt**

Cook's tip
To make this healthier, you could use ready rolled lighter shortcrust pastry by Sainsbury's.

Ready in 20 mins

Thai-style duck salad

This colourful, South East Asian-inspired dish includes lots of fresh, zingy flavours to complement the richness of the leftover roast duck

Serves 4

Prep time: 20 mins

1 head Chinese leaf, coarsely shredded

1/2 cucumber, trimmed, halved lengthways and very thinly shredded

6 spring onions, trimmed and shredded

150g fresh beansprouts

8 radishes, trimmed and very thinly sliced

Small handful fresh coriander

450g leftover roast duck, shredded

25g dry roasted peanuts, roughly chopped

Lime wedges, to serve

FOR THE DRESSING

Zest and juice of 1 large lime

1 tbsp olive oil

1 tbsp toasted sesame oil

1 tbsp soy sauce

1 tsp light brown soft sugar

1 clove garlic, crushed

1 red chilli, deseeded and finely chopped

1 Put the Chinese leaf, cucumber, most of the spring onions, the beansprouts and radishes in a large bowl and toss together. Chop the coriander stalks (reserve the leaves) and add to the bowl.

2 Put all the ingredients for the dressing in a jug and whisk together. Season to taste with salt and freshly ground black pepper. Pour half of the dressing over the salad and toss well.

3 Arrange the dressed salad on a large platter or 4 shallow bowls. Scatter over the shredded duck and the peanuts. Drizzle over the rest of the dressing and garnish with the remaining spring onions and reserved coriander leaves. Serve with the lime wedges.

● Per serving: 371 cals, 22.4g fat, 5.3g saturates, 6.5g sugars, 0.81g salt

lamb

Choosing and roasting
lamb...

Whether you're serving up Sunday lunch or enjoying an Easter roast, lamb makes any meal feel extra special. There are plenty of different cuts you can use for roasting - here are some of our top picks

RACK LOIN

SHOULDER

BREAST

SHANKS

LEG

Leg
This classic cut is a firm favourite for a big family roast, and ideal for a crowd. You'll get lots of lean, meat with plenty of leftovers and it only needs some simple seasoning to bring out its rich, succulent flavour. If you're cooking for a smaller group, you can divide the leg into two joints - the knuckle end and the fillet end - and freeze one of those for another time.

Shanks
A meaty, substantial cut from the lower end of the leg, lamb shanks are less expensive than other joints of lamb, and their smaller size makes them an inexpensive way to serve roast lamb to smaller gatherings. They're full of rich flavour and benefit from longer, slower roasting so that the meat falls away from the bone in tender, delicious chunks.

Rack
Packed full of flavour with lots of lean, flavoursome meat, a rack of lamb is an elegant choice if you're out to impress. It's ideal for serving two people, making it a faultless choice if you're entertaining a loved one. For larger groups try a 'crown roast' - two racks twisted in a circle to look like a crown - or a 'guard of honour', which is two racks placed side by side to create an arch with the bones.

Breast
The fattiest of all the lamb joints, breast is under-used and underrated. When boned and rolled around a well-flavoured stuffing, it makes for a tender and inexpensive roasting joint.

Perfect partners
Rosemary, bay leaves, sage and parsley; anchovies; garlic and lemon.

Accompaniments
Mint sauce and redcurrant jelly.

Cook's tip
If your joint is cold when you put it in the oven, it won't roast evenly. Make sure you allow enough time to take it out of the fridge well before cooking to bring it to room temperature. It will take a couple of hours, depending on the size of the joint.

Roasting tips and tricks...

Q How do I carve a leg of lamb?

Once you've let the lamb rest, transfer it to a board with the thickest, meatiest part turned upright. Steady the joint with a carving fork, and use a carving knife to cut a slim wedge from the centre of the joint. Next, angle your knife along the line of the wedge, and carve down to the bone. Cut across the base to separate the slices from the joint. Finally, flip over the joint and carve the rest of the meat parallel to the bone.

Q What can I do with the leftover bones or carcass of a roast?

Make a tasty stock. Put the bones or carcass in a large stock pot and cover with cold water. Add onion, carrot, celery, garlic, herbs of your choice (try a bouquet garni) and black peppercorns and bring to a gentle boil. Simmer for at least 30 mins, skimming the surface every so often so you get a clear stock. Any remaining meat that is on the bones will fall away with ease. Strain, reserve any meat, and use the strained stock as the basis for soups, stews, risottos and ramen noodle dishes. The stock will keep in an airtight container in the fridge for up to 2 days, and in the freezer for up to 3 months.

Q What should I use to flavour lamb?

Simple flavourings are best – make incisions in the flesh, massage in salt and pepper, and insert slices of garlic and sprigs of fresh rosemary into the cuts. Or, try Moroccan-style spices – ground cumin works well. Mix with olive oil and rub into the meat and marinate in the fridge for 1 hour before roasting.

Mint sauce

What's roast lamb without mint sauce? Make it yourself – it's quick, easy and delicious. Sprinkle a pinch of salt and 1 tbsp caster sugar over a handful of chopped fresh mint leaves. Stir in 4 tbsp boiling water. Let cool then stir in 4 tbsp white wine vinegar to finish. It will keep in the fridge for up to 4 days.

Cooked to perfection

The cooking time for roast lamb will depend on a number of things, including the cut of meat you're roasting, the temperature you're cooking it at, and the size of your joint. The most accurate, and most straightforward way to tell if your joint is cooked as you want it, is to use a meat thermometer, inserted into the centre of the joint at the thickest point. The joint is cooked when it reaches these temperatures:

Medium:	70-75°C
Well done:	75-80°C

Classic roast lamb

This flavoursome and tender roast lamb is so easier to prepare

Serves 4,
with leftovers
Prep time: 15 mins
Cook time:
1 hour 30 mins –
1 hour 45 mins
Rest time: 20 mins

Large (about 2kg) bone-in leg of lamb by Sainsbury's

2 tbsp olive oil
300ml white wine or vegetable stock

1 Preheat the oven to 220°C, fan 200°C, gas 7. Weigh the lamb leg and calculate the cooking time. Allow 15 mins, plus 18 mins per 500g for medium lamb; and 15 mins, plus 20-22 mins per 500g for well-done lamb. Rub the olive oil all over the leg, season with salt and freshly ground black pepper, and put on a rack in a roasting tin.

2 Pour the wine or stock around the lamb in the base of the roasting tin. Roast for 15 mins then reduce the temperature to 200°C, fan 180°C, gas 6, and continue roasting for the remaining calculated time.

3 Baste the lamb frequently, adding a little water to the tin if the juices start to dry up. Use a meat thermometer inserted into the thickest part of the lamb to test if it's done. For medium, it should read 70-75°C, and for well done, 75-80°C.

4 When the lamb's done to your liking, transfer it to a warm platter, cover with foil and let rest for 20 mins before carving. Skim off and discard any fat from the juices in the bottom of the roasting tin and pour them into a warm small jug to serve as a thin gravy.

● Per serving (150g lamb, plus gravy): 350 cals, 18.2g fat, 5.9g saturates, 0.5g sugars, 0.38g salt

Cook's tip
Serve your classic roast lamb with traditional homemade mint sauce – for an easy recipe, go to p49.

An Easter Sunday
classic, roasted leg of
lamb is a real treat

Tamarind & lime roasted leg of lamb

Serves 4,
with leftovers
Prep time:
35 mins, plus
2 hours' marinating
Cook time:
1 hour 30 mins –
1 hour 45 mins
Rest time: 20 mins

Tamarind has a sharp, sour taste, which works wonders with lamb.
Serve it with Thai-style rice for a Sunday roast with a difference

2kg bone-in leg of lamb by Sainsbury's
110g jar tamarind paste
Juice of 2 limes, plus a few extra limes,
cut into wedges, to serve

3 tbsp light brown soft sugar
Steamed basmati and wild rice with
sultanas and chopped fresh coriander
leaves, to serve

1 Put the lamb in a large roasting tin. In a small bowl, whisk together
the tamarind paste, lime juice and brown sugar until combined.
Rub the paste all over the lamb, then cover and put in the fridge to
marinate for at least 2 hours (or overnight). Remove the lamb from
the fridge and leave for 30 mins to come back to room temperature.

2 Preheat the oven to 190°C, fan 170°C, gas 5. Roast the lamb for 1 hour
30 mins for medium or 1 hour 45 mins for well done. Baste the joint
with juices from the roasting tin every 30 mins. If the top of the lamb
starts to caramelise too much, cover it loosely with foil. Use a meat
thermometer inserted into the thickest part of the lamb to test if it's
done. For medium, it should read 70-75°C, and for well done, 75-80°C.

3 When the lamb is cooked to your liking, remove from the oven,
transfer to a warm platter and cover with foil and let rest for 20 mins.
Skim off and discard any fat from the juices in the bottom of the
roasting tin and pour them into a warm small jug to serve as a sauce.
Serve with extra lime wedges, and steamed basmati and wild rice with
sultanas and chopped fresh coriander leaves.

● Per serving (150g lamb): 397 cals, 16g fat, 5.4g saturates,

Serves 4
Prep time: 15 mins
Cook time:
25-40 mins
Rest time: 10 mins

Herb-crusted roast rack of lamb

This springtime roast has so much flavour thanks to a punchy herb crust. We've used thyme, chives and parsley, but you can use any herbs you like

1 ¹/₂ tbsp Dijon mustard
6 tbsp fresh white breadcrumbs
4 tbsp chopped fresh herbs (we used thyme, chives and flat-leaf parsley)

25g unsalted butter
2 x 6-bone racks of lamb by Sainsbury's
Steamed green vegetables, to serve (try our recipe on p164)

1 Mix together the mustard, breadcrumbs, herbs and butter in a small bowl. Season lightly with salt and freshly ground black pepper. Put the lamb racks on a board and spread the breadcrumb mixture in a thin layer onto the skin of each, pressing down firmly.

2 Preheat the oven to 200°C, fan 180°C, gas 6. Place the racks of lamb, coated-side up, in a roasting tin. Roast in the oven for 25-35 mins for rare or 30-40 mins for medium. Cover the racks loosly with foil after 20 mins to prevent the herb crust from over-browning.

3 Remove the roasting tin from the oven and leave covered in a warm place to rest for 10 mins. Carve the racks into cutlets and serve with steamed green veg and pan gravy (see tip below).

● Per serving (3 cutlets): 401 cals, 34.7g fat, 17.3g saturates, 0.5g sugars, 0.67g salt

Cook's tip
For a delicious gravy, stir 4 tbsp redcurrant jelly into the roasting pan juices and heat until the jelly has dissolved. Gradually stir in 300ml red wine or stock, and simmer until reduced by one third.

Serves 4
Prep time: 15 mins
Cook time: 2 hours

Roasted herb & cumin lamb shanks

A brilliant all-in-one spring roast that's great for couples or smaller families – just make as few or as many as you need

80g butter, softened
Large handful fresh flat-leaf parsley, leaves picked and chopped
12 sprigs fresh rosemary, leaves picked
Large handful thyme, leaves picked and chopped
2 cloves garlic, finely chopped
2 tsp ground cumin

400g chantenay carrots, trimmed
350g baby leeks, trimmed
4 lamb shanks by Sainsbury's
200ml white wine
1kg potatoes, peeled and chopped
2 tbsp semi-skimmed milk
Steamed kale, to serve

1 Preheat oven to 180°C, fan 160°C, gas 4. In a bowl, mix 60g of the butter with the herbs, garlic and cumin until combined. Rub the herb butter all over the lamb shanks.

2 Cut 4 foil squares, each measuring 35cm x 35cm, and divide the carrots and leeks between each. Gather up the edges of the foil to make a loose bowl shape. Put the shanks on top of the veg, then carefully pour in the wine. Gather the foil around the bone, pinching it together tightly to seal.

3 Transfer the parcels to a large roasting tin and roast for 2 hours, until the lamb is tender and falling off the bone.

4 Twenty minutes before the lamb is cooked, put the potatoes in a pan of cold water. Bring to the boil then reduce the heat and simmer for 10-12 mins until tender. Drain then mash with the rest of the butter and the milk.

5 Serve the lamb and roasted veg on the mash, with the kale on the side, drizzled all over with the juices from the parcels.

● Per serving: 793 cals, 42.8g fat, 21.6g saturates, 10.7g sugars, 0.46g salt

" A three-herb
butter makes the lamb
meltingly tender "

Serves 4
Prep time: 15 mins
Cook time: 1 hour
30 mins - 2 hours
Rest time: 15 mins

Lamb breast stuffed with mint & pine nuts

An inexpensive cut of lamb made special with a stuffing that's full of fresh and punchy flavours, and a delicious red wine sauce

2 tbsp olive oil
1 onion, finely chopped
50g fresh white breadcrumbs
100g sliced chargrilled sundried aubergines, drained and chopped
75g goats' cheese, crumbled
75g fresh redcurrants

3 tbsp chopped fresh mint
25g toasted pine nuts
700g Sainsbury's basics lamb breast
1 tbsp plain flour
150ml red wine
200ml vegetable stock
1 tbsp mint sauce

1 Preheat the oven to 160°C, fan 140°C, gas 3. To make the stuffing, heat half the oil in a pan over a medium heat. Add the onion and cook gently for 5 mins until soft. Transfer to a bowl and add the breadcrumbs, aubergine, goats' cheese, redcurrants, mint and pine nuts. Season with freshly ground black pepper.

2 Untie the lamb, lay 5 new pieces of kitchen string across a large chopping board. Lay the lamb on top of the string, skin-side down. Spread the stuffing over the lamb, then roll up tightly securing at regular intervals with the string.

3 Heat the remaining oil in a frying pan over a high heat. Add the lamb and sear for 4-5 mins, turning, until browned all over. Transfer to a roasting tin and roast for 1 hour 30 mins - 2 hours, until tender. Check the lamb after 1 hour - if it's looking a bit too brown, cover with foil for the remaining roasting time. Transfer to a warm plate, cover with foil and rest for 15 mins while you make the sauce.

4 Skim the fat from the roasting tin and pour the juices into a pan. Heat over a medium-high heat, stir in the flour, and cook for 1 min. Gradually stir in the wine, bring to the boil and bubble until reduced by half. Stir in the stock and mint sauce. Simmer gently until thickened.

● Per serving: 745 cals, 50.9g fat, 21.2g saturates, 5.8g sugars, 1.46g salt

Ready in 55 mins

Shepherd's pie

Use leftover lamb and a batch of potato and celeriac mash from the recipe on p156 to make this delicious family pie

Serves 4

Prep time: 10 mins

Cook time: 40-45 mins

1 tbsp olive oil

1 onion, finely chopped

300g carrots, peeled and diced

2 cloves garlic, crushed

390g carton Italian chopped tomatoes

100ml lamb stock

1 tbsp cornflour

1 tbsp Worcestershire sauce

75g frozen petits pois

750g leftover roast lamb, chopped

900g potato and celeriac mash from recipe on p156

Steamed green veg, to serve

1 Preheat the oven to 200ºC, fan 180ºC, gas 6.

2 Heat the oil in a large pan, add the onion and carrot and cook for 10 mins. Stir in the garlic, chopped tomatoes and stock, then simmer for 10 mins.

3 In a small bowl, mix the cornflour with 5 tbsp cold water until you have a smooth paste. Stir into the pan, then add the Worcestershire sauce and peas and cook for a further 5 mins. Stir in the leftover roast lamb and season with salt and freshly ground black pepper.

4 Tip into a 2-litre ovenproof dish. Spoon over the potato and celeriac mash and bake for 25-30 mins until the top is golden brown and the filling is bubbling. Serve with steamed green veg.

● Per serving: 679 cals, 24.3g fat, 8.6g saturates, 14.1g sugars, 0.74g salt

Cook's tip
Spice it up by adding a couple of dashes of Tabasco sauce or, alternatively, stir in a couple of finely chopped red chillies.

Moroccan lamb parcels

Make a meal out of leftover lamb with these spicy parcels served with couscous.
They're also perfect for packing in lunchboxes – just serve with a yogurt dipping sauce

Serves 4

Prep time: 15 mins

Cook time: 35-45 mins

1 tbsp olive oil

1 onion, finely chopped

2 cloves garlic, crushed

¼ tsp ground nutmeg

¼ tsp ground cinnamon

½ tsp ground ginger

50g pine nuts

50g raisins

75g dried apricots, finely chopped

200g leftover roast lamb, finely chopped

1 tbsp honey

200ml passata

8 sheets filo pastry

50g unsalted butter, melted

1 tbsp sesame seeds

Couscous, from recipe on p168, to serve

Cook's tip
If you don't have sesame seeds, scatter over poppy seeds instead. Nigella and black mustard seeds work well, too.

1 Preheat the oven to 180°C, fan 160°C, gas 4. Heat the oil in a pan and cook the onion for 5 mins, adding the garlic for the last 1 min.

2 Stir in the spices, the pine nuts, raisins, apricots, lamb and honey. Pour in passata and cook, stirring occasionally, for 3-4 mins.

3 Lay out 1 sheet of filo and halve lengthways. Brush each strip with some of the melted butter. Stack the 2 strips to make 1 long strip. Spoon an eighth of the filling onto one corner. Fold the pastry and filling over at right angles to make a triangle and continue folding to form a neat triangular parcel. Seal with a little melted butter. Repeat with the remaining pastry and lamb mix.

4 Transfer to a baking sheet, brush the tops with the remaining butter, sprinkle over the sesame seeds and bake for 25-35 mins until crisp and golden. Serve with the couscous.

● Per serving: 809 cals, 36.8g fat, 11g saturates, 35.8g sugars, 0.55g salt

Ready in 1 hour 10 mins

Lamb & butter bean couscous

Use leftover roast lamb to make this easy Moroccan-style supper. With authentic North African flavours, it will add a bit of spice and interest to your midweek meals

Serves 4

Prep time: 20 mins

Cook time: 40-50 mins

½ tbsp olive oil

1 onion, chopped

2 tsp harissa paste or ras-el-hanout

390g carton Italian chopped tomatoes in tomato juice

5-6 ripe vine tomatoes, chopped

2 courgettes, trimmed and chopped

100ml vegetable stock

500g leftover roast lamb, diced

410g tin butter beans drained and rinsed

Steamed couscous, to serve

FOR THE GREMOLATA

Zest of 1 lemon

Small handful fresh flat-leaf parsley, roughly chopped

1 red chilli, deseeded and finely chopped

1 Heat the oil in a large heavy-based pan. Add the onion and cook for 4-5 mins until soft but not coloured. Add the harissa or ras-el-hanout, and cook for 1-2 mins.

2 Add all of the tomatoes, the courgettes and stock. Bring to the boil, then reduce the heat and simmer, uncovered, for 20-25 mins until the courgettes are tender and the sauce has thickened slightly. Stir in the lamb and butter beans and cook for 10-15 mins. Season with salt and freshly ground black pepper.

3 Make the gremolata: combine all the ingredients in a bowl and season to taste.

4 To serve, divide the couscous between plates, top with the stew and garnish with the gremolata.

● Per serving: 639 cals, 15.6g fat, 5.2g saturates, 9.2g sugars, 0.80g salt

Ready in 30 mins
Lamb korma

An Indian classic made easy with leftover roast lamb and pre-cooked pilau rice, that's on the table in half an hour – perfect for a Monday night dinner

Serves 4

Prep time: 5 mins

Cook time: 25 mins

1 tbsp olive oil

1 large onion, diced

2 cloves garlic, chopped

350g leftover roast lamb, chopped into bite-size chunks

1/2 x 290g jar korma paste by Sainsbury's

4 mini garlic and coriander naan breads

1/2 x 500g pack Indian three colour pilau rice by Sainsbury's

Small handful fresh coriander, leaves picked and chopped

150g Greek yogurt

260g young leaf spinach

1 Heat the oil in a pan and sauté the onion for 5 mins until soft but not coloured. Add the garlic and lamb and fry for 5 mins. Stir in the korma paste, and cook for a further 3 mins. Pour in 200ml water, bring to the boil then simmer gently for 10 mins.

2 Meanwhile, heat the naan and the rice according to pack instructions and stir the coriander into the rice.

3 Stir the yogurt and spinach through the korma and serve with the rice and naan.

● **Per serving:** 624 cals, 27g fat, 11.3g saturates, 12.8g sugars, 1.84g salt

Cook's tip
Add a bit of extra heat by stirring in 1 or 2 finely chopped chillies to the pan at the same time as you add the garlic.

beef

Choosing and roasting beef...

The quintessential centrepiece to a Sunday lunch, a joint of British beef is guaranteed to please. Choose the best cuts and get the most from your roast with these tips...

Diagram labels: CHUCK, RUMP, TOP-SIDE, SIRLOIN & FILLET, FORE RIB, BRISKET

Topside

By far the most popular choice when it comes to roasting, topside is both lean and succulent. It's also easy to cut into large, generous slices. It's usually covered in a layer of fat to stop it drying out, but you can remove this before roasting, and just baste regularly with the pan juices.

Perfect partners...
Rosemary, parsley, thyme and bay leaves.

Brisket

Tougher than other cuts of beef, and best when slow-roasted, brisket joints are an inexpensive way to serve roast beef at a large gathering. Brisket is usually boned and rolled, and benefits from longer, slower roasting so that the meat falls apart. Use it in pot roasts for the most succulent results and try the leftovers in pies, stews and oriental soups.

Fore rib

Rich in flavour and juicy in texture, rib of beef is a fantastic special-occasion roast as it's usually on the bone and looks spectacular on a platter surrounded by golden Yorkshire puddings and roast potatoes. It's marbled and has a natural layer of fat, which means the meat will stay moist and succulent during roasting as it effectively self-bastes.

Fillet & sirloin

These lean cuts of beef can be roasted whole and are great if you're looking for something with less fat. Sirloin is usually boned and rolled – cut it into smaller joints if you're only cooking for a few people. Fillet is a very lean cut of beef – cooking it in pastry will keep it moist.

Accompaniments...
Horseradish sauce and English mustard.

Cook's tip

Making sure the oven is extra hot when you start roasting will allow the heat to get right to the centre of the joint. Preheat your oven to 240°C, fan 220°C, gas 9, then turn it down to the recommended temperature once you've put your meat in the oven.

Roasting tips and tricks...

Q Beef is quite expensive. Are there any cheaper cuts I can use?

Roasting a large joint of beef may seem like a bit of an indulgence, but leftover beef is delicious cold and there'll be enough to make another family meal or two. Also, the bigger the joint the better it will roast, as smaller joints tend to dry out and be less succulent. However, cheaper cuts are also brilliant. They tend to require slower cooking to keep them tender. Topside and brisket make great roasts. Both are quite lean, so frequent basting with a little liquid added to the tin will help keep them moist.

Cooked to perfection

Rare, medium or well done? Everyone has a preference, but if you're cooking for a number of people, it's best to go for medium. If it's still too rare for some people, you can always wrap slices in foil and return them to the oven for a few minutes. To tell if the meat is cooked the way you want it, use a meat thermometer. Push it into the centre of the thickest part of the meat and check for the following:

Rare:	60°C
Medium:	70°C
Well done:	80°C

Leftovers

As a general rule, leftover roasted meats - including beef - are safest when they're refrigerated or frozen within 2 hours of the end of cooking. Reheat to at least 65°C before serving. To serve meat cold, it should be well cooked to begin with, refrigerated quickly and then served within 2 days straight from the fridge. You can also freeze leftover beef. Wrap it properly to avoid freezer burn and fully defrost before reheating.

Expert carving

The way you carve a joint of beef can make a big difference when it comes to maximising its flavour...

- Let the roasted joint rest for about 20 mins before carving. This allows the juices to be redistributed and reabsorbed throughout the joint. As a result, the meat will retain its juices when you carve it, and will be tender and succulent.
- Transfer the joint to a carving board to make the job easier.
- Steady the joint with a carving fork and use a carving knife to cut. Hold the knife at the same angle for each slice.
- Carve against the grain for the most tender slices.

Classic roast beef

Get this British classic right first time and every time with this recipe

**Serves 4,
with leftovers**
Prep time: 5 mins
Cook time:
1 hour 15 mins –
2 hours 15 mins
Rest time: 20 mins

Large (about 2kg) British beef
roasting joint by Sainsbury's
1 tbsp English mustard

1 tbsp plain flour
400ml beef stock
Splash of dark stout or Guinness (optional)

1 Take the joint out of the fridge 30 mins before cooking to bring it up to room temperature. Preheat the oven to 220°C, fan 200°C, gas 7. Weigh the joint and calculate the cooking time. Allow 15 mins per 500g, plus 15 mins for rare; 18 mins per 500g plus 20 mins for medium and 22-27 mins per 500g plus 25 mins for well done.

2 If your joint is wrapped in a net, remove and discard then tie at regular intervals with kitchen string. Put the joint in a flameproof roasting tin, fat-side up. Smear the mustard over the fat and season with a little salt and freshly ground black pepper – the hot mustard helps to form a tasty crust on the beef, but the flavour will mellow during roasting. Roast for 30 mins, then reduce the oven temperature to 180°C, fan 160°C, gas 4 for the remaining calculated cooking time. Cover the joint with foil during roasting if the surface starts to brown too quickly.

3 When the roast is done, leave to rest covered in the foil for 20 mins while you make the gravy. Spoon any excess fat out of the roasting tin then put on the hob over a medium heat. Sprinkle over the flour. Cook, stirring, for about 1 min. Gradually stir in the beef stock and stout (if using) and bring to the boil, stirring and scraping all the meaty residues from the bottom of the roasting tin. Let it bubble for a minute or so then strain and serve alongside the beef.

● Per serving (150g beef, plus gravy): 861 cals, 80.9g fat, 37.4g saturates, 0.5g sugars, 0.38g salt

Cook's tip
Serve your classic roast beef with traditional homemade Yorkshire puddings – for an easy recipe, go to p72.

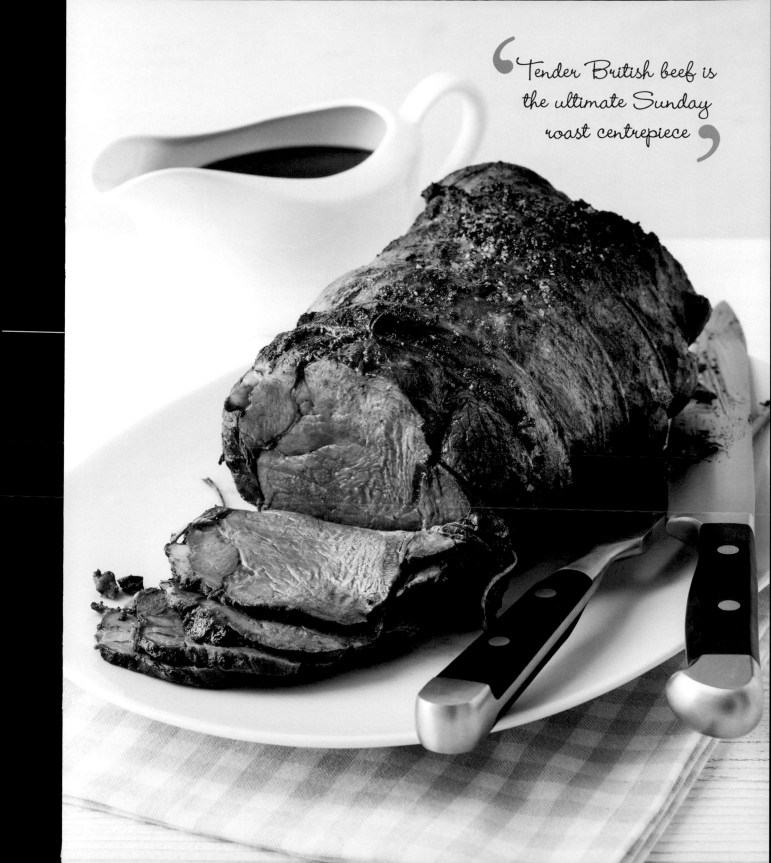

Tender British beef is the ultimate Sunday roast centrepiece

Maple-glazed roast beef with sesame veg

For roast beef with a difference, try this sticky and sweet joint

Serves 4, with leftovers
Prep time: 15 mins
Cook time:
1 hour 30 mins –
1 hour 45 mins
Rest time: 30 mins

2 onions, cut into thick wedges
3 tbsp olive oil
1.5kg British beef topside roasting joint by Sainsbury's
40g butter
3 tbsp maple syrup
2 tbsp soy sauce

1kg Maris Piper potatoes, peeled, halved, larger potatoes quartered
4 carrots, peeled and cut into chunks on the diagonal
4 parsnips, peeled and cut into quarters lengthways
1 tbsp sesame seeds

1 Preheat the oven to 200ºC, fan 180ºC, gas 6. Put the onions in a large roasting tin. Rub 1 tbsp of the oil over the beef and season with salt and freshly ground black pepper. Put the beef on top of the onions and roast for 1 hour for medium-rare or 1 hour 15 mins for medium.

2 To make the glaze, put the butter, maple syrup and soy sauce in a small pan. Bring to the boil then simmer for 2-3 mins until thickened and syrupy. Brush the beef with the glaze for the final 15 mins of cooking time, reserving a little to serve.

3 Meanwhile, boil the potatoes in a large pan of lightly salted water for 15 mins until almost tender, adding the carrots and parsnips after 8 mins. Drain well and set aside.

4 Transfer the beef to a large warm platter, cover with foil and let rest while you roast the vegetables. Increase the oven temperature to 220ºC, fan 200ºC, gas 7. Leave the onions in the tin and stir in the remaining oil. Add the vegetables to the tin and toss to coat in the oil and meat juices. Return to the oven and roast for 30 mins until golden and tender. Scatter the sesame seeds over the vegetables after 20 mins and turn gently to coat.

6 Brush the meat with the remaining glaze and serve with the sesame roasted vegetables.

● Per serving (150g beef, plus vegetables): 838 cals, 39.1g fat, 15.2g saturates, 28.1g sugars, 1.21g salt

beef

Roast rib of beef with Yorkshire puddings

Nothing adds succulence to a beef joint than roasting it on the bone

Serves 6,
with leftovers
Prep time: 30 mins
Cook time:
2 hours 20 mins –
3 hours 15 mins
Rest time: 20 mins

3kg rib of beef (with 3 bones)
1 tbsp plain flour
4 shallots, thinly sliced
1 tbsp English mustard powder
5 tbsp wholegrain mustard

FOR THE YORKSHIRE PUDDINGS
3 tbsp vegetable oil
150g plain flour
$1/4$ tsp salt
4 medium eggs, beaten
200ml semi-skimmed milk

1 Remove the joint from the fridge and bring to room temperature. Preheat the oven to 230°C, fan 210°C, gas 8. Weigh the joint and calculate the roasting time. Allow 15 mins per 450g plus 15 mins for rare, or 20 mins per 450g plus 20 mins for medium. Sprinkle the flour in the centre of a large roasting tin and put the shallots on top. Sit the joint - with the bones on the underside - on the shallots.

2 Mix together the mustard powder and mustard. Spread over the layer of fat on the joint. Season with salt and ground black pepper.

3 Roast for 10 mins, then reduce the oven temperature to 180°C, fan 160°C, gas 4. Cover the mustard crust with oiled foil to prevent it over-browning, and roast for the remaining calculated time. Baste the joint during roasting with the pan juices. Remove from the oven, cover and let rest for 20 mins while you make the Yorkshire puddings.

4 Increase the oven temperature to 220°C, fan 200°C, gas 7. Pour 1 tsp oil into each hole of a 12-hole muffin tray. Put in the oven for 5 mins until sizzling. Meanwhile, sift the flour and salt into a bowl and make a well in the centre. Whisk in the eggs until smooth, then gradually whisk in the milk to make a smooth batter. Transfer to a jug.

5 Remove the hot tin from the oven and pour the batter into the holes. Return to the oven and cook for 15-20 mins until risen and golden.

6 Serve the beef with the Yorkshires and pan gravy (see p68 for a recipe).

● Per serving (150g beef, plus 2 Yorkshires): 478 cals, 22.7g fat, 6.5g saturates, 2.6g sugars, 1.49g salt

'Roasting beef on the bone gives tender, juicy, flavoursome results'

Beef Wellington

A restaurant classic, this is a great way to roast beef for a special occasion

Serves 8
Prep time: 20 mins,
plus 1 hour chilling
Cook time: 1 hour
Rest time: 15 mins

1.25kg whole beef fillet, cut from the
middle, trimmed of excess sinew
2 tsp vegetable oil
500g block all-butter puff pastry
(use lighter pastry, if you like)
1 medium egg, beaten

FOR THE MUSHROOM DUXELLE
25g unsalted butter
125g chestnut mushrooms, thinly sliced
1 large clove garlic, crushed
100g smooth chicken liver pâté
1 tbsp chopped fresh thyme leaves

1 Season the beef all over with salt and freshly ground black pepper. Heat the oil in a large frying pan over a medium heat. Brown the beef all over for 5 mins, then transfer to a plate and set aside until completely cold.

2 Meanwhile, make the mushroom duxelle. Wipe out the frying pan with kitchen paper, then melt the butter over a low heat. Add the mushrooms and garlic, increase the heat, and cook for 7-8 mins until the mushrooms are tender and starting to brown. Remove from the heat and set aside to cool.

3 Put the chicken liver pâté in a bowl and stir in the thyme leaves. Add the cold mushroom mixture and stir gently until combined.

4 Roll out a third of the pastry on a lightly floured surface to a thickness of 2-3mm, and measuring 3cm longer and wider than the beef fillet.

5 Transfer the pastry to a baking sheet lined with baking parchment, and brush all over with egg. Spread ½ of the duxelle in a thin layer over the pastry, leaving a 1.5cm border all round. Place the beef on top, then spread the remaining duxelle over the top and sides. Roll out the rest of the pastry to a thickness of 2-3 mm, measuring roughly 30cm x 35cm. Drape the pastry over the beef, and press the edges together to form a seal. Cut any leftover pastry trimmings into leaves and attach to the pastry with egg. Brush all over with any remaining egg. Chill in the fridge for at least 1 hour, or overnight.

6 Preheat the oven to 220°C, fan 200°C, gas 7. Bake the chilled Wellington for 45 mins for medium. Remove from the oven and leave to stand in a warm place for 15 mins before serving.

● Per serving: 595 cals, 40.6g fat, 24g saturates, 1.3g sugars, 0.81g salt

Slow-roast brisket

Meltingly tender, this hearty pot roast uses an inexpensive cut of beef

1.6kg beef brisket joint by Sainsbury's	2 tbsp flour
1 tsp English mustard	500ml beer or brown ale
2 tbsp olive oil	300ml beef stock
250g shallots, peeled	2 tbsp Worcestershire sauce
225g baby or small turnips, halved	1 sachet bouquet garni
225g carrots, cut into chunks	400g potatoes, cut into chunks
1 clove garlic, chopped	Fresh thyme sprigs, plus extra to garnish

1 Preheat the oven to 160°C, fan 140°C, gas 3. Spread the mustard over the brisket joint. Heat half of the oil in a large frying pan. Add the beef and brown on all sides. Transfer to a large deep roasting tin or casserole.

2 Add the rest of the oil to the pan and fry the shallots, turnips and carrots for 3-4 mins, adding the garlic for the last 1 min. Sprinkle over the flour and cook, stirring, for 1 min then gradually stir in the beer or brown ale, stock and Worcestershire sauce. Bring to the boil, add the bouquet garni then remove from the heat.

3 Spoon the vegetables and all the liquid around the beef. Season with salt and freshly ground black pepper. Cover tightly with a double thickness of foil or casserole lid and cook in the oven for 1 hr 45 mins.

4 Remove from the oven and add the potato chunks and thyme sprigs. Cover and cook for a further 35-40 mins until the beef and all the vegetables are very tender.

5 For a thicker gravy, carefully pour off the cooking liquid from the tin or casserole into a pan (remove and discard the bouquet garni and leave the beef and vegetables covered). Skim off any excess fat and bring to the boil over a high heat. Boil for 5-10 mins until the liquid has reduced and thickened slightly. Pour back over the vegetables and serve garnished with the extra thyme leaves.

● Per serving: 479 cals, 28g fat, 10.6g saturates, 8.4g sugars, 0.31g salt

A great roast for warming you up on chilly, wintry days

Ready in 1 hour 20 mins

Vietnamese pho

An aromatic beef noodle soup (pronounced 'fer'), that can be as mild or spicy as you like – simply stir in more chilli for added heat

Serves 4

Prep time: 10 mins

Cook time: 1 hour 10 mins

2 litres beef stock, made with 1 stock cube

1 onion, sliced

3cm piece root ginger, peeled and sliced

2 dried cloves

1 tsp black peppercorns

1/2 cinnamon stick

1 1/2 tbsp hoisin sauce

2 tbsp fish sauce

2 red chillies, sliced

200g beansprouts

300g rice noodles

200g leftover rare roast beef, thinly sliced

Handful of fresh coriander, roughly chopped

1/2 x bunch spring onions, trimmed and finely sliced

1 lime, cut into wedges

Cook's tip
You can use any leftover roast beef in this recipe – chunks of brisket that have been slow-cooked so they're falling apart are perfect, too.

1 Put the stock, onion, ginger, dried cloves, peppercorns and cinnamon in a large pan. Bring to the boil, then reduce the heat and simmer, covered, for 1 hour.

2 Strain the stock then stir in the hoisin and fish sauces, and half the chillies. Return to the heat, then add the beansprouts, and simmer until cooked through.

3 Divide the noodles between 4 bowls and top with the beef slices. Ladle over the hot stock and serve with the coriander, spring onions, remaining chillies and lime wedges to stir into the hot broth as desired.

● Per serving: 228 cals, 4.7g fat, 1.3g saturates, 6g sugars, 1.83g salt

Ready in 30 mins

Spicy beef & potato sauté

Use up leftover roast beef, potatoes and cabbage to make this quick and easy midweek meal. If you don't want to poach eggs, you can fry them instead

Serves 4

Prep time: 10 mins

Cook time: 20 mins

---

1 tbsp olive oil

1 tsp ground cumin

1 tsp garam masala

1 onion, finely chopped

800g leftover roast potatoes, cut into chunks

250g frozen garden peas, defrosted

300g leftover cooked cabbage, chopped

300g leftover roast beef, cut into chunks

4 medium eggs

1 tsp white wine vinegar

1 In a large frying pan, heat the oil and add the cumin, garam masala and onion. Gently cook for 5 mins until softened. Add the potatoes and fry for 5 mins. Stir in the peas, cabbage and beef and season with salt and freshly ground black pepper. Fry for a further 5 mins until piping hot.

2 Meanwhile, bring a large, deep pan of water to a simmer and add the vinegar. Carefully crack each egg into the pan and simmer gently for 2 mins for a runny yolk or 4 mins for a firm yolk.

3 Using a slotted spoon, remove the eggs from the pan and serve on top of the sauté, seasoned with freshly ground black pepper.

● Per serving: 636 cals, 22.9g fat, 4.8g saturates, 6.7g sugars, 0.39g salt

Ready in 40 mins

Ultimate roast beef sandwiches

A chunky roast beef sandwich perked up with caramelised onions and a horseradish mayonnaise, served with crunchy, golden chips

Makes 4

Prep time: 10 mins

Cook time: 30 mins

1 tbsp olive oil

15g butter

2 large onions, thinly sliced

Pinch of brown sugar

8 thick slices white bread
(taken from a large
farmhouse loaf)

4 tbsp horseradish sauce

8 tbsp mayonnaise

75g baby leaf watercress

25g wild baby leaf rocket

500g leftover roast beef,
thinly sliced

Chunky chips, to serve

1 Heat the olive oil and butter in a large frying pan until the butter has melted. Add the onions and sugar and cook gently for about 30 mins or until the onions are soft and caramelised, stirring frequently. Season with salt and freshly ground black pepper.

2 Meanwhile, mix the horseradish sauce and mayonnaise together in a small bowl and season to taste.

3 Spread the horseradish mayonnaise on 4 of the slices of bread. Top with the watercress and rocket leaves then pile on the leftover roast beef and warm caramelised onions. Top with the remaining slices of bread. Halve each sandwich and serve with chunky chips.

● Per serving: 521 cals, 38.4g fat, 7.2g saturates, 10.3g sugars, 1.08g salt

Cook's tip
If you don't have horseradish sauce, mix some hot English mustard through the mayo. Caramelised red onions also work brilliantly with this.

Hearty beef & prune stew

The natural sweetness of the prunes makes this a dish with a difference. It's a large stew, but can easily be halved if you don't have enough leftover beef

Serves 6

Prep time: 20 mins

Cook time: 1 hour 40 mins

2 tbsp olive oil

1 large onion, finely chopped

4 carrots, roughly chopped

250g chestnut mushrooms, cut into quarters

2 tbsp plain flour

750ml beef stock, made with 1 stock cube

1 tsp gravy browning mix

1 tsp Dijon mustard

1 tbsp tomato purée

150g soft, stoneless, ready to eat prunes, halved

4 sprigs fresh thyme, leaves picked, plus extra to garnish

1 fresh bay leaf

900g leftover roast beef, cut into large chunks

❄ Freezer tip
Cool completely, then freeze for up to 3 months. Defrost completely (overnight in the fridge) before reheating in a pan until piping hot.

1 Heat the oil in a large casserole, add the onion and cook for 4-5 mins until softened. Increase the heat to high and stir in the carrots and chestnut mushrooms. Cook for a further 5 mins.

2 Sprinkle over the flour and cook, stirring for 1-2 mins. Gradually pour in the stock and gravy browning mix along with the Dijon mustard and tomato purée. Bring to the boil. Add the prunes, thyme and bay leaf then cover and simmer gently over a very low heat for 1 hour until the carrots are tender.

3 Stir in the beef and simmer gently, uncovered, for 30 mins until the sauce is thick and glossy.

4 Garnish with the extra thyme leaves and serve with mashed potato.

● Per serving: 447 cals, 13.6g fat, 4.6g saturates, 15.5g sugars, 0.36g salt

pork & gammon

Choosing and roasting
pork & gammon...

Whether you're enjoying a classic pork roast with crackling, or celebrating with a whole gammon, you can't go wrong with this guide to one of the more versatile roasts

Pork leg

A whole leg is great for a crowd, but you can buy it deboned and cut into smaller joints. It's leaner than other cuts of pork, so take care not to overcook it.

Pork shoulder

Although it can be roasted on the bone, it's tricky to carve. More often, it's boned, then rolled and tied so it lends itself well to stuffing. It has dry skin with a layer of fat beneath, which makes it a fantastic joint for crackling.

Pork belly

A great-tasting cut with a good amount of fat, so it stays moist and succulent throughout roasting. Great for crackling - make sure the skin is well scored - and if it's deboned, it can be stuffed and rolled.

Pork tenderloin

A lean cut of pork and, as the name suggests, a tender, one too. Because it has so little fat, it's often wrapped in bacon or pancetta to protect it during roasting. Its shape means it can be sliced into small, neat slices that look tempting on the plate.

Perfect partners...
Rosemary, sage and thyme; fennel, ginger, coriander seeds, caraway seeds, cloves and cinnamon; apples, apricots and prunes.

Pork ribs

Bought as a rack and slow cooked with a sticky glaze, pork ribs make a really flavoursome roast. Since they're a less expensive cut, they're good for large numbers of people.

Pork shanks

A great alternative roast, shanks are another less expensive cut, and benefit from long, slow cooking, after which the tender meat will fall off the bone. They work well in a pot roast.

Gammon

This British classic is often rolled out as the perfect partner to a Christmas turkey, but there's no reason not to enjoy it year round. It has a reputation for being on the salty side, but if prepared properly, it makes a juicy centrepiece for any dinner table, with the most delicious leftovers.

Roasting tips and tricks...

Q How do I glaze a gammon joint?

Using a sharp knife, remove the rind, leaving as much fat as possible. Score the fat in a diamond pattern and the smear with your glaze.

Q How do I make gammon less salty?

Soaking a gammon joint beforehand will help remove the salt - for best results, soak for 24 hours before roasting and change the water a couple of times.

Q How long can I keep leftovers for?

Pork keeps in the fridge for 2 days, and in the freezer for up to 3 months.

Cooked to perfection

With pork, slow, gentle roasting always produces the best results. Cook it too fast and you'll end up with stringy, dry meat. Secondly, always cook pork thoroughly. The most accurate way to test it's fully cooked is with a meat thermometer. Pierce the centre of the joint – it needs to read 75°C-80°C. Or, use a skewer. Insert it into the centre of the joint – the juices that emerge when the skewer is removed should be clear. If there are traces of pink, roast it for another 10-15 mins.

Gammon versus ham

Confused about the difference between gammon and ham? A ham is a whole raw leg that is then cured, whereas gammon is cut from an already cured leg. These days, you'll rarely find raw ham sold in stores. Gammon, however, is sold raw and needs to be cooked or roasted, whereas ham is almost always already cooked or dry-cured.

How do I get the perfect crackling?

Roast pork with bubbly, crunchy crackling is the ultimate roast indulgence - but achieving it can be tricky. Get crispy crackling every time you roast with these insider tips...

1 Carefully wipe the skin dry, using kitchen paper.
2 Resist the temptation to oil the skin – simply rub in a teaspoon of coarse salt.
3 Keep the skin completely dry and don't be tempted to baste it during cooking. If it's not crisp enough at the end of cooking time, pop it under a hot grill for just a couple of minutes.

1

2

3

Classic roast pork

Tender pork with crisp crackling and apple sauce is a winning roast

**Serves 4,
with leftovers**
Prep time: 5 mins
Cook time: 3 hours
Rest time: 15 mins

Large (about 2.5kg) crackling pork shoulder joint by Sainsbury's, skin scored
1 tsp sea salt
1 tbsp plain flour

400ml medium cider or good-quality vegetable stock
Pinch of caster sugar
Easy apple sauce, to serve (see below)

1 Preheat the oven to 190°C, fan 170°C, gas 5. Carefully wipe the skin of the pork dry, using kitchen paper, and rub the salt into the scored skin.

2 Weigh the joint and calculate the cooking time allowing 30 mins per 500g, plus an extra 30 mins. Set the joint on a rack over a roasting tin, put in the oven and roast for 30 mins. Reduce the temperature to 170°C, fan 150°C, gas 3, and continue cooking for the remaining calculated time – for how to tell when it's cooked, see p85. Remove from the oven and let rest for 15 mins, covered in foil to keep warm.

3 While the pork is resting, make the gravy and apple sauce. Spoon any excess fat out of the roasting tin then place it on the hob. Sprinkle over the flour and cook, stirring, for 1 min. Add the cider and sugar, and bring to the boil, stirring and scraping all the meaty residues from the bottom of the tin. Let the liquid bubble for a minute then strain and serve with the pork – remove the crackling to make carving easier.

● Per serving (150g roast pork, plus gravy): 511 cals, 29.7g fat, 11.6g saturates, 26.9g sugars, 2.19g salt

Easy apple sauce

Peel, core and chop 500g Bramley apples and put in a pan with 150ml water, 1 tsp cider vinegar and 50g caster sugar. Put the lid on, bring to a simmer over a low-medium heat, and cook for 5-8 mins, stirring until the apples are soft. Remove the lid to let any remaining water to evaporate. Take off the heat and stir in 25g butter. Serve hot or cold. It will keep in the fridge for 3-4 days.

Serves 4, plus leftovers Prep time: 5 mins Cook time: 8-10 mins

Per serving: 37 cals, 1.3g fat, 0.8g saturates, 5.9g sugars, 0.02g salt

A succulent pork joint with loads of crisp crackling

Apricot-glazed pork

You won't be able to resist this sticky, crunchy roasted leg of pork

Serves 4,
with leftovers
Prep time: 25 mins,
plus cooling
Cook time:
1 hour 30 mins
Rest time: 15 mins

15g butter	2 tbsp chopped fresh flat-leaf parsley
2 tsp olive oil	1.3kg boned and rolled leg of pork with
1 small leek, trimmed and finely chopped	crackling by Sainsbury's, skin scored
30g pine nuts	1 tsp sea salt
40g dried apricots, finely chopped	4 tbsp apricot jam
80g fresh white breadcrumbs	2 tbsp clear honey
A few fresh sage leaves, chopped	1 tbsp red wine vinegar

1 Heat the butter and oil in a large frying pan over a medium heat. Add the leek and cook for 5 mins until soft. Add the pine nuts and apricots and cook for a further 2-3 mins. Stir in the breadcrumbs, remove from the heat and let cool. Stir in the sage.

2 Preheat the oven to 190°C, fan 170°C, gas 5. Open out the pork shoulder joint, skin-side down, on a board. Spoon the stuffing lengthways down the middle of the pork, heaping it up into a cylindrical shape, then bring the sides of the joint up and around the stuffing so that they meet tightly. Tie tightly at intervals with kitchen string. Transfer to a large roasting tin, and rub the salt all over the skin and into the cuts. Cover loosely with foil and roast for 1 hour.

4 Heat the jam, honey and vinegar in a small pan over a low heat, stirring until the mixture turns syrupy – about 4-5 mins. Remove the roasting tin from the oven and transfer the pork to a board. Untie the string, remove the crackling in 1 piece and set aside. Re-roll and re-tie the pork and return to the roasting tin. Increase the oven temperature to 200°C, fan 180°C, gas 6. Brush the joint all over with the glaze and roast for 20 mins, basting once, until the glaze is sticky and caramelised and the pork is cooked. Set aside to rest for 30 mins before carving.

5 While the pork is resting, preheat the grill to high. Put the crackling in a roasting tin and cook under the grill for 15 mins until crisp. Break the crackling into pieces and serve with the roast pork.

● Per serving (150g pork): 501 cals, 31.5g fat, 10.1g saturates, 17.3g sugars, 1.86g salt

**Serves 4,
with leftovers**
Prep time: 20 mins
Cook time: 2 hours
30 mins
Rest time: 15 mins

Slow-roasted pork belly with five spice

With its crisp crackling, tender meat and fragrant spicy flavours, this roasted pork belly joint is absolutely irresistible

1.5kg boneless pork belly joint by Sainsbury's, skin deeply scored
$1/2$ tsp Szechuan peppercorns
$1/2$ tsp black peppercorns

$1/2$ tsp caster sugar
$1/2$ tsp Chinese five spice
1 tbsp sea salt
175ml dry white wine

1 Preheat the oven to 220°C, fan 200°C, gas 7. Place the pork belly on a rack over a roasting tin and pour over a kettle of boiling water (this helps to ensure a crispy skin). Pat dry thoroughly with kitchen towel, then place on a board. Remove the rack from the tin and discard the water.

2 Toast the peppercorns in a small pan over a low heat, until fragrant, then transfer to a pestle and mortar and crush to a coarse powder. Stir in the sugar, five spice and sea salt and rub the mixture all over the pork, making sure you work it into the cuts in the skin.

3 Pour the wine into the roasting tin. Put the pork belly in the tin and roast for 20 mins. Reduce the heat to 160°C, fan 140°C, gas 3 and roast for a further 2-2$1/2$ hours, or until meltingly tender. If the skin isn't as crisp as you'd like, increase the heat to 220°C, fan 200°C, gas 7 for the final 15 mins' cooking time.

4 Let the pork rest in a warm place for 15 mins and brush all over with the tray juices just before serving.

● Per serving (150g pork): 336 cals, 24.5g fat, 8.3g saturates, 0.6g sugars, 2.78g salt

Cook's tip
Try serving this with roasted fennel (see p162) and steamed basmati rice flavoured with finely chopped spring onions.

Rolled pork shoulder with fennel & cumin

Get great results by stuffing and rolling a pork shoulder before roasting

Serves 6, with leftovers
Prep time: 20 mins, plus 10 mins cooling
Cook time: 2 hours 25 mins – 3 hours 5 mins
Rest time: 30 mins

15g unsalted butter
1 tbsp olive oil
1 tsp cumin seeds
1 onion, finely chopped
1 fennel bulb, trimmed and finely chopped (feathery fronds chopped and reserved)
75g fresh white breadcrumbs
Zest and juice of 1 unwaxed lemon
1 medium egg, beaten

2 tbsp chopped fresh flat-leaf parsley
2kg boned pork shoulder joint by Sainsbury's, skin scored
1 tsp salt
4 red apples, cored and cut into wedges
2 tbsp plain flour
150ml cider
200ml chicken stock, made with 1 stock cube
Fresh sage leaves (optional), to garnish

1 Heat the butter and oil in a frying pan. Stir in the cumin, onion and fennel, and cook gently for 8-10 mins until softened. Remove from the heat and stir in the breadcrumbs, lemon zest and juice. Cool for 10 mins, then stir in the egg, fennel fronds and parsley. Season.

2 Preheat the oven to 230°C, fan 210°C, gas 8. Open the pork, skin-side down, on a board. Spoon the stuffing down the middle of the pork, then bring the sides of the joint up and around the stuffing so that they meet. Tie tightly at intervals with kitchen string. Transfer to a large roasting tin, and rub the salt all over the skin and into the cuts.

3 Roast for 25 mins then reduce the heat to 180°C, fan 160°C, gas 4, and roast for a further 2-2^1/2 hours, until the pork is cooked and the crackling is crisp. Add the apple wedges for the last 30 mins of roasting time. Transfer to a warm platter, cover and rest for 30 mins.

4 While the pork is resting, make the gravy. Transfer the pan juices to a small pan. Heat until sizzling, then add the flour and stir to form a paste. Pour in the cider, bring to the boil and bubble until reduced by half. Add the stock, bring to the boil and reduce by half again. Transfer to a jug and serve with the pork and apples. Garnish with the sage, if using.

● Per serving (150g pork, plus apples and gravy): 431 cals, 27.9g fat, 9.6g saturates, 6.8g sugars, 15.6g salt

Pulled pork

A delicious slow-roasted joint that melts in the mouth

**Serves 4,
with leftovers**
Prep time:
10 mins, plus
5 hours' chilling
Cook time:
4-4¹/2 hours

1/2 tbsp ground cumin
1/2 tbsp mild chilli powder
1 tbsp paprika
1/2 tbsp light brown soft sugar
Pinch of onion powder
Pinch of garlic powder
1.4kg medium boneless pork shoulder crackling joint by Sainsbury's, skin and most of the fat removed and discarded
2 tbsp vegetable oil

FOR THE BARBECUE SAUCE
300ml passata
5 tbsp clear honey
2 tbsp cider vinegar
2 tbsp Worcestershire sauce
1 1/2 tbsp Dijon mustard
1 tbsp soy sauce
2 tsp garlic purée

1 Combine the spices, sugar, onion and garlic powder in a small bowl. Season with salt and freshly ground black pepper.

2 Rub the pork all over with the spice mixture, making sure it is well coated. Put in a roasting tin lined with foil. Cover with cling film and marinate in the fridge for at least 5 hours or overnight.

3 Remove the pork from the fridge about 45 mins before you want to roast it. Preheat the oven to 150°C, fan 130°C, gas 2. Heat the oil in a large frying pan over medium-high heat and brown the pork all over.

4 Put the pork back into the lined roasting tin and cover tightly with foil. Roast in the oven for 4-4 1/2 hours, turning the joint over after 2 hours and basting it occasionally with any tin juices. The pork is done when it can easily be shredded with two forks.

5 To make the sauce, put all the ingredients in a small pan. Simmer gently over a low heat for 25 mins, stirring frequntly, until thickened. Season with freshly ground black pepper.

● Per serving (150g pulled pork, plus sauce): 459 cals, 28.8g fat, 8.3g saturates, 19.5g sugars, 1.34g salt

Serves 4
Prep time: 30 mins
Cook time: 2 hours

Pot roast pork shanks with leeks & shallots

Take your Sunday lunch to a whole new level with a flavour-packed pot roast of tender pork shanks with cider and root vegetables

---

2 tbsp olive oil

4 pork shanks

400g shallots, peeled

4 leeks, trimmed and cut into chunks

2 medium parsnips, cut into chunks

1 tbsp fennel seeds, lightly crushed

2 tsp coriander seeds, lightly crushed

2 heaped tbsp plain flour

300ml cider

300ml chicken stock

Large handful fresh flat-leaf parsley, leaves picked and chopped

---

1 Preheat the oven to 180°C, fan 160°C, gas 4. Heat 1 tbsp of the oil in a large ovenproof pan or casserole. Add the pork shanks and brown all over. Remove from the pan or casserole and set aside.

2 Heat the remaining oil in the pan or casserole, add the shallots, leeks and parsnips and cook gently for 10 mins until softened. Stir through the fennel and coriander seeds and the flour and cook for 1 min over a medium heat. Stir in the cider and stock then bring to the boil.

3 Return the pork shanks to the pan or casserole, cover with a lid and roast in the oven for 1 hour 15 mins until the meat is tender and coming away from the bone.

4 Garnish with the parsley and serve straight from the pot.

● Per serving: 485 cals, 30.3g fat, 9g saturates, 11.6g sugars, 0.37g salt

Serves 4
Prep time: 10 mins
Cook time:
1 hour 15 mins

Roasted sticky pork rib racks

Impressive on the plate and full of flavour, these sticky roast rib racks are sure to become a family favourite

---

2 x 600g British pork rib
racks by Sainsbury's
4 tbsp maple syrup
4 1/2 tbsp dark brown soft sugar
1 1/2 tsp ground cinnamon

2 tsp mild chilli powder
1/2 tsp cayenne pepper
1 tsp garlic granules
Cooked corn on the cob, to serve

---

1 Preheat the oven to 180°C, fan 160°C, gas 4. Line a large roasting tin with foil and put the ribs in the tin.

2 Put the maple syrup, sugar, cinnamon, chilli powder and garlic granules in a small bowl. Add a generous pinch of salt and some freshly ground black pepper and whisk in 2 tbsp water until thoroughly combined. Transfer 4 tbsp of this mixture to a small pan and set aside. Brush the rest of the mixture all over the racks and cover the roasting tin with foil. Roast in the oven for 45 mins.

3 Increase the oven temperature to 200°C, fan 180°C, gas 6. Remove the foil and return the roasting tin to the oven for a further 30 mins, basting the racks with any juices. About 5 mins before the end of the cooking time, put the small pan with the remaining sauce over a high heat and let it bubble for 2-3 mins until it is thick and syrupy.

4 Remove the ribs from the oven and brush the thickened sauce all over them. Transfer to a serving board or platter, drizzle any sticky marinade from the tin onto the ribs and serve with the corn cobs.

● Per serving: 432 cals, 23.8g fat, 8.2g saturates, 26.3g sugars, 0.23g salt

Cook's tip
Ribs are a great warm-weather roast. As well as corn on the cob, coleslaw is a good dish to serve on the side. Try our recipe on p102.

"Meaty, sticky pork ribs with a sweet and spicy glaze"

Serves 4
Prep time:
20 mins, plus 30
mins' chilling and
15 mins' cooling
Cook time:
45-50 mins
Rest time: 15 mins

Roast pork tenderloin wrapped in pancetta

For a quicker way to enjoy a pork roast, try tender, juicy pork loins

1 tbsp vegetable oil
Knob of butter
1 onion, finely chopped
1 tbsp chopped fresh sage, plus extra
leaves to garnish

50g fresh white breadcrumbs
2 x 350g British pork tenderloin
fillets by Sainsbury's
210g smoked pancetta
Cranberry sauce, to serve

1 Heat the oil and butter in a frying pan and fry the onion for 5-6 mins until softened. Remove from the heat and stir in the chopped sage and breadcrumbs. Season with salt and freshly ground black pepper and leave to cool for 15 mins.

2 Put the pork tenderloins on a board and thoroughly pat dry with kitchen paper. Remove any sinew from the meat. Place a sheet of greaseproof paper over the tenderloins and bash them with a rolling pin until slightly flattened. Spoon the stuffing in a line down the centre of one of the flattened tenderloins. Put the second tenderloin on top, pressing down to sandwich the stuffing.

3 Stretch each pancetta rasher with the back of a knife and arrange them, overlapping, on a large sheet of greased foil to make a rectangle measuring about 25cm x 30cm. Put the stuffed pork tenderloins in the centre of the rectangle and bring the pancetta rashers up each side of the pork to completely enclose it. Wrap tightly in the foil and chill in the fridge for 30 mins.

4 Preheat the oven to 200ºC, fan 180ºC, gas 6. Unwrap the pork and place in a foil-lined roasting tin, making sure the joins of pancetta are underneath. Roast for 40-45 mins or until the pancetta is crisp and the pork is cooked through. Cover loosely with foil after 30 mins if the pancetta is over-browning. Transfer to a warm platter, cover and let rest for 15 mins. Garnish with sage leaves and serve with cranberry sauce.

● Per serving: 606 cals, 33.4g fat, 10g saturates, 2.9g total sugars, 2.24g salt

Ready in 15 mins
Pulled pork & coleslaw rolls

Better than a burger and tastier than a sandwich. Tender pork and crunchy coleslaw combine for a mouthwatering lunchtime option

Serves 4

Prep time: 15 mins

1 carrot, finely grated

1 Braeburn apple, cored and finely grated

Zest and juice of 1 lemon

100g red cabbage, shredded

1/2 red onion, finely sliced

2 tbsp mayonnaise

3 tbsp natural yogurt

1/2 tsp Dijon mustard

Handful of fresh flat-leaf parsley, chopped

4 ciabatta rolls

400g leftover pulled pork (see recipe p94), shredded

4 tbsp barbecue sauce

1 To make the coleslaw, put the grated carrot and apple in a bowl along with the lemon zest and juice, cabbage, onion, mayonnaise, yogurt and Dijon mustard. Season with salt and freshly ground black pepper and mix together. Stir through the parsley.

2 Halve the ciabatta rolls, and fill with the shredded pork and coleslaw. Drizzle over the sauce then sandwich together. Serve any remaining coleslaw in a bowl on the side.

● Per serving: 507 cals, 15.1g fat, 3.5g saturates, 14.2g sugars, 1.38g salt

Cook's tip
Bring the leftover pulled pork to room temperature before filling the roll.

Ready in 20 mins

Pork & egg fried rice

This speedy supper is made even speedier by using microwaveable rice. If you don't have any, use regular rice – cook to pack instructions before getting started on the stir-fry

Serves 4

Prep time: 10 mins

Cook time: 10 mins

---

1 tbsp toasted sesame oil

2cm piece fresh root ginger, peeled and finely grated

1 clove garlic, crushed

6 spring onions, trimmed and finely chopped

250g leftover roast pork, diced

125g frozen peas, defrosted

2 x 250g packs microwaveable long grain rice, cooked to pack instructions

2 tbsp light soy sauce, plus extra to serve

2 medium eggs, beaten

1 Heat 2 tsp of the sesame oil in a large wok or non-stick frying pan until almost smoking. Add the ginger, garlic and nearly all the spring onions, and stir-fry over a high heat for 1 min.

2 Add the diced pork and stir-fry for a further 1-2 mins until crisp and browned. Add the peas, rice and soy sauce and stir-fry for 2-3 mins until the rice is piping hot.

3 Move the rice mixture to one side of the wok and add the rest of the sesame oil. Pour in the beaten egg and leave for a few seconds until cooked through. Using chopsticks or a fork, break up the egg and quickly stir it into the rice. Serve in warmed bowls, garnished with the remaining spring onion and with extra soy sauce to taste.

● Per serving: 421 cals, 12.2g fat, 3.3g saturates, 2.6g sugars, 1.65g salt

Cook's tip
Use the edge of a teaspoon to peel root ginger – it gently scrapes away the papery skin, but leaves the flesh intact.

Ready in 40 mins
Pork quesadillas

A bright and flavoursome leftover roast pork recipe that will bring a little taste of Mexico to your plate – and it couldn't be easier to make

Serves 4

Prep time: 15 mins

Cook time: 25 mins

1 tbsp olive oil

1 large onion, sliced

1 red, 1 yellow and 1 orange pepper, deseeded and thinly sliced

2 tbsp chipotle chilli paste by Sainsbury's

1 tsp ground cumin

300g leftover roast pork, roughly shredded

200g cherry tomatoes, quartered

8 flour tortillas

6 spring onions, trimmed and finely sliced

Large handful of fresh coriander, roughly chopped

100g be good to yourself Cheddar, grated

Green salad, to serve

100g cucumber, sliced into rounds and halved, to serve

Smoky chipotle & lime salsa by Sainsbury's (optional), to serve

1 Heat the oil in a large frying pan, add the onion and peppers and sauté for 5 mins. Stir through the chipotle and cumin and cook for 30 secs. Add the pork and tomatoes and cook for 2-3 mins until the pork is piping hot. Remove from the heat and keep warm.

2 Put another large non-stick frying pan over a medium heat and add a tortilla to the pan. Spoon over a quarter of the pork mixture then scatter over a quarter each of the spring onions, coriander and Cheddar. Top with another tortilla and press down firmly. Cook for 1 1/2 mins then flip the quesadilla over and cook for a further 1 1/2 mins until the tortilla is crisp and golden and the cheese has melted. Slide onto a plate and cover to keep warm. Repeat with the remaining tortillas and filling so you have 4 quesadillas.

3 Cut into quarters and serve with the salad and salsa, if using.

● Per serving: 563 cals, 19g fat, 7.5g saturates, 14.6g sugars, 1.82g salt

Pork ragù with tagliatelle

This rustic pasta dish is hearty and filling – and using leftover roast pork cuts down
on the cooking time of a traditional ragù, too

Serves 4

Prep time: 10 mins

Cook time: 45 mins

---

2 tbsp olive oil

1 onion, chopped

2 cloves garlic, finely chopped

2 fresh bay leaves

200ml red wine

2 x 390g cartons Italian
chopped tomatoes in
tomato juice

1 tsp caster sugar

A few fresh thyme sprigs, leaves
picked, plus extra to garnish

500ml vegetable stock, made
with 1 stock cube

500g leftover roast pork,
roughly chopped

350g tagliatelle

Parmesan shavings, to serve

❄ Freezer tip
Leave the ragù to
cool completely then
freeze in an airtight
container for up to
3 months. Defrost
completely (overnight
in the fridge) before
reheating in a pan
until piping hot.

1 Heat the oil in a large pan over a medium heat. Add the onion
and fry for 2-3 mins, until softened. Add the garlic and bay
leaves and cook for a further 2 mins.

2 Pour in the red wine, bring to the boil and bubble for 2 mins, or
until reduced by about half. Add the chopped tomatoes, sugar
and thyme leaves and stir well. Season with salt and freshly
ground black pepper and cook for a further 5 mins.

3 Stir in the stock and the leftover pork. Simmer, covered, for about
30 mins, until the ragù is quite thick, stirring occasionally.

4 Meanwhile, cook the tagliatelle according to pack instructions
and drain well. Toss the pork ragù through the tagliatelle until
coated all over. Divide between 4 bowls and serve garnished with
the extra thyme and the parmesan shavings.

● Per serving: 520 cals, 17.3g fat, 6.5g saturates, 9.4g sugars, 1.10g salt

**Serves 6,
with leftovers**
Prep time: 25 mins
Cook time: 2 hours
Rest time: 15 mins

Classic roast gammon

This spiced gammon can be served warm or cold with homemade chutney

2kg gammon joint, boned and rolled

1 onion, peeled and quartered

2 dried bay leaves

12 black peppercorns

500ml clear apple juice

40g demerara sugar

$1/4$ tsp dried chilli flakes

$1/2$ tsp coriander seeds, lightly crushed

$1/2$ tsp cumin seeds, lightly crushed

1 tbsp Dijon mustard

FOR THE CHUTNEY

1 tsp coriander seeds, lightly crushed

$1/2$ tsp cumin seeds, lightly crushed

$1/4$ tsp dried chilli flakes

1 tbsp sunflower oil

1 medium onion, finely chopped

2 medium mangoes, peeled, destoned
and finely diced

3 tbsp light soft brown sugar

4 tbsp white wine vinegar

1 Put the gammon in a deep pan, cover with cold water and bring
to the boil. Drain off the water and add the onion, bay leaves,
peppercorns and apple juice to the pan. Top up with cold water
to cover the gammon, and bring to the boil. Reduce the heat and
simmer for 1 $1/2$ hours, topping up the water level as needed.

2 Remove the gammon, discard the stock and cool slightly. Preheat the
oven to 220°C, fan 200°C, gas 7. Cut away the skin and discard, leaving
a layer of fat on the gammon. Score the fat in diamond shapes.

3 Mix the demerara sugar with the chilli and coriander and cumin seeds.
Using a pastry brush, smear the mustard over the gammon fat, then
pat on the sugar mixture. Put on a baking tray lined with greaseproof
paper, and roast for 20 mins until the skin is glazed and golden.

4 Meanwhile, make the chutney. Mix the coriander and cumin seeds
with the chilli flakes. Put the spices in heavy-based pan and dry-fry
until the aromas are released, then remove from the pan. Add the
oil and onion to the pan and cook over a medium heat for 5 mins.
Add the spices, mango, sugar, vinegar and 200ml water. Simmer
for 20 mins until thickened. Transfer to a bowl and let cool before
serving with slices of the warm or cold gammon.

● Per serving (150g gammon, plus chutney): 453 cals, 18.3g fat,
6g saturates, 5.87g sugars, 33.3g salt

Ginger beer & pear glazed gammon

Serves 6,
with leftovers
Prep time: 25 mins
Cook time:
2 hours 30 mins –
2 hours 40 mins
Rest time: 15 mins

This warming ginger beer-glazed ham topped with overlapping slices of pear is the perfect centrepiece for Boxing Day buffets

2kg gammon joint by Sainsbury's
1 fresh bay leaf
Few black peppercorns
1 small onion, halved
150ml runny honey
4 tbsp wholegrain mustard

200ml ginger beer
2 large pears, cored and very thinly sliced using a mandoline if you have one
Potato and celeriac mash (see recipe p156), to serve
Steamed broccoli, to serve

1 Put the gammon in a large deep pan and cover with cold water. Add the bay leaf, peppercorns and onion and bring to the boil. Skim off any scum that forms on the surface then cover and simmer gently for 1 hour, topping up with boiling water, if needed.

2 Preheat the oven to 180ºC, fan 160ºC, gas 4. Remove the gammon from the liquid and set aside until it's cool enough to handle. Cut away and discard the skin and nearly all the fat. Wrap the joint loosely in lightly oiled foil, put in a large roasting tin and roast for 1 hour.

3 Meanwhile, make the glaze. Put the honey, mustard and ginger beer in a pan and bring to the boil. Reduce the heat and simmer for 40-45 mins until thickened, sticky and reduced by half. Leave to cool for 10 mins.

4 Remove the roasting tin from the oven and uncover the gammon. Brush liberally with some of the glaze. Arrange the pear slices, overlapping slightly, all over the top of the gammon joint. Carefully brush with more of the glaze then return to the oven. Roast, uncovered, for 30-40 mins until the pears are tender and golden, basting occasionally with any remaining glaze.

5 Remove the gammon from the oven. Cover and leave to rest for 15 mins before carving. Serve with potato and celeriac mash and broccoli.

● Per serving (150g gammon): 365 cals, 16.8g fat, 5.8g saturates, 16.7g sugars, 6.04g salt

Ready in 1 hour

Gammon & leek pie

Leftover roast gammon is delicious with pastry, and because the meat is already cooked, you'll cut down on the time you'd normally spend making a pie

Serves 4
Prep time: 10 mins, plus cooling
Cook time: 45-50 mins

30g unsalted butter

1 large onion, roughly chopped

3 leeks, trimmed and sliced

2 potatoes, peeled and diced

3 cloves garlic, crushed

2 tbsp plain flour, plus extra

100ml white wine

200ml chicken stock, made with 1 stock cube

150ml half-fat crème fraîche

1 tbsp wholegrain mustard

250g leftover roast gammon, roughly chopped

198g tin sweetcorn, drained

400g puff pastry (use lighter if you prefer)

1 medium egg, lightly beaten

1 Melt the butter in a pan over a medium heat then add the onion, leeks and potatoes. Cook for 10 mins, stirring occasionally, until softened. Add the garlic and cook for a further 1 min.

2 Stir in the flour and cook for 30 secs. Gradually stir in the wine and stock, and simmer for 5 mins.

3 Remove from the heat, season with salt and freshly ground black pepper and stir in the crème fraîche, mustard, gammon and sweetcorn. Spoon into a 1.5-litre pie dish and cool for 10 mins.

4 Preheat the oven to 220°C, fan 200°C, gas 7. Dust a work surface with flour and roll out the pastry to a 3mm thickness. Brush the rim of the pie dish with egg, then drape the pastry over the top. Trim off any excess pastry and crimp the edge with a fork to seal. Brush with beaten egg and bake for 25-30 mins.

● Per serving: 840 cals, 43.4g fat, 22.2g saturates, 11.6g sugars, 3.87g salt

Ready in 30 mins

Pea & gammon soup

A great winter warmer, this comforting soup is on the table in half an hour.
Serve with plenty of crusty bread for a really satisfying meal

Serves 4

Prep time: 10 mins

Cook time: 20 mins

1 tbsp olive oil

1 onion, finely chopped

1 clove garlic, crushed

250g potatoes, peeled
and diced

400ml ham or chicken stock,
made with 1 stock cube

500g frozen petits pois

200ml whole milk

1 tbsp chopped fresh mint
leaves, plus a few extra
whole leaves to garnish

150g leftover roast gammon,
half finely chopped and half
roughly torn

Crusty bread, to serve

1 Heat the oil in a large pan and gently sauté the onion for
   5 mins until softened but not coloured, adding the garlic for
   the final 1 minute of the cooking time.

2 Stir in the potatoes, pour over the stock and bring to the boil.
   Reduce the heat and simmer for 10 mins until the potatoes are
   tender. Stir in the peas, bring to the boil and cook for 2 mins.

3 Remove from the heat and season with salt and freshly ground
   black pepper. Stir in the milk and chopped mint and leave to cool
   slightly. Using a hand-held blender, whiz the soup until smooth.

4 Stir the chopped gammon through the soup and divide between
   4 bowls. Garnish with the torn gammon pieces and mint leaves
   and serve with the crusty bread.

● Per serving: 400 cals, 8.6g fat, 2.9g saturates, 9g sugars, 2.75g salt

Cook's tip
For a really decadent
soup, you could stir
through single cream
instead of milk.

fish

Choosing and roasting
fish...

Roasted fish is a pretty special addition to the dinner table. It's the perfect dish for warmer weather, and is also good if you're looking to enjoy a roast dinner with fewer calories than a meat or poultry roast, but still want the wow factor

White fish
Delicate and flaky, white fish is great for roasting. It is naturally lower in fat than other types of fish, and tends to work better with subtle, delicate flavours. Classic choices include cod, sea bass and sea bream, but there are plenty more options to experiment with. You could try meatier monkfish, which can handle more robust flavours than its counterparts, or sustainable and less expensive fish like pollock and coley. They all roast well either on the bone, or filleted.

Perfect partners...
Black pepper; parsley and dill; lemons, oranges, grapefruit, and tomatoes; white wine.

Oily fish
The perfect choice if you're looking for a fish that can hold its own against rich, bold flavours. A whole roast salmon stuffed with fresh breadcrumbs and herbs looks fantastic, while mackerel has enjoyed a surge in popularity. Oily fish is a source of Omega-3 fatty acids, and vitamins A and D, and it's recommended that we eat 1 portion a week.

Perfect partners...
Black pepper; garlic, ginger and chilli; fennel and citrus fruits.

Sustainable fish
Conserving the world's fish stocks has become an increasingly important issue in recent years. Responsible fishing practices help to ensure that fish stocks remain healthy for future generations. To ensure the fish you buy is from sustainable sources, look for the Marine Stewardship Council logo on packacking. As part of our ongoing commitment to sustainable fishing, Sainsbury's is aiming to sell only MSC-certified fish by 2020.

Cook's tip
Before cooking fish, rub it all over with lemon juice. Not only will this add to the flavour, it will also help to keep the colour bright.

Roasting tips and tricks...

Q **How do I know when fish is cooked?**

When fish is cooked, the flesh is opaque and will have lost all translucence. For a fillet, press the thickest part - it should have lost the firmness it had prior to roasting. When checking that a whole fish is cooked, make a small slit next to the dorsal fin (the one on top of the fish) and lift the flesh with the flat of the knife – it should be opaque all the way through and still moist.

Q **Is it possible to get a crisp skin without overcooking the fish?**

Roasting whole fish should give you a lovely crisp skin, but when a fish is small the flesh may be cooked before the skin's had a chance to crisp up. Before roasting, cut a few slashes in the top so that the cut edges catch some colour, brush all over with oil, and season. If the fish is small, or if it hasn't crisped up when nearing the end of roasting time, pop it under a hot grill for the last few minutes of cooking.

Q **What's the best way to marinate whole fish?**

Cutting slits in the skin before brushing on the marinade will help the flavours infuse all the way into the fish. Season, and add a little oil to compensate for any moisture that might be lost during cooking. Marinate for 30 minutes only - any longer and the acidity you find in most marinades can make the fish soft and mushy in texture.

Q **Will roasting fish dry it out?**

When roasting fish, there's a fine line between cooking it perfectly and overcooking it completely. If you're roasting steaks, fillets or loins, they are susceptible to drying out. Brush with melted butter and, unless they have a crust or topping, cover them with a piece of lightly buttered foil. As for whole fish, it will be succulent if you stuff the cavity and brush it all over with butter or oil.

Q **How should I store fresh fish after buying?**

After purchasing, rewrap fresh fish tightly in plastic wrap or put in an airtight container, and store in the coldest part of the fridge. Cook as soon as you can.

Roasting on the bone

Bones can put a lot of people off roasting whole fish, but you'll get far greater flavour if you do...

- A fish that's roasted with the skin and bones, head and tail intact will have a greater concentration of flavours. These also protect the flesh and keep it moist and tender. Plus, there's a very thin layer of healthy fat just below the skin, which also helps keep flesh tender.
- Stuffing the cavity of a whole fish is great way to infuse the delicately flavoured flesh. Go for herbs and citrus slices.
- To serve, gently lift the top fillet off the bone then flip over the fish to serve the other fillet.

Serves 4,
with leftovers
Prep time: 15 mins
Cook time: 40 mins

Stuffed roast salmon

An impressive but easy way to roast whole sides of salmon

50g unsalted butter
2 red onions, finely chopped
1 clove garlic, crushed
140g sundried tomatoes, drained
and chopped
225g fresh white breadcrumbs

6 tbsp chopped fresh flat-leaf parsley,
plus extra leaves to garnish
2 tbsp olive oil
2 x 700g salmon fillets
Lemon wedges, to garnish
Steamed asparagus and beans, to serve

1 Melt the butter in a large frying pan, add the onions and garlic and
cook for 6-8 mins until softened. Transfer to a large bowl and add the
sundried tomatoes, breadcrumbs and chopped parsley. Season with
salt and freshly ground black pepper and mix until combined. Let cool.

2 Preheat the oven to 180°C, fan 160°C, gas 4. Drizzle 1 tbsp of the
olive oil in a large roasting tin. Lay 3 long pieces of kitchen string in
the roasting tin and place 1 of the salmon fillets, skin-side down, on
top of the string.

3 Spread the cooled breadcrumb mixture over the top of the salmon,
pressing down firmly so that it's compact. Score the skin of the
second fillet using a sharp knife and position it, skin-side up, on top
of the stuffing. Tie the kitchen string to secure the salmon pieces
together and drizzle all over with the remaining oil. Season with a
little salt and freshly ground black pepper and roast for 30 mins or
until the salmon flakes easily and the skin is beginning to crisp (for
extra-crisp skin, pop under a hot grill for 1-2 mins).

4 Carefully transfer to a large serving plate, garnish with the extra
parsley and the lemon wedges. Serve with steamed asparagus and
fine beans, if you like.

● Per serving (230g salmon, plus stuffing): 693 cals, 39.4g fat, 12.3g saturates,
7.4g sugars, 0.54g salt

Tender salmon with crisp skin is perfect for special occasions

Salmon en croute

A stunning centrepiece that's easier to make than you might think

280g plain flour
140g unsalted butter, chilled and cubed
1 medium egg, beaten with 1 tbsp water
200g young leaf spinach
250g ricotta
50g toasted pine nuts

Zest 1 unwaxed lemon
Freshly grated nutmeg
500g skinless, boneless salmon fillet,
about 25cm long, cut from the middle
of the fish

1 Put the flour and butter in a food processor; whiz until the mixture resembles breadcrumbs. Add most of the egg mixture and pulse until a soft dough forms – if it's too dry, add more of the egg. Remove from the bowl, wrap in cling film and chill in the fridge for 30 mins.

2 Put the spinach in a pan with 1 tbsp water, cover with a lid and cook over a medium heat for 2 mins until wilted. Drain in a colander, then press out as much water as possible, using a wooden spoon. Chop the spinach finely and put in a bowl with the ricotta, pine nuts, lemon zest and a little grated nutmeg. Season well and mix until combined.

3 Preheat the oven to 190°C, fan 170°C, gas 5. Cut the pastry dough in half, then roll out each piece on a lightly floured surface into a rectangle measuring about 35cm x 22cm (or about 6cm longer and 6cm wider than the salmon) to the thickness of a £1 coin. Transfer to a baking sheet lined with baking parchment. Spread the ricotta mixture down the centre of the pastry, to the same size as the salmon, leaving a 3cm border all around.

4 Lay the salmon on top of the ricotta mixture, brush the pastry border with some of the remaining egg, and top with the remaining pastry sheet. Press the edges together with a fork to seal. Trim off the excess, leaving a 2cm edge around the salmon. Brush all over with the remaining egg, then score a fish scale pattern into the pastry using the edge of a spoon. Bake for 35-40 mins until golden.

● Per serving: 646 cals, 41.8g fat, 19.3g saturates, 3g total sugars, 0.31g salt

Roast lemon sole with caper sauce

Serves 4
Prep time: 10 mins
Cook time:
15-20 mins

Whole fish roasts really well, and it looks spectacular on the plate, too. Bring out the delicate flavour of lemon sole with this easy roast

4 whole lemon sole
1 tbsp olive oil
2 small unwaxed lemons, quartered
150ml soured cream

1 tsp Dijon mustard
2 tbsp capers, drained and rinsed
3 tbsp chopped fresh flat-leaf parsley

1 Preheat the oven to 200°C, fan 180°C, gas 6. Put the sole on a lightly greased baking tray and cut slashes into the flesh of each. Drizzle over the oil and squeeze over all but 1 of the lemon quarters, then add them to the tray. Roast for 15-20 mins or until the fish flakes easily.

2 Meanwhile, put the soured cream, mustard, capers and half the parsley in a pan and heat gently. Squeeze in the juice from the last lemon quarter and season with freshly ground black pepper.

3 Pour the sauce over the fish and garnish with the rest of the chopped parsley and more freshly ground black pepper.

● Per serving: 210 cals, 11.5g fat, 4.9g saturates, 2.4g sugars, 1.06g salt

Roast sea bass

Preheat the oven to 200°C, fan 180°C, gas 6. Cut 1 lemon and 1/2 a fennel bulb into thin slices and stuff into the cavities of 2 whole sea bass, reserving 2 lemon slices. Season with salt and freshly ground black pepper. Top with the reserved lemon slices and a fresh bay leaf, and tie with kitchen string to secure. In a medium roasting tin, toss together 250g cherry tomatoes (halved), 1 red onion (cut into wedges), 100g pitted black olives, 6 cloves garlic (unpeeled) and 1 lemon (cut into wedges). Drizzle with 1 tbsp olive oil. Put the fish on top of the veg, brush all over with olive oil and roast for 20 mins.

Serves 6 Prep time: 10 mins Cook time: 20 mins

Per serving: 309 cals, 12.6g fat, 1.9g saturates, 5.3g sugars, 1.14g salt

Roast monkfish tails with mushrooms

Monkfish is great to roast as it's quite meaty. It's robust, too, so holds its own against the strong flavour of roasted pancetta and mushrooms

---

2 x 350g whole monkfish tails, skin and fine membrane removed (leave bone in)
1 tbsp olive oil
15g butter
1/2 x 260g pack cubetti di pancetta

2 cloves garlic, crushed
300g mini portabella mushrooms
Few sprigs fresh thyme
175ml white wine

---

1 Preheat the oven to 200°C, fan 180°C, gas 6. Pat the monkfish tails dry with kitchen paper then season all over with salt and freshly ground black pepper.

2 Heat the oil and butter in a large frying pan and add the monkfish. Sear over a high heat for 1-2 mins, turning once. Transfer to a roasting tin.

3 Add the pancetta to the frying pan and fry for 3-4 mins until just starting to go brown and crisp. Remove with a slotted spoon and set aside. Add the garlic to the pan and fry for 1-2 mins until softened then add the mushrooms and thyme and toss to coat in the garlicky mixture. Spoon into the roasting tin around the monkfish then pour over the wine. Scatter over the fried pancetta.

4 Roast for 30-35 mins until the monkfish is firm and cooked through and the mushrooms are tender. To serve, separate each tail along the bone so you have 4 portions in total.

● Per serving: 271 cals, 14.8g fat, 5.6g saturates, 0.5g total sugars, 1.04g salt

Roast cod loins

Meaty cod loins – and alternative white fish like coley and pollock – roast well. This quick and easy dish is overflowing with rustic Italian flavours

Serves 4
Prep time: 15 mins
Cook time: 30 mins

450g new potatoes, scrubbed and sliced
3 tbsp olive oil
Zest and juice of 1 unwaxed lemon
2 courgettes, trimmed and thickly sliced
225g red cherry tomatoes on the vine
100g yellow pomodorino tomatoes

Handful of pitted black olives
75g white bread, torn
4 tbsp chopped fresh flat-leaf parsley, plus extra to garnish
4 x 150g skinless and boneless cod loins
Lemon wedges, to serve

1 Preheat the oven to 220°C, fan 200°C, gas 7. In a medium roasting tin, toss the potatoes with half of the oil, the lemon juice and some salt and freshly ground black pepper. Roast for 15 mins. Add the courgettes, tomatoes and olives, and roast for a further 15 mins.

2 Meanwhile, put the bread, remaining oil, zest and parsley in a food processor. Season and pulse until you have a crumb mixture. Put the cod in a roasting tin; top with the breadcrumbs. Roast alongside the veg for 8-10 mins until the crumbs are golden and the fish is cooked through.

3 Serve the cod garnished with the extra parsley and the roasted veg and lemon wedges on the side.

● Per serving: 355 cals, 11.6g fat, 1.7g saturates, 4.7g sugars, 0.97g salt

Crispy cod & pesto parcels

Preheat the oven to 200°C, fan 180°C, gas 6. Lay a filo pastry sheet on a work surface, with the shortest end facing you. Brush all over with melted butter, then fold in half. Place a 150g skinless and boneless cod fillet at the end nearest to you, season with pepper and spread with 1 tsp pesto. Fold the sides of the pastry over the fish to completely enclose, and brush all over with melted butter. Repeat to make 6 parcels in total. Transfer the parcels to a baking sheet and bake for 20-25 mins until crisp and golden. Serve with steamed green beans tossed with toasted sesame seeds and lemon wedges.

Serves 6 Prep time: 20 mins Cook time: 20-25 mins

Per parcel: 299 cals, 12.7g fat, 6.2g saturates, 2.6g sugars, 0.56g salt

Ready in 1 hour 15 mins

Potato-topped salmon pie

Leftover roast fish works perfectly in this crowd-pleasing family pie. We've used salmon, but you could use any leftover fish – just check for bones beforehand

Serves 4

Prep time: 20 mins

Cook time: 45-55 mins

100g young leaf spinach

40g unsalted butter

1 onion, finely chopped

1 clove garlic, crushed

40g plain flour

568ml semi-skimmed milk

4 hardboiled eggs, peeled and cut into quarters

240g leftover roast salmon, cut into bite-size chunks

40g capers, drained and roughly chopped

Handful of fresh dill, chopped

400g Maris Piper potatoes, sliced into thin rounds, using a mandoline if you have one

1 tbsp olive oil

1 Preheat the oven to 200°C, fan 180°C, gas 6.

2 In a large pan over a medium heat, wilt the spinach with a little water. Drain and squeeze out any excess water. Set aside.

3 In another large pan, melt the butter. Add the onion and cook for 5 mins, adding the garlic for the last minute. Stir in the flour and cook for 1-2 mins. Remove from the heat and slowly whisk in the milk. When all the milk has been added, return the pan to the heat. Simmer for 5 mins, stirring, until thickened. Season.

4 Gently stir in the eggs, salmon, capers, cooked spinach and dill. Tip into a 1.5-litre pie dish. Arrange the potatoes over the top, and brush all over with the oil. Bake for 30-40 mins until the potato top is crisp and golden.

● Per serving: 519 cals, 27.9g fat, 10.6g saturates, 10.3g sugars, 1.32g salt

Cook's tip
Make this even easier to prepare by topping with a couple of packs of ready-made mashed potato before putting into the oven.

Salmon, spinach & lemon risotto

Midweek meals don't get simpler than this one-pot dish – it uses leftover roast salmon flakes and is packed with zesty flavours

Serves 4

Prep time: 10 mins

Cook time: 30 mins

---

1 tbsp olive oil

2 leeks, trimmed and sliced

1 clove garlic, finely chopped

250g arborio risotto rice

50ml white wine (optional)

1.25 litres hot vegetable stock, made using 1 stock cube

Zest and juice of 1 unwaxed lemon

200g young leaf spinach

25g parmesan, grated

240g leftover roast salmon, flaked into pieces with a fork

Cook's tip
To get a really glossy finish on your risotto, stir a knob of butter through the rice at the same time as you add the lemon juice.

1 Heat the oil in a large pan, add the leeks and cook for 10 mins until translucent. Add the garlic and risotto rice for the last minute. Stir until the rice is coated, then pour in the wine (if using) and let bubble until the liquid has almost disappeared.

2 Gradually add the hot stock, a ladleful at a time. When the rice absorbs the liquid, you can add another ladle or so, stirring often. Continue cooking until the rice is plump and creamy but still has a little bite left in it – this should take about 20 mins. Stir in the lemon juice and most of the zest, the spinach and the grated parmesan. Season with freshly ground black pepper.

4 Gently stir the flaked salmon pieces through the risotto, scatter over the remaining lemon zest and serve.

● Per serving: 438 cals, 14.1g fat, 3.9g saturates, 2.1g sugars, 0.30g salt

vegetarian mains

Ideas for

vegetarian mains...

Make a vegetarian dish the centrepiece of your roast dinner. With a little inspiration and great fresh produce, you can create a vegetarian main that everyone will love

Nut roasts

Nut roasts haven't always had the best reputation, but these days they're a world away from their dry, bland image. Served with all the trimmings, they really look the part for a special occasion such as Christmas. Try using a variety of nuts and seeds, and add flavour with herbs and spices, or other flavoursome ingredients, such as artichokes and shallots.

Perfect partners...
Parsley and sage; garlic; cranberries; traditional roasted vegetables; vegetarian gravy.

Pastries and tarts

Pastry parcels can be packed full of goodies like spinach and mushroom, while tarts look colourful and vibrant on the plate. They're easy to make and incredibly versatile. Make an individual tart for a single guest, or create a family-sized one for sharing. Strong flavours work well – try ingredients like blue cheese, asparagus, aubergines, caramelised onions or roasted tomatoes.

Stuffed vegetables

Simple and satisfying, stuffed and roasted vegetables make a filling supper that can be customised in so many different ways. From butternut squash to peppers, aubergines to courgettes, there are plenty of options. Popular stuffing ingredients include rice and breadcrumbs, but try couscous, barley, quinoa and nuts for variety. Pack in plenty of flavour with lots of fresh herbs, or for a Mediterranean twist, add olives, sundried tomatoes and toasted pine nuts.

Perfect partners...
A fresh green salad is a great accompaniment for most vegetarian dishes.

Cook's tip
Make tarts more interesting by layering flavours and textures – try a layer of roasted pumpkin, then a layer of ricotta cheese, followed by spinach and caramelised onions.

Roasting tips and tricks...

Q How do I stop my nut roast falling apart when I cut it?

One method is to roast your loaf in advance and pop it in the fridge. Take it out of the fridge before serving and slice while still cool – it will be much firmer than when it's hot. Once sliced, you can reheat and serve.

Q How can I add texture to my dish?

If your vegetarian main doesn't seem particularly exciting, try adding nuts or seeds to give it some extra bite. Plus, they'll add lots of extra flavour, too. Try flaked almonds, pine nuts, pistachios and sunflower seeds. Toast them lightly before adding them to release the flavours.

Q How do I get the pastry on my tarts to be crisp?

Vegetables tend to release a lot of liquid, so for chunkier veg, or dishes like quiches, a shortcrust pastry is best. Blind bake the pastry case in the tin (without the filling) for 20 mins to partially cook the pastry before putting the filling in and then baking again. Puff pastry is great for lighter, thinly cut veg such as mushrooms, or vegetables that have already been roasted. Brush the pastry with beaten egg before putting the topping on – this will help seal it against moisture. Also, make sure your oven is hot enough, and don't underbake.

Veggie tip

Mushrooms are a favourite choice for veggie dishes because, as well as having loads of flavour, they also have an interesting, almost meaty texture. Try roasting large, flat mushrooms, then topping with a herb-flavoured butter, or use them as the base for a tart filling.

Cooking for vegetarians

If you're not used to making meat-free meals, cooking for a vegetarian can be a little daunting, especially when you're making a meat-based roast dinner for others. Here are some basics to remember.

- Keep things separate. Use different utensils and work surfaces, and wash your hands thoroughly after handling meat.
- Keep an eye on the ingredients you use. Make alternative gravy with a meat-free stock and don't roast your potatoes in animal fat. Check the packaging of your ingredients if you're unsure.
- Try to make sure there's a protein element to vegetarian dishes – nuts, eggs, soya and pulses are all good ways to add protein.

Serves 6
Prep time: 30 mins
Cook time: 35 mins
Rest time: 10 mins

Classic nut roast

The addition of toasted seeds makes this nut roast extra special

2 tbsp olive oil
1 large onion, chopped
2 cloves garlic, chopped
250g closed cup mushrooms, chopped
150g walnut halves, chopped, plus an extra 50g left whole
150g shelled pistachios, chopped, plus an extra 50g left whole
100g fresh wholemeal breadcrumbs
50g toasted sunflower seeds
50g toasted pumpkin seeds
1 tsp chopped fresh thyme

1 medium egg, beaten
1 tbsp soy sauce
75g extra-mature Cheddar, grated
20g butter
Chopped fresh curly parsley, to garnish

FOR THE VEGGIE GRAVY
20g butter
20g plain flour
1 tsp yeast extract by Sainsbury's
1 tbsp redcurrant jelly
400ml vegetable stock

1 Preheat the oven to 180°C, fan 160°C, gas 4. Grease a 1.5-litre loaf tin and line the base with a strip of greaseproof paper. Heat the oil in a frying pan over a medium heat, add the onion, garlic and mushrooms and cook gently for 8-10 mins until softened

2 Mix together the mushroom mixture, chopped nuts, breadcrumbs, seeds, thyme, egg, soy sauce and cheese until combined. Season.

3 Tip into the loaf tin, pressing down firmly. Roast for 35 mins, or until the loaf is set. Rest for 10 mins while you make the gravy.

4 In a medium pan, melt the butter and stir in the flour. Cook over a medium heat for 2-3 mins until the mixture is thick and smells biscuity. Stir in the yeast extract and redcurant jelly. Remove from the heat and stir in the vegetable stock. Return the pan to the hob and bring to a simmer. Cook for 5 mins until you have a smooth and velvety gravy. Season with salt and freshly ground black pepper.

5 Turn the nut loaf out onto a serving plate. Toss the whole nuts in a frying pan over a low heat for 1-2 mins then stir in the butter until melted. Scatter the nuts over the top of the loaf, and garnish with parsley. Serve sliced with the gravy and your choice of roasted veg.

● Per serving: 741 cals, 61.4g fat, 12.4g saturates, 5.9g sugars, 0.86g salt

Roasted aubergine

Aubergines roast well and are a satisfying vegetarian main course

2 large aubergines
3¹/₂ tbsp olive oil
1 small onion, chopped
2 cloves garlic, finely chopped
400g tin cherry tomatoes
1 tsp caster sugar
100g orzo pasta
2 tbsp green pesto

2 tbsp pitted black olives, drained
and roughly chopped
125g buffalo mozzarella, drained and torn
2 tbsp coarse ciabatta breadcrumbs
2 tbsp finely grated vegetarian parmesan
or Italian hard cheese
Extra-virgin olive oil, to drizzle
Fresh basil leaves, to garnish

1 Preheat the oven to 200°C, fan 180°C, gas 6. Cut the aubergines in
   half lengthways, and score a crisscross pattern over the cut side of
   each half, taking care not to cut through to the skin. Arrange, cut-side
   up, on a roasting tray and drizzle with 2 tbsp of the oil. Roast for
   30 mins, until tender. Remove from the oven and let cool slightly.

2 Meanwhile, heat 1 tbsp of the oil in large frying pan. Add the onion
   and cook for 8 mins until softened. Stir in the garlic and cook for a
   further 2 mins. Add the cherry tomatoes and the sugar. Bring to the
   boil, then reduce the heat and simmer, uncovered, for 15 mins.

3 Cook the orzo to pack instructions until al dente. Drain, then toss
   together with the pesto and olives. When the aubergine has cooled
   slightly, scoop the flesh out of the middle and transfer to a board.
   Roughly chop and add to the tomato sauce. Season with salt and
   freshly ground black pepper, to taste.

4 Add the orzo mixture to the tomato mixture and mix everything
   together. Divide equally between the aubergine shells then top each
   with some torn mozzarella. Mix the breadcrumbs with the parmesan
   and the remaining olive oil, and sprinkle over the filled aubergines.

5 Return to the oven and roast for 10-15 mins until the cheese is melted
   and the breadcrumbs golden. Finish with a drizzle of extra-virgin oil
   and a few basil leaves.

● Per serving: 450 cals, 26.9g fat, 8.8g saturates 12.4g sugars, 0.74g salt

Serves 4
Prep time: 10 mins,
plus 1 hour chilling
Cook time: 15 mins

V 1 of 5 A-DAY

Polenta with roasted tomatoes & mushrooms

A brilliant roast for anyone who's vegetarian, or has a wheat intolerance

800ml vegetable stock
200g one-minute-cook polenta
2 tbsp grated parmesan
Handful of chopped fresh chives, plus extra to garnish

300g vine tomatoes
12 mini portabella mushrooms
2 tbsp balsamic vinegar
3 tbsp olive oil
150g vegetarian Roquefort (optional)

1 Line a 20cm square baking tin with cling film. Bring the stock to the boil in a large pan. Pour the polenta into the stock in a steady stream, stirring all the time. Keep stirring and cook for 5 mins, then add the parmesan and chives. Season. Transfer the polenta to the prepared tin, let cool and then put in the fridge to chill for 1 hour.

2 Heat the oven to 180°C, fan 160°C, gas 4. Arrange the tomatoes (on their vines) and the mushrooms on a baking tray. Drizzle with the balsamic vinegar and 2 tbsp of the oil. Season. Roast for 10 mins until the tomatoes are starting to split and the mushrooms are cooked.

3 While the vegetables are roasting, heat a griddle pan over a high heat. Turn the polenta out of the baking tin, cut into 4 squares and brush all over with the remaining oil. Griddle for 3 mins each side.

4 Arrange the polenta on plates and top with the roasted tomatoes, mushrooms and a drizzle of the warm pan juices. Crumble over the vegetarian Roquefort, if using, and garnish with the remaining chives.

● Per serving: 304cals, 22.5g fat, 11.8g saturates, 4.3g sugars, 1.92g salt

Cook's tip
You can prepare the polenta in advance – it will keep in the fridge for a couple of days. For a smooth mixture, use a whisk until the liquid and polenta are combined and then change to a wooden spoon.

‘ A sophisticated veggie
roast that looks restaurant-quality
when it's on the plate ,

Serves 4
Prep time: 15 mins
Cook time: 50 mins
– 1 hour 5 mins

Roasted vegetable tart

Roasting the vegetables gives this tart a gorgeous caramelised flavour

225g butternut squash, peeled, deseeded and cut into chunks
1 courgette, trimmed and cut into chunks
1 red pepper, deseeded and sliced
1 yellow pepper, deseeded and sliced
1 red onion, cut into wedges
5 sage leaves, chopped, plus a few extra

leaves, to garnish (optional)
1 tbsp olive oil
375g pack ready rolled puff pastry
2 tbsp sundried tomato purée
25g walnut pieces
60g pack goats' cheese, sliced
1 medium egg, beaten, to glaze

1 Preheat the oven to 200°C, fan 180°C, gas 6. In a large roasting tin, toss the veg with the chopped sage and the oil. Roast for 30-40 mins.

2 Increase the oven temperature to 220°C, fan 200°C, gas 7. Unroll the pastry onto a dampened baking sheet. Spread over the tomato purée, leaving a 2-3cm border. Top with the roasted veg, walnuts and cheese.

3 Fold the border in, leaving the centre uncovered, then brush the pastry border with the egg. Bake for 20-25 mins, until the pastry is risen and golden. Serve garnished with the extra sage leaves, if using.

● Per serving: 605 cals, 38.6g fat, 15.8g saturates, 12.4g sugars, 0.35g salt

Squash & blue cheese tarts

Preheat the oven to 200°C, fan 180°C, gas 6. Peel, deseed and dice 1kg butternut squash. Put in a roasting tin, drizzle with olive oil and roast for 25 mins. Meanwhile, cut 3 filo sheets into 8 rectangles so you have 24. Brush 6 x 12cm x 2cm loose-bottomed tart tins with olive oil. Line each with a filo rectangle, brush with oil and lay the remaining filo rectangles on top, at angles, to fully line the tins. Put on a baking sheet and bake for 5 mins or until golden. Add 50g dried cranberries, 50g chopped pecans, 1 tbsp chopped fresh sage and 100g crumbled vegetarian blue cheese to the squash. Season, mix well and divide between the tart shells. Bake for a further 5 mins. Remove from the tin and garnish with a fried sage leaf to serve.

Serves 4 Prep time: 25 mins Cook time: 35 mins

Per serving: 395 cals, 20.5g fat, 6.2g saturates, 21.9g sugars, 0.67g salt

Serves 4
Prep time: 20 mins
Cook time: 20 mins

Lentil, ricotta & spinach filo parcels

These crisp vegetarian pies are packed with flavours of the Med – serve with a simple herb salad for a delicious warm-weather roast

60g unsalted butter	150g feta, crumbled
2 onions, thinly sliced	50g toasted pine nuts
2 cloves garlic, crushed	260g tinned green lentils, drained
260g young leaf spinach, chopped	12 sheets filo pastry
200g ricotta	Herb salad, to serve

1 Preheat the oven to 200°C, fan 180°C, gas 6. Melt 20g of the butter in a large frying pan and fry the onions and garlic for 3-4 mins until softened. Add the spinach and cook for a further minute. Let cool.

2 Transfer the cooled spinach mixture to a bowl and fold in the ricotta, feta, pine nuts and lentils. Mix well.

3 Melt the remaining butter and use it to brush 8 of the pastry sheets. Layer 2 of the buttered sheets on top of each other. Repeat 3 more times to make 4 parcels in total. Top each with 1 of the remaining 4 pieces of unbuttered pastry. Spoon the spinach mixture into the centre of each. Pick up all corners and twist together to make a parcel. Transfer to a baking tray, brush with any remaining melted butter and bake for 12-14 mins until crisp and golden.

4 Serve seasoned with freshly ground black pepper with the herb salad on the side.

● Per serving: 643 cals, 36.4g fat, 18.6g saturates, 10.1g sugars, 1.75g salt

Cook's tip
Make a sauce to drizzle over your parcels – whisk Greek yogurt, chopped fresh mint and a little lemon zest and juice together until smooth. Season with a little salt and some freshly ground black pepper.

Serves 4
Prep time: 5 mins
Cook time: 25 mins
Rest time: 40 mins

Couscous stuffed butternut squash

Bursting with colour and flavour, these golden roasted squash halves taste as good as they look

2 x large butternut squash, halved lengthways and deseeded
2 tbsp olive oil
125g couscous
1 vegetable stock cube
50g feta, chopped

8 cherry tomatoes, chopped
1/2 green pepper, deseeded and finely diced
5 pitted black olives, chopped
1 tbsp chopped fresh mint
1 tbsp freshly squeezed lemon juice
Herb salad, to serve

1 Preheat the oven to 200°C, fan 180°C, gas 6. Cut criss-cross patterns into the flesh of each butternut squash half, then brush all over with 1 tbsp of the oil. Put on a baking tray and roast for 40 mins.

2 Meanwhile, prepare the couscous to pack instructions, adding the stock cube to the boiling water before pouring over the couscous.

3 Stir the feta, cherry tomatoes, green pepper, black olives and mint into the couscous. Season and stir in the lemon juice and the remaining olive oil.

4 Spoon the couscous mixture onto the roasted squash halves and serve with a herb salad on the side.

● Per serving: 443 cals, 11.1g fat, 3.7g saturates, 24g total sugars, 0.81g salt

Serves 4
Prep time: 20 mins
Cook time: 30 mins

Herby stuffed roasted courgettes

Courgettes are inexpensive and plentiful – make the most of them with this easy vegetarian roast

---

6 courgettes

2 tbsp olive oil

2 cloves garlic, finely chopped

2 large carrots, grated

100g fresh breadcrumbs

4 tbsp raisins

2 medium eggs, lightly beaten

4 tbsp finely shredded fresh basil leaves

4 sprigs fresh thyme, leaves picked

100g mild Cheddar, grated

---

1 Preheat the oven to 200°C, fan 180°C, gas 6. Cook the courgettes whole in a large pan of boiling water for 5 mins. Drain then leave to cool slightly. Halve the cooked courgettes lengthways and scoop out the flesh. Set aside the hollowed-out halves and roughly chop the cooked flesh.

2 Heat the oil in a large frying pan, add the chopped courgette flesh and garlic, and cook for about 5 mins, until golden. Transfer the mixture to a large bowl and mix in the grated carrot, breadcrumbs, raisins, beaten eggs, basil, thyme and most of the grated Cheddar.

3 Arrange the courgettes, side by side, in two large baking dishes. Spoon the courgette mixture back into the hollowed-out courgette halves and scatter the reserved grated Cheddar over the top. Roast in the oven for 20 mins, until the tops are a lovely golden brown.

● Per serving: 343 cals, 17.6g fat, 7.1g sat fat, 17.7g sugars, 0.80g salt

Cook's tip
For this recipe, choose firm and heavy courgettes with glossy skins. For an extra flavour boost, you could add in a handful of toasted pine nuts to the stuffing mixture, and top with a mature Cheddar.

Tender roasted courgettes with a veggie and herb filling

side dishes

Making the perfect
side dishes...

A roast wouldn't be the same without an array of sumptuous sides. Whether you want to stick to the classics, or spice things up with some tasty alternatives, there's something for every roast

Potatoes

A warming dish of roasties that are crisp and golden on the outside and fluffy on the inside is a must-have side for a family feast. For best results, use Desirée, Maris Piper or Kind Edward varieties. If you do fancy a change, there are loads of other potato dishes you can try, too. Indulge in a creamy dauphinois or whip up a buttery bowl of mash.

Perfect partners...

Rosemary, sage and thyme; garlic; salt and black pepper.

Other vegetables

Vegetables are a great way to bring a bit of colour to your table, and keep your meal balanced – and roasting them is one of the best ways to bring out all that rich flavour. Popular choices include carrots and parsnips, but you can also give your meal an exotic twist with some spiced sweet potatoes or by using Mediterranean flavours. Experiment with different herbs and spices from your storecupboard. Other great veg for roasting are fennel, courgettes, tomatoes, peppers, red onions and butternut squash.

Alternative side dishes

There's no need to stick to the traditional two veg with your roast - make your Sunday roast more contemporary with some less obvious sides. Make your own coleslaw (it's great with pork and chicken), or bring new flavours to a classic dish like mash by using celeriac or cauliflower in place of potato. Instead of just one green veg, serve a medley of three or four, steamed and topped with a flavoured butter (see opposite). And if you're serving a joint that you've flavoured with spices, why not serve a couscous or rice dish with it, instead of the usual potatoes.

Great gravy

Want to turn everyday gravy into something special? Add a splash of red wine (perfect for beef), or make mint sauce and gravy in one for lamb by stirring in chopped fresh mint. For chicken or pork, try stirring in a spoonful of Dijon mustard and a splash of brandy.

Roasting tips and tricks...

Q How do I make my roast potatoes really crisp?

Parboil the potatoes, drain in a colander, then give them a good shake. This will rough up the edges – vital if you want the outsides to catch some colour and become crunchy. Sprinkle them with flour or even semolina and put in a tin of hot fat, turning to coat evenly before roasting. Turn halfway through cooking. For a rich flavour, roast in duck fat or beef dripping.

Q How can I make sure my vegetables are roasted evenly?

It's all about preparation – cut your veg to a uniform size to help them roast evenly. Turn them halfway through cooking so they colour at the same rate.

Q How can I avoid lumpy mash?

Before you mash, ensure your potatoes are fork tender – there shouldn't be any resistance in the middle. Use a potato ricer rather then a masher, and then whip in hot milk and butter using a wooden spoon.

Try this...

For roasties with a difference, try Swedish hasselback roast potatoes. Peel 1kg Desirée potatoes, then cut thin, even slices into them, stopping about 1cm from the base. Slot a bay leaf into each potato, then stand in a roasting tin, drizzle with 2 tbsp olive and pour in 350ml veg stock. Roast at 220°C, fan 200°C, gas 7 for 40-50 mins, basting with the stock.

Buttered up

Give plain steamed vegetables a boost with flavoured butter. Just whiz 100g of cold diced butter in a food processor, along with your chosen flavourings. When everything's combined, tip it onto a square of cling film, roll it up like a sausage and refrigerate until firm. Cut it into thin rounds to melt on top of your veg. Why not make a batch - it will freeze for up to 1 month. Try these combinations:

- **Garlic and herb** - use 1 clove of garlic and about 2 tbsp chopped fresh herbs of your choice - parsley, chives, dill and tarragon all work. Add more or less garlic and herbs if you prefer, and season.
- **Ginger, chilli and lemon** - use half a deseeded and chopped red chilli, the grated zest of 1 lemon and a 4cm piece of fresh ginger, finely chopped. This goes well with steamed broccoli.
- **Basil and parmesan** - use 2 tbsp chopped fresh basil, 50g grated parmesan, a squeeze of lemon juice and 1 chopped clove of garlic. This is delicious with steamed or roasted asparagus.
- **Mint** - use 2 tbsp chopped fresh mint, a squeeze of lemon juice and some freshly ground black pepper. Add a chopped clove of garlic, too, if you like. Serve with peas or broad beans.

Classic roast side dishes

A traditional Sunday roast is nothing without this supporting cast

Honey-glazed carrots & parsnips

Preheat the oven to 220°C, fan 200°C, gas 7. Peel, trim and quarter 200g of thin carrots and 200g thin parsnips and put in a roasting tin. Dot with 25g butter and pour in 50ml white wine. Season with salt and freshly ground black pepper and roast for 15 mins until just tender. Remove from the oven and drizzle over 2 tbsp warm honey. Return to the oven and roast for 8-10 mins, until caramelised.

Serves 4 Prep time: 10 mins Cook time: 25 mins

Per serving: 139 cals, 5.8g fat, 3.5g saturates, 15.1g sugars, 0.05g salt

Perfect roast potatoes

Preheat the oven to 220°C, fan 200°C, gas 7. Peel 2kg King Edward potatoes and cut into large chunks. Put in a pan and cover with cold water. Bring to the boil, then reduce the heat and simmer for 10-12 mins. Drain. Return to the pan over a low heat, cover and shake the pan for 1 min to fluff up the edges of the potatoes. Season with 1 tsp sea salt. Meanwhile, put 100g goose or duck fat in a large roasting tin and heat in the oven for 10 mins, until sizzling hot. Carefully spoon the potatoes into the tin, turning to coat in the hot fat. Sprinkle with 2 tsp finely chopped fresh rosemary. Roast for 30-40 mins, turning occasionally, until crisp and golden.

Serves 10 Prep time: 15 mins Cook time: 45-55 mins

Per serving: 242 cals, 10.1g fat, 3.3g saturates, 1.4g sugars, 0.49g salt

Tenderstem broccoli with garlic & shallots

Heat 1 tbsp olive oil and a knob of butter in a frying pan. Add 4 halved and sliced shallots and 2 chopped cloves of garlic. Cook for 1 min. Add 400g tenderstem broccoli and cook for 1 min then pour in 150ml hot vegetable stock. Cover and cook for 5-8 mins until tender. Remove the broccoli and stir 1/4 tsp English mustard into the liquid. Heat for 1 min then pour over the broccoli, season and serve.

Serves 4 Prep time: 5 mins Cook time: 8-11 mins

Per serving: 85 cals, 5.2g fat, 1.8g saturates, 2.4g sugars, 0.18g salt

Braised red cabbage with apple

Preheat the oven to 160°C, fan 140°C, gas 3. Melt 25g butter in a large flameproof casserole. Add 2 sliced red onions and cook for 10 mins. Stir in 1 cored and chopped red cabbage, 2 peeled, cored and chopped apples, 50ml red wine vinegar, 50g brown sugar and 200ml red wine. Bring to the boil, then add 1 halved orange studded with 4 cloves, 1 bay leaf, 1 cinnamon stick and 2 thyme sprigs. Cover and cook in the oven for 1 1/2 hours, stirring halfway. Stir in 2 tbsp redcurrant jelly until melted then season to taste with salt and freshly ground black pepper. Remove orange halves before serving.

Serves 6 Prep time: 20 mins Cook time: 1 hour 45 mins

Per serving: 160 cals, 4g fat, 2.3g saturates, 20.7g sugars, 0.05g salt

Alternative roast side dishes

If you've given your roast meat a twist, why not do the same with your veg!

Roasted Mediterranean vegetables

Preheat the oven to 180°C, fan 160°C, gas 4. Deseed and slice 1 red, 1 yellow and 1 green pepper. Trim and slice 1 aubergine and 1 courgette, and cut 1 red onion into wedges. Put all the vegetables in a large roasting tin and toss with 4 tbsp olive oil. Add 1 tbsp chopped fresh basil and 2 tsp each of dried oregano and marjoram. Season with salt and freshly ground black pepper and roast for 30-40 mins until tender, turning once.

Serves 8 Prep time: 10 mins Cook time: 30-40 mins

Per serving: 86 cals, 5.6g fat, 0.9g saturates, 5g sugars, 0.01g salt

Steamed oriental veg with chilli dressing

Put 200g each sugar snap peas and mange tout in the base of a steamer basket then top with 200g pak choi, trimmed and leaves separated. Set the basket over a pan of simmering water, cover tightly with a lid and steam for 4-5 mins until the vegetables are just tender. Meanwhile, put 2 tbsp each of soy sauce and rice wine vinegar in a small pan, along with 2 tsp caster sugar and 1 tbsp water. Heat gently, stirring to dissolve the sugar. Stir in 1 deseeded and diced red chilli, leave for 1 min to infuse, then drizzle over the steamed vegetables.

Serves 4 Prep time: 10 mins Cook time: 5 mins

Per serving: 63 cals, 0.5g fat, 0.1g saturates, 8.4g sugars, 0.95g salt

Spiced roasted sweet potato

Preheat the oven to 200°C, fan 180°C, gas 6. In a small bowl, mix 2 tsp garam masala, 1 tsp crushed chillies and 2 tbsp olive oil. Cut 800g peeled sweet potatoes into chunky wedges and put in a large roasting tin. Drizzle over the spice mix and toss to coat the wedges. Roast for 30-35 mins, turning once, until tender and crisp at the edges.

Serves 4 Prep time: 10 mins Cook time: 30-35 mins

Per serving: 246 cals, 5.9g fat, 0.9g saturates, 11.4g sugars, 0.20g salt

Roasted cauliflower with cumin

Preheat the oven to 180°C, fan 160°C, gas 4. Cut 1 head of cauliflower into small florets, and put in a roasting tin. Toss with 2 tbsp olive oil and 2 tsp cumin seeds and season with salt and freshly ground black pepper. Roast for 25 mins until tender. Garnish with 1 tbsp chopped fresh coriander.

Serves 4 Prep time: 10 mins Cook time: 25 mins

Per serving: 96 cals, 6.4g fat, 1g saturates, 3.1g sugars, 0.03g salt

Cauliflower cheese

A classic side dish everyone loves – it goes especially well with roast beef

30g butter
30g plain flour
325ml semi-skimmed milk
75g lighter mature Cheddar, grated

20g parmesan, grated
1 tsp English mustard
1 head cauliflower, cut into small florets
200g leeks, trimmed and sliced

1 Preheat the oven to 200°C, fan 180°C, gas 6. Melt the butter in a pan and stir in the flour. Cook for 1 min before whisking in the milk, a little at a time. Bring the mixture to the boil and simmer for 2 mins before stirring in 50g of the Cheddar, 15g of the parmesan and the mustard.

2 Meanwhile, cook the cauliflower in a pan of boiling water for 5 mins, adding in the leeks for the last 3 mins. Drain. Transfer to a 1-litre baking dish, pour over the cheese sauce, and scatter over the remaining Cheddar and parmesan.

3 Bake in the oven for 15-20 mins, until golden and bubbling.

● Per serving: 252 cals, 14.4g fat, 8.7g saturates, 7.9g sugars, 0.64g salt

Cook's tip
Don't throw away the cauliflower leaves when you cut off the florets. They're full of flavour and add extra crunch and colour to the dish. Simply add them to the pan at the same time as the leeks.

Melting, bubbling cheese and tender cauliflower are perfect partners

Serves 4
Prep time: 20 mins
Cook time:
1 hour 5 mins

Potato dauphinois

Oozing with flavour, this creamy, decadent potato dish goes beautifully with all roast meats, but especially with velvety slices of rare beef

---

25g butter, softened
300ml double or single cream
150ml milk
1 clove garlic, crushed
900g Desirée potatoes, sliced very thinly

(use a mandoline if you have one) and put into a bowl of cold water
50g Gruyère, finely grated
Pinch of grated nutmeg (optional)

---

1 Preheat the oven to 190°C, fan 170°C, gas 5. Use some of the butter to grease a shallow 1-litre ovenproof dish.

2 Pour the cream and milk into a large pan. Add the garlic and slowly bring to the boil. Drain the potatoes and pat dry with kitchen paper. Add to the pan and simmer gently for 5 mins, stirring to separate the slices. Season lightly with salt and freshly ground black pepper.

3 Transfer the potato to the prepared dish, pressing firmly with the back of the spoon. Pour over the rest of the cream mixture. Dot with the remaining butter, sprinkle over the cheese and nutmeg, if using, and bake for 1 hour until tender and the topping is golden.

● Per serving: 623 cals, 45.8g fat, 28.5g saturates, 5.4g sugars, 0.24g salt

Potato & celeriac mash

Put 1.5kg Maris Piper potatoes, peeled and cut into large chunks, and 500g peeled and chopped celeriac in a large pan of water. Bring to the boil, then reduce the heat and simmer for 10 mins until tender. Drain, then mash with 50ml semi-skimmed milk and 30g butter. Season and serve. This mash works brilliantly with roasted lamb, and also makes a more interesting topping for a shepherd's pie than just plain mashed potato. You could make a double batch and use the rest in the recipe on p60.

Serves 8 Prep time: 15 mins Cook time: 15 mins

Per serving: 189 cals, 3.6g fat, 1.9g saturates, 2.8g sugars, 0.22g salt

Makes 8
Prep time: 20 mins
Cook time: 25 mins

Savoy cabbage & potato wraps with cheese

An unusual – and impressive – way to serve potatoes and cabbage together. They're also a great way to entice children to eat their greens

1 medium savoy cabbage
500g Maris Piper potatoes, peeled and cut into small chunks

1 leek, trimmed and thinly sliced
100g mature Cheddar, grated

1 Bring a pan of water to the boil. Remove 8 large cabbage leaves and blanch for 3 mins. Drain and put straight into a bowl of cold water. Drain when cool.

2 Cut the remaining cabbage in half, then remove and discard the core. Shred the cabbage finely and set aside.

3 Put the potatoes in a pan, cover with cold water and bring to the boil. Cook for about 10 mins, until tender, adding the shredded cabbage and sliced leek for the last 5 mins of cooking time. Drain well, return to the pan and mash everything together. Stir in 80g of the Cheddar and season with a little salt and freshly ground black pepper.

4 Preheat the oven to 200°C, fan 180°C fan, gas 6. Lay out the blanched cabbage leaves and divide the potato mixture between each. Gather each cabbage leaf together to create a little package, with some of the potato mixture still exposed. Secure each package with a piece of kitchen string and transfer to a large baking tray.

5 Sprinkle with the remaining Cheddar and roast in the oven for 10-15 mins until the cheese is golden and bubbling.

● Per wrap: 136 cals, 4.7g fat, 2.7g saturates, 4.7g sugars, 0.24g salt

Makes 8
Prep time: 15 mins,
plus cooling
Cook time: 50 mins

Stuffed roast onions

A flavoursome side dish that goes especially well with roast pork

8 medium red onions, peeled
2 tbsp olive oil
100g fresh white breadcrumbs
2 tbsp fresh chopped sage

50g dried apricots, chopped
4 thick Lincolnshire pork sausages
(about 270g)

1 Bring a large pan of lightly salted water to the boil and add the onions. Boil for 10 mins until almost tender. Drain (reserving 250ml of the cooking liquid) and rinse the onions under cold water to cool.

2 Slice ½ cm off the top of each onion and a sliver off each base so the onions stand upright when roasting. Using a small knife and teaspoon, cut and scoop out the inner core of each onion, leaving three outer layers intact. Stand the onion shells in a shallow roasting tin. Chop the inner cores of three of the onions.

3 Heat half the oil in a frying pan and fry the chopped onion for 5 mins until golden. Transfer to a bowl and stir in the breadcrumbs, sage and apricots. Set aside to cool.

4 Preheat the oven to 180°C, fan 160°C, gas 4. Squeeze the sausages from their skins and add the sausagemeat to the breadcrumb mixture. Stir with a fork until thoroughly combined. Season with a little salt and freshly ground black pepper.

5 Spoon the stuffing into the onion shells (don't worry if some of the stuffing spills out into the tin). Pour the reserved cooking liquid around the onions and drizzle over the rest of the oil.

6 Roast for 30-35 mins until the onions are caramelised and the stuffing is golden. Cover loosely with foil after 25 mins if they begin to overbrown.

● Per serving: 234 cals, 11.4g fat, 3.5g saturates, 11.4g sugars, 0.61g salt

Cook's tip
Finely chop the leftover onion and freeze – it's handy to have at the ready for adding to soups, pasta sauces and stir-fries.

Slow-roasted fennel

Serves 4
Prep time: 10 mins
Cook time: 40 mins

Roasting delicately fragrant fennel intensifies its aniseed flavour. It goes especially well with fish and pork, but try it with other roast meats, too

2 large fennel bulbs (shoots and roots removed and discarded), each cut vertically into 6 pieces

1 tbsp olive oil
1 tsp caraway seeds
2 cloves garlic, finely sliced

1 Preheat the oven to 200°C, fan 180°C, gas 6.

2 Arrange the fennel in a single layer on a baking tray and drizzle all over with the olive oil. Sprinkle over the caraway seeds and season with salt and freshly ground black pepper. Add the garlic to the tray and roast for 40 mins until the fennel is soft.

● Per serving: 31 cals, 2.7g fat, 0.4g saturates, 0.9g sugars, 0.01g salt

Roasted balsamic beetroot

Put 500g trimmed fresh beetroot into a medium pan, cover with water, bring to the boil and cook for 20-25 mins until tender. Drain and peel under running water. Preheat the oven to 200°C, fan 180°C, gas 6. Cut the beetroot into wedges, place in a roasting tin and gently toss with 1 tbsp extra virgin olive oil, the zest of 1 orange and 1 tbsp fresh thyme leaves. Season and roast for 10 mins. Make a dressing by whisking together 1 tbsp balsamic vinegar, 1 tbsp extra virgin olive oil and a squeeze of orange juice. Put the roasted beetroot into a serving bowl, pour over the dressing and leave to marinate for 30 mins before serving.

Serves 4 Prep time: 10 mins plus marinating Cook time: 40 mins

Per serving: 109 cals, 5.2g fat, 0.7g saturates, 11g sugars, 0.21g salt

The sweet aniseed flavour of fennel goes well with roast pork

Steamed green veg with flavoured butter

A flavoursome combination of wonderfully fresh green veg and herbs

Serves 6
Prep time:
10 mins, plus 2-3
hours' chilling
Cook time:
6-8 mins

75g butter, softened
Zest of 1 unwaxed lemon
2 tbsp fresh chopped mixed herbs
2 leeks, trimmed and thickly cut on
the diagonal

200g green beans, trimmed
200g baby courgettes, trimmed
and halved lengthways
200g green or savoy cabbage,
cored and shredded

1 Put the butter in a bowl and beat in the lemon zest and chopped mixed herbs. Season with salt and freshly ground black pepper. Spoon the butter onto a small sheet of greaseproof paper, then wrap and shape into a 12cm long roll. Twist the ends of the paper together and chill in the fridge for 2-3 hours or until the butter is firm enough to slice.

2 Put the leeks, beans and courgettes in a steamer or metal colander and set it over a pan of simmering water. Cover and steam for 4 mins. Add the shredded cabbage and steam for a further 2-4 mins until all the vegetables are just tender.

3 Transfer to a warmed serving bowl. Slice half the butter into 6 x 1cm rounds. Add 2 of the slices to the hot vegetables and toss together gently until the butter has melted. Serve topped with the remaining 4 slices of herb butter and serve. The remaining butter will keep in the fridge for 4-5 days, or the freezer for up to 1 month.

● Per serving: 134 cals, 10.9g fat, 6.9g saturates, 3.7g sugars, 0.01g salt

Cook's tip
You can use any combination of 2-3 fresh herbs to flavour the butter –
dill, parsley, mint, chives, basil and tarragon all work well. Or you can
just use 1 herb for a more defined flavour.

Fresh lemon zest adds a burst of citrusy freshness to this veg dish

Serves 6
Prep time: 10 mins
Cook time: 10 mins

Zesty medley of spring vegetables

If you're roasting spring lamb for Easter, this vibrant side dish will go beautifully, along with the glazed carrots, below

100g fresh or frozen broad beans
350g asparagus, trimmed
200g baby courgettes, sliced widthways
50g fresh or frozen peas

Zest and juice of 1 unwaxed lemon
Knob of butter
25g toasted almond flakes

1 Cook the broad beans in a medium pan of lightly salted boiling water for 4-5 mins, until tender. Drain and set aside until cool enough to handle, then peel the skins off to reveal their green colour.

2 Put the asparagus and courgettes in a steamer and set over a pan of boiling water. Steam for 3-4 mins, adding the peas to the pan below the steamer for the final 2 mins of cooking. Remove the steamer from the heat and drain the peas.

2 Toss all the vegetables together until the beans are warmed through. Season and sprinkle over the lemon zest and juice and toss together with the knob of butter. Serve garnished with the flaked almonds.

● Per serving: 84 cals, 4.8g fat, 1.6g saturates, 2.4g sugars, 0.01g salt

Glazed baby carrots

Scrub and trim 500g bunched baby carrots and cook in a large pan of lightly salted boiling water for 6-8 mins or until tender. Drain well and set aside. Heat 20g butter and 1 tbsp clear honey in a pan over a low heat until melted and bubbling. Add the carrots to the pan and toss through the glaze. Tip onto a serving plater, drizzle with any glaze left in the pan and season.

Serves 6 Prep time: 10 mins Cook time: 12 mins

Per serving: 75 cals, 3.2g fat, 1.9g saturates, 10.3g total sugars, 0.41g salt

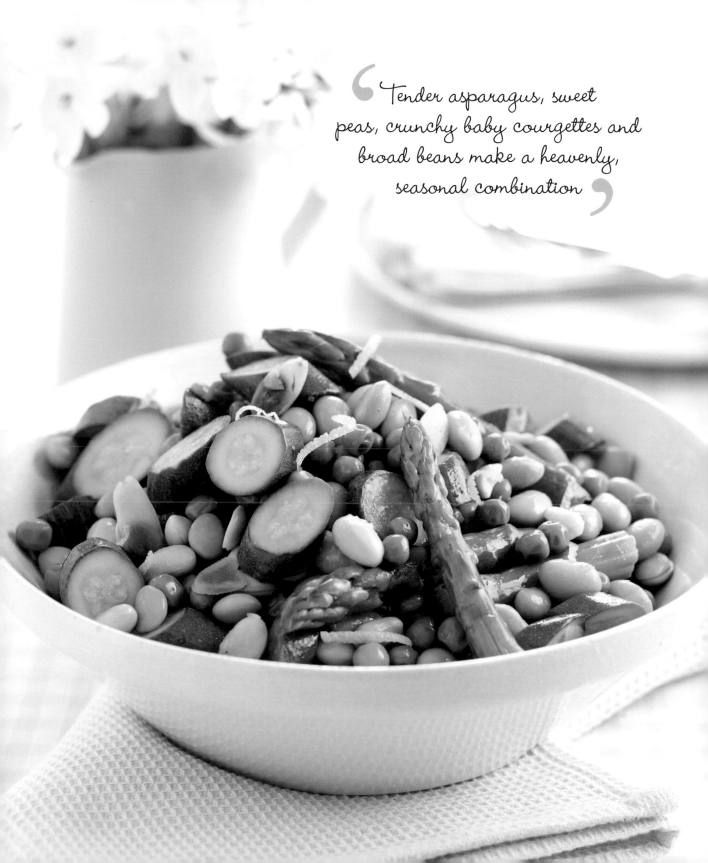

'Tender asparagus, sweet peas, crunchy baby courgettes and broad beans make a heavenly, seasonal combination'

Pomegranate & fig couscous

A great side for roast lamb and duck, this fruity, nutty couscous is simple to prepare and ready to eat in just 20 minutes

200g couscous
1-2 tsp ras-el-hanout spice mix
Knob of butter
250ml hot chicken or vegetable stock, made using 1 stock cube

50g dried figs, roughly chopped
50g toasted hazelnuts, chopped
Seeds of 1 pomegranate
Handful of chopped fresh mint

1 Put the couscous in a heatproof bowl and stir in the ras-el-hanout. Season, add the butter and pour over the stock. Cover with cling film and leave to stand for 10 mins.

2 Fluff the grains up with a fork and stir through the figs, hazelnuts and pomegranate seeds. Sprinkle over the mint and serve.

● Per serving: 322 cals, 8.7g fat, 1.1g saturates, 9.6g sugars, 0.19g salt

Celeriac & green apple coleslaw

In a large bowl, whisk together 1 tbsp wholegrain mustard, 55ml lighter mayonnaise, 2 tsp chopped capucines capers, and 2 tbsp cold water. Add 325g peeled and coarsely grated celeriac and toss well in the dressing. Mix through 1 cored and coarsely grated Granny Smith apple and a small handful of chopped fresh flat-leaf parsley until completely combined.

Serves 4 Prep time: 15 mins

Per serving: 53 cals, 1.3g fat, 1g saturates, 5.4g sugars, 0.70g salt

desserts

And to finish?

desserts...

A proper roast wouldn't be complete without pudding, even if everyone swears they don't have room for it! While the meat is resting and the oven's still on, whip up something sweet for afters. It will cook while you're enjoying your roast, and be ready to serve when the plates have been cleared

What to serve

Crumbles and cobblers, fruit pies, fools and trifles – they're all popular, traditional desserts to serve with a classic roast. Whether you fancy something warm and comforting in winter, or light and refreshing in summer, roasted fruit is a great choice. Served straight from the roasting tin with yogurt or ice cream, it's a simple, elegant dessert. Or, it can be used as the basis for countless other desserts.

Choosing fruit

Stone fruits are right for roasting, as the juices are drawn out and the flesh becomes soft and succulent. The sugars in the fruit caramelise, adding a layer of rich, intense flavour. When in season, try plums, peaches, apricots and nectarines. Cut them in half, remove the stones, and spread them out in a single layer in a roasting tin with just a sprinkling of sugar, a knob of butter and a squeeze of lemon juice. Roast at 200°C, fan 180°C, gas 6 for 20 mins until soft. Don't stop at stone fruits – experiment with figs, rhubarb, pears, bananas, pineapple, mangoes and even strawberries.

What to add

Be adventurous with flavourings when roasting fruits – add spices such as cinnamon, nutmeg or ginger, or even aromatic herbs, such as rosemary, or lemon thyme. A vanilla pod or grated lemon, lime or orange zest will also work wonders. Leave out the sugar and splash in some sweet wine or a drizzle of honey to give a little added sweetness and a burst of extra flavour.

Finally...

A little extra liquid in the roasting tin will give you a lovely syrupy sauce – try a splash of wine, rum or even beer. For a stickier sauce, add an extra sprinkling of brown sugar.

Cook's tip

Use any leftover pastry to make a fruit pie – put the fruit in a dish, cover with a pastry lid, brush with beaten egg and bake until golden.

Sweet ideas...

Q My kids aren't keen on fruit - what else can I use?

Chocolate! Try a miraculous self-saucing choc-mint pudding on p184, or whip up a chocolate trifle using leftover chocolate cake or brownies, instant chocolate pudding and chopped nuts. You might even get away with sneaking in berries!

Q How can I make a pouring custard?

Beat 6 egg yolks in a bowl with 2 tbsp caster sugar, a few drops of vanilla extract and 1 tsp plain flour. Pour over 600ml of hot milk, whisking all the time, then pour into a pan and heat, stirring constantly with a wooden spoon, until the custard thickens to the consistency of pouring cream - it should coat the back of the spoon. Freeze the egg whites in sealable plastic bags for later.

The perfect crumble

Desserts don't get much simpler - or yummier - than crumble, and part of its appeal lies in its versatility. Perfect for serving with roasts, you can use just about any fruit, even frozen, and a variety of toppings. Mix things up a bit with these three variations on the traditional crumble topping. Each one will cover a 20cm x 20cm baking dish. Sprinkle them over your chosen fruit base and bake for 25 mins at 180°C, fan 160°C gas 4, until golden.

- **Pecan & maple** - blend 100g diced, unsalted butter in a food processor with 125g plain flour and 50g chopped pecan nuts. Drizzle over 1 tbsp maple syrup once cooked.
- **Chocolate and oat** - blend 100g porridge oats in a food processor with 50g caster sugar, 75g diced, unsalted butter, 25g plain flour and 30g chopped dark chocolate.
- **Macadamia and cinnamon** - blend 75g diced, unsalted butter with 50g caster sugar, 100g plain flour, 1 tsp cinnamon and 50g chopped macadamia nuts.

Q Help! I need an easy standby pudding.

If you've got rice, sugar and milk, you've got rice pud! To serve 6, mix together 100g short grain or pudding rice, 50g sugar, 1/2 tsp mixed spice and 1.2 litres of milk in an ovenproof dish. Cook in an oven heated to 150°C, fan 130°C, gas 2 for 1 hour. If you don't like spice, leave it out, and add raisins, fresh berries or choc chips.

Strawberry shortcake

An easy but impressive pud to serve with your favourite roast

Serves 8
Prep time: 30 mins,
plus 1 hour cooling
Cook time:
15-20 mins

500g strawberries, hulled and halved

2 tbsp caster sugar

300g self-raising flour

1 tsp baking powder

150g butter, chilled and cubed

75ml buttermilk

1 medium egg, lightly beaten

300ml double cream

3 tbsp icing sugar, plus a
little extra for dusting

1 Preheat the oven to 190°C, fan 170°C, gas 5. Put the strawberries in a bowl with the caster sugar, cover and chill in the fridge for approximately 1 hour to release the juices.

2 Sieve the flour, baking powder and a pinch of salt into a large mixing bowl. Add the butter and rub everything together with your fingertips until you have a mixture that resembles fine breadcrumbs.

3 Make a well in the middle of the flour mixture, then pour in the buttermilk and the beaten egg. Gently stir the mixture with a fork until it just comes together to form a soft, sticky dough.

4 Transfer the dough to a lightly floured surface, knead gently, then cut into two pieces. Roll each piece into a ball, then pat them out into 2 rounds, each measuring approximately 18cm in diameter.

5 Transfer the rounds to a lightly greased large baking sheet. Bake for 15-20 mins until risen and golden. Carefully transfer the shortcake to a wire rack and set aside to cool.

6 In a bowl, whip the cream and icing sugar together until soft peaks form.

7 To assemble the shortcake, spread half of the cream over the top of 1 shortcake, then scatter over half of the strawberries and drizzle with some of the strawberry juices. Top with the second shortcake, then layer the remaining cream, strawberries and juices. Dust with the icing sugar before serving.

● Per serving: 508 cals, 34.5g fat, 21.6g saturates, 15.7g sugars, 0.49g salt

Makes 4
Prep time: 20 mins
Cook time: 50 mins

Salted caramel & date steamed puds

An up-to-date twist on a classic sticky toffee pudding, these individual desserts taste even better with a generous scoop of vanilla ice cream

50g ready-to-eat dates, chopped
115g butter, softened, plus a little
extra for greasing
115g light brown soft sugar
2 medium eggs, beaten
1/2 tsp vanilla extract
115g self-raising flour

1/4 tsp baking powder

FOR THE SALTED CARAMEL SAUCE
50g unsalted butter
75g light brown soft sugar
75ml double cream
1/4 tsp sea salt flakes

1 Preheat the oven to 190°C, fan 170°C, gas 5. Butter and line the bases of 4 x 175ml metal pudding basins. Put the dates in a heatproof bowl and pour over 50ml of boiling water. Soak for 5 mins.

2 Put the butter and sugar in a bowl and, using an electric whisk, beat until pale and fluffy. Beat in the eggs and the vanilla extract. Sift over the flour and baking powder and fold in gently. Purée the dates and water, or mash with a fork, and fold into the sponge mixture.

3 Divide the mixture between the pudding basins and cover each with a square of pleated, buttered foil, scrunching it tightly around the sides of each basin. Transfer to a roasting tin and pour in enough boiling water to reach halfway up the sides of the basins. Bake for 45-50 mins, until risen, firm to the touch and a skewer inserted into one of the puddings comes out clean.

4 Meanwhile, make the sauce. Put the butter and sugar in a small pan and heat gently, stirring, until the sugar has dissolved. Simmer for 2 mins, stirring occasionally. Remove from the heat and stir in the cream and half the salt flakes. Taste the sauce (taking care as the mixture will be hot) and add the remaining salt, if needed. Turn the puds out onto warmed serving plates and drizzle over the sauce.

● Per serving: 753 cals, 46.3g fat, 28.8g saturates, 55.4g sugars, 0.73g salt

Plum cobbler

Serves 6
Prep time: 20 mins
Cook time:
40-55 mins

Not quite a crumble, not quite a pie, this classic pud from America's deep south works with any combo of fresh or tinned stone fruits and berries

500g red plums, destoned and thickly sliced
1 tsp vanilla extract
75g light brown soft sugar
225g self-raising flour

Pinch of salt
55g butter, diced, plus extra for greasing
150-175ml semi-skimmed milk
2 tsp demerara sugar
Whipped cream or crème fraîche, to serve

1 Preheat the oven to 200°C, fan 180°C, gas 6. Put the plums, vanilla extract and 40g of the sugar in a pan and simmer gently for 5-10 mins until the plums begin to soften.

2 Meanwhile, sift the flour and salt into a bowl and rub in the butter until the mixture resembles fine breadcrumbs. Stir in the remaining sugar and then 150ml of the milk to get a soft, spoonable mixture, adding the rest of the milk if needed.

3 Tip the plums into a lightly buttered 1-litre ovenproof dish. Spoon the cobbler mix on top of the fruit, leaving smallish gaps so you can see some of the fruit between the topping. Sprinkle over the demerara sugar.

4 Bake for 35-45 mins until the plums are very soft and the cobbler topping is crisp and golden. Leave to cool for a few mins before serving with the whipped cream or crème fraiche.

● Per serving: 301 cals, 8.6g fat, 5.3g saturates, 23.3g sugars, 0.49g salt

When in season, use ripe, fresh, peaches or apricots instead of plums

Baked apples

Fill your kitchen with fruity, almond aromas with these baked treats

Serves 6
Prep time: 20 mins
Cook time:
40-45 mins

50g unsalted butter
75g light muscovado sugar
6 tbsp Amaretto
100g dried figs, chopped

100g sultanas, raisins or dried cherries
50g blanched almonds, roughly chopped
6 large firm eating apples, such as
Braeburns, cored

1 Preheat the oven to 180°C, fan 160°C, gas 4. Melt the butter in a medium pan, add the sugar and Amaretto and heat gently, stirring, until the sugar has dissolved. Stir in the dried fruit and almonds. Remove from the heat and set aside to cool slightly.

2 Make the apple cavities a bit bigger by cutting away a little more from the middle of each apple, using a small sharp knife. Transfer to a lightly greased baking dish. Spoon the fruit mixture into the apples, piling any excess on top. Cover loosely with foil and bake for 30 mins, then remove the foil and bake for a further 10-15 mins until tender. Serve with warm custard and the syrupy pan juices.

● Per serving: 305 cals, 11.9g fat, 5g saturates, 31.7g sugars, 0.03g salt

Fruit crumble with chocolate

Preheat the oven to 180°C, fan 160°C, gas 4. Peel, core and chop 4 apples and 4 pears, and peel and grate a 1.5cm piece of root ginger. Put in a pan, cover and cook over a medium heat for 5 mins, stirring occasionally, until softened. Tip into a large, shallow, ovenproof dish and scatter over 75g chopped dark chocolate. In a separate bowl, mix together 50g porridge oats, 50g golden caster sugar, 100g diced unsalted butter, 75g plain flour and 1 tsp vanilla extract, rubbing the butter with your fingertips until the mixture is crumbly. Sprinkle over the fruit and bake for 25-30 mins until golden brown. Melt 25g dark chocolate and drizzle over the hot crumble to serve.

Serves 6   Prep time: 10 mins   Cook time: 30-35 mins

Per serving: 404 cals, 20.2g fat, 12.6g saturates, 35.1g sugars, 0.01g salt

Baked custard pots

An easy, versatile dessert that can be doubled or halved easily

Makes 4
Prep time:
10 mins, plus
30 mins' infusing
Cook time:
35-40 mins

250ml whole milk
125ml single cream
1 vanilla pod
1 fresh bay leaf

3 medium eggs, plus 1 extra egg yolk
55g caster sugar
Freshly grated nutmeg

1 Pour the milk and cream into a pan. Halve the vanilla pod lengthways and scrape the sticky black vanilla seeds into the pan with the point of a knife. Drop the scraped pod in, too, along with the bay leaf. Bring the mixture almost to the boil then turn off the heat. Leave for 30 mins, for the vanilla to flavour the mixture. Discard the pod and the bay leaf.

2 Preheat the oven to 150°C, fan 130°C, gas 2. In a jug, whisk together the whole eggs, the egg yolk and the caster sugar. Gradually pour into the infused milk, whisking as you go. Strain into a jug then pour into 4 x 100ml ramekins. Sprinkle with nutmeg.

3 Put the ramekins in a roasting tin, pour in enough hot water to come halfway up the sides of the ramekins, and bake for 30-35 mins until just set, but with a slight wobble.

● Per serving: 224 cals, 13g fat, 6.5g saturates, 18.6g sugars, 0.29g salt

Roasted Yorkshire forced rhubarb with maple syrup

Preheat the oven to 200°C, fan 180°C, gas 6. Trim and slice 450g Yorkshire forced rhubarb into 7.5cm lengths and arrange in a single layer in a roasting tin. Drizzle over 50ml maple syrup and roast for 12 mins until just tender. Serve drizzled with the syrupy juices from the roasting tin, with yogurt and lemon zest on the side.

Serves 4 Prep time: 5 mins Cook time: 12 mins

Per serving: 112 cals, 5.1g fat, 3.1g saturates, 12.4g sugars, 0.11g salt

Serves 6
Prep time: 10 mins
Cook time:
35-45 mins

Self-saucing choc-mint pudding

This super-simple pudding produces its own sauce! The method may seem a bit strange, but don't worry – it'll come out perfectly

A little butter, for greasing
150g caster sugar
250g self-raising flour
1/2 tsp baking powder
75g cocoa powder, plus extra for dusting
3 medium eggs
100g unsalted butter, melted

150ml semi-skimmed milk
1 tsp Taste the Difference American peppermint extract
167g pack crunchy mint sticks by Sainsbury's, roughly chopped
200g light brown soft sugar
Icing sugar, for dusting

1 Preheat the oven to 180°C, fan 160°C, gas 4. Lightly grease a 1.5-litre shallow baking dish with butter.

2 Put the caster sugar in a mixing bowl, then sift in the flour, baking powder, 50g of the cocoa powder and a pinch of salt.

3 In a jug, whisk together the eggs, melted butter, milk and peppermint extract, then add to the flour mixture. Stir to combine, then fold though half of the chopped mint sticks. Pour into the prepared baking dish.

4 For the sauce, mix together the light brown soft sugar, remaining cocoa powder and 300ml of boiling water in a jug. Stir well to combine, then pour over the chocolate batter.

5 Scatter with the remaining mint chocolate sticks and transfer to the oven to cook for 35-45 mins until the top is crisp and set – take care not to overcook, though, or you'll lose the lovely sauce. Cover loosely with foil after 30 mins if the top starts to over-brown. Dust with icing sugar and serve immediately.

● Per serving: 740 cals, 27.8g fat, 16.4g saturates, 77.4g sugars, 1.21g salt

Cook's tip
If you're not a fan of the chocolate and mint combination, you can just leave out the peppermint essence and mint sticks from the recipe.

Roasted peach fool

Juicy, sweet and caramelised - roasted peaches are well worth a try

Serves 4
Prep time: 5 mins,
plus 1 hour chilling
Cook time: 10 mins

4 ripe peaches, destoned and chopped	500g tub natural fromage frais
2 tbsp clear honey	1 tbsp icing sugar
1 vanilla pod, seeds only	6 amaretti biscuits

1 Preheat the oven to 170°C, fan 150°C, gas 3. Arrange the peach pieces in a roasting tin. Mix the honey with the vanilla seeds and drizzle over the peaches. Roast for 10 mins until just becoming juicy and golden.

2 Use a whisk to whip together the fromage frais and icing sugar. Gently stir in the roasted peaches and any of the roasting juices. Divide the peach fool between 4 glasses or small bowls and chill in the fridge for 1 hour.

3 To serve, crumble the amaretti biscuits and sprinkle over the top of each fool. Serve immediately before the biscuits go soggy.

● Per serving: 203 cals, 1.3g fat, 0.1g saturates, 33.7g sugars, 0.56g salt

Tropical fruit trifle

Soak 175g sponge fingers in 2 tbsp each of dark rum and Malibu; set aside. Whip 200ml double cream to stiff peaks; add 1 tbsp caster sugar. Fold in 200ml half-fat crème fraîche then cover and chill in the fridge. Peel, core and chop 1 pineapple; peel and chop 3 kiwi fruit; scoop the pulp from 2 passionfruit; peel and chop 1 banana; and peel, destone and chop 1 mango. In a blender, blitz 200g of the pineapple, 1 of the kiwi fruit, $1/2$ the passionfruit pulp, the banana and the juice of 1 lime (keep the zest). Cover the base of a 2-litre trifle bowl with soaked sponge fingers, followed by a layer of fruit pulp. Top with a layer of the chopped fruit. Repeat until the sponge, pulp and fruit are used up. Top with the cream and chill in the fridge for 1 hour. To serve, scatter over the lime zest, the remaining passionfruit pulp and 50g toasted coconut flakes.

Serves 10 Prep time: 30 mins, plus at least 1 hour's chilling

Per serving: 294 cals, 16.3g fat, 10.7g saturates, 27g sugars, 0.06g salt

This easy pud is great for crowds — just double or triple the quantities depending on what you need

Timed to perfection

Serve a classic Sunday roast with all the trimmings on time, every time, with these helpful timing plans...

Chicken
Based on a 2kg whole chicken served with roast potatoes, tenderstem broccoli with garlic and shallots, steamed vegetables and pan gravy.

Turkey
Based on a 4.8kg whole turkey served with roast potatoes, braised red cabbage, honey-glazed carrots and parsnips, steamed vegetables and pan gravy.

Lamb
Based on a 2kg medium-roasted leg of lamb served with roast potatoes, steamed vegetables with lemon and herb butter, pan gravy and mint sauce.

Beef
Based on a 2kg medium-cooked joint of beef served with roast potatoes, steamed vegetables, Yorkshire puddings and pan gravy.

Pork
Based on a 2.5kg joint served with roast potatoes, braised red cabbage, steamed vegetables, pan gravy and apple sauce.

Chicken

Three hours to go...
Take the chicken out of the fridge and allow it to come to room temperature.

Two hours 10 mins to go...
● Preheat the oven to 200°C, fan 180°C, gas 6. Prepare the chicken following the recipe on p14.

Two hours to go...
● Roast the chicken following the recipe until cooked through.

1 hour 15 mins to go...
● While the chicken is roasting, prepare the potatoes. Follow the recipe on p150, boiling the potatoes for an extra 2-3 mins. Heat the fat in the roasting tin for 12 mins, then add the potatoes. Roast on a shelf underneath the chicken for 40 mins, turning occasionally.

40 mins to go...
● Prepare the vegetables for the tenderstem broccoli side dish following the recipe on p150. Cover and set aside. If you wish to serve any other steamed vegetables with the roast, then prepare them now, too.

15-20 mins to go...
● When the chicken is cooked, take it out of the oven, cover tightly with foil and let rest in a warm place. Turn the oven up to 220°C, fan 200°C, gas 7 and continue roasting the potatoes for 15-20 mins or until crisp and golden. Meanwhile, make the gravy with the pan juices following the recipe on p14. Cook the tenderstem broccoli recipe and put in a warmed serving bowl.

10 mins to go...
● If you are serving extra steamed vegetables with the roast, put in a steamer set over a pan of simmering water. Cover and steam for 5-10 mins until just tender.

To serve...
● Remove the roast potatoes from the oven and serve with the chicken, vegetables and gravy.

Turkey

The day before...
Cook the braised red cabbage following the recipe on p150. Leave to cool completely, then cover and put in the fridge.

Five hours to go...
● Take the turkey out of the fridge and allow it to come to room temperature.

Four hours to go...
● Preheat the oven to 190°C, fan 170°C, gas 5. Prepare the turkey following the recipe on p30.

Three hours 30 mins to go...
● Roast the turkey following the recipe until cooked: the juices should run clear when a skewer is inserted into the thigh.

1 hour 30 mins to go...
● Prepare the potatoes, carrots and parsnips following the recipes on p150. Cover and set aside. If you wish to serve steamed vegetables with the roast, prepare them now, too.

50 mins to go...
● Parboil the potatoes. At the same time put the goose or duck fat in a roasting tin and heat in the oven for 15 mins until sizzling.

30-35 mins to go...
● When the turkey is cooked, take it out of the oven, cover with foil and rest in a warm place. Turn the oven up to 220°C, fan 200°C, gas 7 and roast the potatoes in the hot fat for 30-40 mins until golden. Roast the carrots and parsnips at the same time. Meanwhile, make the gravy with pan juices following the recipe on p14 but doubling the quantities (without the garlic). Gently reheat the red cabbage on the hob for 20-25 mins, until piping hot.

10 mins to go...
● If you are serving extra steamed vegetables with the roast, put in a steamer set over a pan of simmering water. Cover and steam for 5-10 mins until just tender.

To serve...
● Remove the roast vegetables from the oven and serve with the turkey, braised red cabbage, steamed vegetables and gravy.

Lamb

3 hours to go...
Take the lamb out of the fridge and allow it to come to room temperature. Make the lemon and herb butter for the steamed vegetables following the recipe on p164, and chill in the fridge.

2 hours to go...
● Preheat the oven to 220°C, fan 200°C, gas 7. Prepare the lamb following the recipe on p50.

1 hour 50 mins to go...
● Roast the lamb following the recipe until cooked to your liking.

1 hour 15 mins to go...
● While the lamb is roasting, prepare the roast potatoes. Follow the recipe on p150, boiling the potatoes for an extra 2-3 mins. Heat the fat in the roasting tin for 12 mins, then add the potatoes. Roast on a shelf underneath the lamb for 40 mins, turning occasionally.

45 mins to go...
● Prepare the vegetables for steaming (see recipe p164) and cover and set aside. Make the mint sauce following the recipe on p49.

15-20 mins to go...
● When the lamb is cooked, take it out of the oven, cover tightly with foil and let rest in a warm place. Turn the oven up to 220°C, fan 200°C, gas 7 and continue roasting the potatoes for 15-20 mins or until crisp and golden.

10 mins to go...
● Cook the steamed vegetables with herb butter following the recipe on p164.

To serve...
● Remove the roast potatoes from the oven and serve with the lamb, steamed vegetables with herb butter, and mint sauce.

Beef

3 hours to go...
Take the beef out of the fridge and allow it to come to room temperature.

2 hours to go...
● Preheat the oven to 220°C, fan 200°C, gas 7. Prepare the beef following the recipe on p68.

1 hour 50 mins to go...
● Roast the beef following the recipe until cooked to your liking, reducing the oven temperature to 180°C, fan 160°C, gas 4 after 30 mins.

1 hour 25 mins to go...
● While the beef is roasting, prepare the potatoes. Follow the recipe on p150, boiling the potatoes for an extra 2-3 mins. Heat the fat in the roasting tin for 12 mins, then add the potatoes. Roast on a shelf underneath the beef for 50 mins, turning occasionally. If you wish to serve any other steamed vegetables, then prepare them now too.

45 mins to go...
● Make the batter for the Yorkshire puddings following the recipe on p72. Cover; set aside.

20 mins to go...
● When the beef is cooked, take it out of the oven, cover tightly with foil and let rest in a warm place for up to 30 mins. Turn the oven up to 220°C, fan 200°C, gas 7 and continue roasting the potatoes for 15-20 mins or until crisp and golden. Cook the Yorkshire puddings following the recipe. Meanwhile, make the gravy with the pan juices following the recipe on p68.

10 mins to go...
● If you are serving extra steamed vegetables with the roast, put in a steamer set over a pan of simmering water. Cover and steam for 5-10 mins until just tender.

To serve...
● Remove the roast potatoes and Yorkshire puddings from the oven and serve with the beef, steamed vegetables and gravy.

Pork

The day before...
● Cook the braised red cabbage following the recipe on p150. Leave to cool completely, then cover and put in the fridge.

4 hours 20 mins to go...
● Take the pork out of the fridge and allow it to come to room temperature.

3 hours 20 mins to go...
● Preheat the oven to 190°C, fan 170°C, gas 5. Prepare the pork following the recipe on p86.

3 hours 15 mins to go...
● Roast the pork following the recipe until cooked.

1 hour 30 mins to go...
● While the pork is roasting, prepare the potatoes following the recipe on p150. Cover and set aside. If you wish to serve any other steamed vegetables with the roast, then prepare them now too. Make the apple sauce following the recipe on p86.

50 mins to go...
● Parboil the potatoes for 15 mins. At the same time, put the goose or duck fat in a roasting tin and heat in the oven for 15 mins until sizzling.

30-40 mins to go...
● When the pork is cooked, take it out of the oven, cover tightly with foil and let rest in a warm place. Turn the oven up to 220°C, fan 200°C, gas 7 and roast the potatoes in the hot fat for 30-40 mins or until crisp and golden. Gently reheat the red cabbage on the hob for 20-25 mins, stirring frequently, until hot. Make the gravy following the recipe on p86.

10 mins to go...
● If you are serving extra steamed vegetables, put in a steamer set over a pan of simmering water. Cover and steam for 5-10 mins until just tender.

To serve...
● Remove the roast potatoes from the oven and serve with the pork, braised red cabbage, steamed vegetables, gravy and apple sauce.

A-Z Index

FOOD SAFETY & HEALTH INFORMATION
- Refer to packaging for full preparation and cooking instructions.
- Wash fresh vegetables, fruit and herbs before use.
- Public health advice is to avoid consumption of raw or lightly cooked eggs, especially for those vulnerable to infections, including pregnant women, babies and the elderly.
- Use separate equipment and surfaces for raw and ready-to-eat food, or wash thoroughly in between use.
- Wash hands thoroughly before and after handling raw food.
- Cover raw meat and store at the bottom of the fridge separate from ready-to-eat food.
- When reheating leftover food, make sure it is piping hot throughout before consuming.

Conversion table

Weights		Volume		Measurements		Oven temperatures		
							fan	gas
15g	½oz	25ml	1floz	2mm	⅟₁₆in	110ºC	90ºC	
25g	1oz	50ml	2floz	3mm	⅛in	120ºC	100ºC	½
40g	1½oz	75ml	3floz	4mm	⅛in	140ºC	120ºC	1
50g	2oz	100ml	4floz	5mm	¼in	150ºC	130ºC	2
60g	2½oz	150ml	5floz (¼pint)	1cm	½in	160ºC	140ºC	3
75g	3oz	175ml	6floz	2cm	¾in	180ºC	160ºC	4
100g	3½oz	200ml	7floz	2.5cm	1in	190ºC	170ºC	5
125g	4oz	225ml	8floz	3cm	1¼in	200ºC	180ºC	6
150g	5oz	250ml	9floz	4cm	1½in	220ºC	200ºC	7
175g	6oz	300ml	10floz (½pint)	4.5cm	1¾in	230ºC	210ºC	8
200g	7oz	350ml	13floz	5cm	2in	240ºC	220ºC	9
225g	8oz	400ml	14floz	6cm	2½in			
250g	9oz	450ml	16floz (¾pint)	7.5cm	3in			
275g	10oz	600ml	20floz (1 pint)	9cm	3½in			
300g	11oz	750ml	25floz (1¼pints)	10cm	4in			
350g	12oz	900ml	30floz (1½pints)	13cm	5in			
375g	13oz	1 litre	34floz (1¾pints)	13.5cm	5¼in			
400g	14oz	1.2 litres	40floz (2 pints)	15cm	6in			
425g	15oz	1.5 litres	52floz (2½pints)	16cm	6½in			
450g	1lb	1.8 litres	60floz (3 pints)	18cm	7in			
500g	1lb 2oz			19cm	7½in			
650g	1lb 7oz			20cm	8in			
675g	1½lb			23cm	9in			
700g	1lb 9oz			24cm	9½in			
750g	1lb 11oz			25.5cm	10in			
900g	2lb			28cm	11in			
1kg	2lb 4oz			30cm	12in			
1.5kg	3lb 6oz			32.5cm	13in			
				35cm	14in			

seven.co.uk

© Produced by Seven Publishing on behalf of Sainsbury's Supermarkets Ltd, 33 Holborn, London EC1N 2HT.
Published December 2013. All rights reserved. No part of this publication may be reproduced, stored in a retrieval system or transmitted in any form by any means, electronic, mechanical, photocopying, recording or otherwise, without the prior written permission of Seven Publishing. Printed and bound by Butler Tanner & Dennis Ltd, Frome and London. ISBN-13: 978-0-9566303-9-1

Credits

Food
Food editors Angela Drake, Angela Romeo
Food assistant Lottie Covell
Recipes & food styling Sophie Austin-Smith,
Fergal Connolly, Silvana Franco, Emma
Franklin, Katy Greenwood, Sue Henderson,
Sal Henley, Catherine Hill, Lucy Jessop,
Jenna Leiter, Lucy McKelvie, Bianca Nice,
Ros Plummer, Jack Sargeson, Mima Sinclair,
Joy Skipper , Jenny White, Mari Williams

Editorial
Editors Christine Faughlin, Ward Hellewell
Editorial assistant Emma Brooke

Design & photography
Senior art directors
David Jenkins, Pamela Price
Senior designer Dan Perry
Prop stylist Morag Farquhar
Photography Craig Robertson,
Jonathan Kennedy
Additional photography
Carolyn Barber, Terry Benson, Michael Hart,
Amanda Heywood, Bill Kingston, Richard
Jung, Claire Miller, Gareth Morgans, David
Munns, William Lingwood, William Shaw,
James Tse, Philip Webb
Additional stylists Jenny Iggleden, Emma
Lahaye, Robert Merrett, Roisin Neild

Account management
Account executive Jo Brennan
Consultant Lynne de Lacy
Client director Andy Roughton
Head of content Helen Renshaw

For Sainsbury's
Book team Phil Carroll, Mavis Sarfo,
Lee Scott, Louise Ward
Nutrition Annie Denny

Print & production
Production manager Mike Lamb
Colour origination F1 Colour Ltd
Printers Butler Tanner & Dennis Ltd

Special thanks to... Patricia Baker,
Miranda Keyes, Kat Mead, Julie Stevens,
Sasha Turnbull, Hannah Yeadon

seven.co.uk

FSC
www.fsc.org

MIX
Paper from
responsible sources
FSC® C023561

GREAT BRITISH BOOKS
PUBLISHED & PRINTED IN THE UK

The Greatest Sport of All
The Boxing Scene
An Unforgiving Sport
Boxing Is …
Box: The Face of Boxing
The Legend of Muhammad Ali (with Bart Barry)
Winks and Daggers
And the New …
Straight Writes and Jabs
Thomas Hauser on Boxing
A Hurting Sport
Muhammad Ali: A Tribute to the Greatest

FICTION

Ashworth & Palmer
Agatha's Friends
The Beethoven Conspiracy
Hanneman's War
The Fantasy
Dear Hannah
The Hawthorne Group
Mark Twain Remembers
Finding the Princess
Waiting for Carver Boyd
The Final Recollections of Charles Dickens
The Baker's Tale

FOR CHILDREN

Martin Bear & Friends

AUTHOR'

Muhammad Ali: His Life and Tim
is often referred to as the definit
of Ali's life. This is the companic
version was published in the U
title *Muhammad Ali: The Lost L*
of the essays and articles I'd w
Tribute to the Greatest contains
the previously unpublished es

HarperSpor

An imprint of HarperC

1 London Bridge

London SE1 9

www.harpercolli

A catalogue record

available from the B

ISBN 978-0-00-

Printed and bound in

Clays Ltd, St

Find out more about HarperC

www.harpercolli

CONTENTS

PART I

ESSAYS

THE IMPORTANCE OF MUHAMMAD ALI

(1996)

Cassius Marcellus Clay Jr, as Muhammad Ali was once known, was born in Louisville, Kentucky, on 17 January 1942. Louisville was a city with segregated public facilities; noted for the Kentucky Derby, mint juleps, and other reminders of southern aristocracy. Blacks were the servant class in Louisville. They raked manure in the backstretch at Churchill Downs and cleaned other people's homes. Growing up in Louisville, the best on the socio-economic ladder that most black people could realistically hope for was to become a clergyman or a teacher at an all-black school. In a society where it was often felt that might makes right, 'white' was synonymous with both.

Ali's father, Cassius Marcellus Clay Sr, supported a wife and two sons by painting billboards and signs. Ali's mother, Odessa Grady Clay, worked on occasion as a household domestic. 'I remember one time when Cassius was small,' Mrs Clay later recalled. 'We were downtown at a five-and-ten-cents store. He wanted a drink of water, and they wouldn't give him one because of his colour. And that really affected him. He didn't like that at all, being a child and thirsty. He started crying, and I said, "Come on; I'll take you someplace and get you some water." But it really hurt him.'

When Cassius Clay was 12 years old, his bike was stolen. That led him to take up boxing under the tutelage of a Louisville policeman named Joe Martin. Clay advanced through the amateur ranks, won a gold medal at the 1960 Olympics in Rome, and turned pro under the guidance of The Louisville Sponsoring Group, a syndicate comprised of 11 wealthy white men.

'Cassius was something in those days,' his long-time physician, Ferdie Pacheco, remembers. 'He began training in Miami with Angelo Dundee, and Angelo put him in a den of iniquity called the Mary Elizabeth Hotel, because Angelo is one of the most innocent men in the world and it was a cheap hotel. This place was full of pimps, thieves and drug dealers. And here's Cassius, who comes from a good home, and all of a sudden he's involved with this circus of street people. At first, the hustlers thought he was just another guy to take to the cleaners; another guy to steal from; another guy to sell dope to; another guy to fix up with a girl. He had this incredible innocence about him, and usually that kind of person gets eaten alive in the ghetto. But then the hustlers all fell in love with him, like everybody does, and they started to feel protective of him. If someone tried to sell him a girl, the others would say, "Leave him alone; he's not into that." If a guy came around, saying, "Have a drink," it was, "Shut up; he's in training." But that's the story of Ali's life. He's always been like a little kid, climbing out onto tree limbs, sawing them off behind him and coming out okay.'

In the early stages of his professional career, Cassius Clay was more highly regarded for his charm and personality than for his ring skills. He told the world that he was 'The Greatest', but the brutal realities of boxing seemed to dictate otherwise. Then, on 25 February 1964, in one of the most stunning upsets in sports history, Clay knocked out Sonny Liston to become heavyweight champion of the world. Two days later, he shocked the world again by announcing that he had accepted the teachings of a black separatist religion known as the Nation of Islam. And on 6 March 1964, he took the name 'Muhammad Ali', which was given to him by his spiritual mentor, Elijah Muhammad.

For the next three years, Ali dominated boxing as thoroughly and magnificently as any fighter ever. But outside the ring, his persona was being sculpted in ways that were even more important. 'My first impression of Cassius Clay,' author Alex Haley later recalled, 'was of someone with an incredibly versatile personality. You never knew quite where he was in psychic posture. He was almost like that shell game, with a pea and three shells. You know: which shell is the pea under? But he had a belief in himself and convictions far stronger than anybody dreamed he would.'

As the 1960s grew more tumultuous, Ali became a lightning rod for dissent in America. His message of black pride and black resistance to white domination was on the cutting edge of the era. Not everything he preached was wise, and Ali himself now rejects some of the beliefs that he adhered to then. Indeed, one might find an allegory for his life in a remark he once made to fellow Olympian Ralph Boston. 'I played golf,' Ali reported, 'and I hit the thing long, but I never knew where it was going.'

Sometimes, though, Ali knew precisely where he was going. On 28 April 1967, citing his religious beliefs, he refused induction into the United States Army at the height of the war in Vietnam. Ali's refusal followed a blunt statement, voiced 14 months earlier – 'I ain't got no quarrel with them Vietcong.' And the American establishment responded with a vengeance, demanding, 'Since when did war become a matter of personal quarrels? War is duty. Your country calls – you answer.'

On 20 June 1967, Ali was convicted of refusing induction into the United States Armed Forces and sentenced to five years in prison. Four years later, his conviction was unanimously over-turned by the United States Supreme Court. But in the interim, he was stripped of his title and precluded from fighting for three and a half years. 'He did not believe he would ever fight again,' Ali's wife at that time, Belinda Ali, said of her husband's 'exile' from boxing. 'He wanted to, but he truly believed that he would never fight again.'

Meanwhile, Ali's impact was growing – among black Americans, among those who opposed the war in Vietnam, among all people with grievances against The System. 'It's hard to imagine that a sports figure could have so much political influence on so many people,' observes Julian Bond. And Jerry Izenberg of the *Newark Star-Ledger* recalls the scene in October 1970, when at long last Ali was allowed to return to the ring.

'About two days before the fight against Jerry Quarry, it became clear to me that something had changed,' Izenberg remembers. 'Long lines of people were checking into the hotel. They were dressed differently than the people who used to go to fights. I saw men wearing capes and hats with plumes, and women wearing next to nothing at all. Limousines were lined up at the curb. Money was being flashed everywhere. And I was confused, until a friend of mine who was black said to me, "You don't get it. Don't you understand? This is the heavyweight champion who beat The Man. The Man said he would never fight again, and here he is, fighting in Atlanta, Georgia.'"

Four months later, Ali's comeback was temporarily derailed when he lost to Joe Frazier. It was a fight of truly historic proportions. Nobody in America was neutral that night. 'It does me good to lose about once every ten years,' Ali jested after the bout. But physically and psychologically, his pain was enormous. Subsequently, Ali avenged his loss to Frazier twice in historic bouts. Ultimately, he won the heavyweight championship of the world an unprecedented three times.

Meanwhile, Ali's religious views were evolving. In the mid-1970s, he began studying the Qur'an more seriously, focusing on Orthodox Islam. His earlier adherence to the teachings of Elijah Muhammad – that white people are 'devils' and there is no heaven or hell – was replaced by a spiritual embrace of all people and preparation for his own afterlife. In 1984, Ali spoke out publicly against the separatist doctrine of Louis Farrakhan, declaring, 'What he teaches is not at all what we believe in. He represents the time of our struggle in the dark and a time of confusion in us, and we don't want to be associated with that at all.'

Ali today is a deeply religious man. Although his health is not what it once was, his thought processes remain clear. He is, still, the most recognisable and the most loved person in the world.

But is Muhammad Ali relevant today? In an age when self-dealing and greed have become public policy, does a 54-year-old man who suffers from Parkinson's syndrome really matter? At a time when an intrusive worldwide electronic media dominates, and celebrity status and fame are mistaken for heroism, is true heroism possible?

In response to these questions, it should first be noted that, unlike many famous people, Ali is not a creation of the media. He used the media in an extraordinary fashion. And certainly, he came along at the right time in terms of television. In 1960, when Cassius Clay won an Olympic gold medal, TV was crawling out of its infancy. The television networks had just learned how to focus cameras on people, build them up, and follow stories through to the end. And Ali loved that. As Jerry Izenberg later observed, 'Once Ali found out about television, it was, "Where? Bring the cameras! I'm ready now."'

Still, Ali's fame is pure. Athletes today are known as much for their endorsement contracts and salaries as for their competitive performances. Fame now often stems from sports marketing rather than the other way around. Bo Jackson was briefly one of the most famous men in America because of his Nike shoe commercials. Michael Jordan and virtually all of his brethren derive a substantial portion of their visibility from commercial endeavours. Yet, as great an athlete as Michael Jordan is, he doesn't have the ability to move people's hearts and minds the way that Ali has moved them for decades. And what Muhammad Ali means to the world can be viewed from an ever deepening perspective today.

Ali entered the public arena as an athlete. To many, that's significant.

'Sports is a major factor in ideological control,' says sociologist Noam Chomsky. 'After all, people have minds; they've got to be involved in something; and it's important to make sure they're involved in things that have absolutely no significance. So professional sports is perfect. It instils the right ideas of passivity. It's a way of keeping people diverted from issues like who runs society and who makes the decisions on how their lives are to be led.'

But Ali broke the mould. When he appeared on the scene, it was popular among those in the vanguard of the civil rights movement to take the 'safe' path. That path wasn't safe for those who participated in the struggle. Martin Luther King Jr, Medgar Evers, Viola Liuzzo, and other courageous men and women were subjected to economic assaults, violence and death when they carried the struggle 'too far'. But the road they travelled was designed to be as non-threatening as possible for white America. White Americans were told, 'All that black people want is what you want for yourselves. We're appealing to your conscience.'

Then along came Ali, preaching not 'white American values', but freedom and equality of a kind rarely seen anywhere in the world. And as if that wasn't threatening enough, Ali attacked the status quo from outside politics and outside the accepted strategies of the civil rights movement.

'I remember when Ali joined the Nation of Islam,' Julian Bond recalls. 'The act of joining was not something many of us particularly liked. But the notion he'd do it; that he'd jump out there, join this group that was so despised by mainstream America, and be proud of it, sent a little thrill through you.'

'The nature of the controversy,' football great Jim Brown (also the founder of the Black Economic Union) said later, 'was that white folks could not stand free black folks. White America could not stand to think that a sports hero that it was allowing to make big dollars would embrace something like the Nation of Islam. But this young man had the courage to stand up like no one else and risk, not only his life, but everything else that he had.'

Ali himself down-played his role. 'I'm not no leader. I'm a little humble follower,' he said in 1964. But to many, he was the ultimate symbol of black pride and black resistance to an unjust social order.

Sometimes Ali spoke with humour. 'I'm not just saying black is best because I'm black,' he told a college audience during his exile from boxing. 'I can prove it. If you want some rich dirt, you look for the black dirt. If you want the best bread, you want the whole wheat rye bread. Costs more money, but it's better for your digestive system. You want the best sugar for cooking; it's the brown sugar. The blacker the berry, the sweeter the fruit. If I want a strong cup of coffee, I'll take it black. The coffee gets weak if I integrate it with white cream.'

Other times, Ali's remarks were less humorous and more barbed. But for millions of people, the experience of being black changed because of Muhammad Ali. Listen to the voices of some who heard his call:

> Bryant Gumbel: One of the reasons the civil rights movement went forward was that black people were able to overcome their fear. And I honestly believe that, for many black Americans, that came from watching Muhammad Ali. He simply refused to be afraid. And being that way, he gave other people courage.

Alex Haley: We are not white, you know. And it's not an anti-white thing to be proud to be us and to want someone to champion. And Muhammad Ali was the absolute ultimate champion.

Arthur Ashe: Ali didn't just change the image that African-Americans have of themselves. He opened the eyes of a lot of white people to the potential of African-Americans; who we are and what we can be.

Abraham Lincoln once said that he regarded the Emancipation Proclamation as the central act of his administration. 'It is a momentous thing,' Lincoln wrote, 'to be the instrument under Providence of the liberation of a race.'

Muhammad Ali was such an instrument. As commentator Gil Noble later explained, 'Everybody was plugged into this man, because he was taking on America. There had never been anybody in his position who directly addressed himself to racism. Racism was virulent, but you didn't talk about those things. If you wanted to make it in this country, you had to be quiet, carry yourself in a certain way and not say anything about what was going on, even though there was a knife sticking in your chest. Ali changed all of that. He just laid it out and talked about racism and slavery and all of that stuff. He put it on the table. And everybody who was black, whether they said it overtly or covertly, said "Amen."'

But Ali's appeal would come to extend far beyond black America. When he refused induction into the United States Army, he stood up to armies everywhere in support of the proposition that, 'Unless you have a very good reason to kill, war is wrong.'

'I don't think Ali was aware of the impact that his not going in the army would have on other people,' says his long-time friend, Howard Bingham. 'Ali was just doing what he thought was right for him. He had no idea at the time that this was going to affect how people all over the United States would react to the war and the draft.'

Many Americans vehemently condemned Ali's stand. It came at a time when most people in the United States still supported the war. But as Julian Bond later observed, 'When Ali refused to take the symbolic step forward, everybody knew about it moments later. You could hear people talking about it on street corners. It was on everyone's lips.'

'The government didn't need Ali to fight the war,' Ramsey Clark, then the Attorney General of the United States, recalls. 'But they would have loved to put him in the service; get his picture in there; maybe give him a couple of stripes on his sleeve, and take him all over the world. Think of the power that would have had in Africa, Asia and South America. Here's this proud American serviceman, fighting symbolically for his country. They would have loved to do that.'

But instead, what the government got was a reaffirmation of Ali's earlier statement – 'I ain't got no quarrel with them Vietcong.'

'And that rang serious alarm bells,' says Noam Chomsky, 'because it raised the question of why poor people in the United States were being forced by rich people in the United States to kill poor people in Vietnam. Putting it simply, that's what it amounted to. And Ali put it very simply in ways that people could understand.'

Ali's refusal to accept induction placed him once and for all at the vortex of the 1960s. 'You had riots in the streets; you had assassinations; you had the war in Vietnam,' Dave Kindred of the *Atlanta Constitution* remembers. 'It was a violent, turbulent, almost indecipherable time in America, and Ali was in all of those fires at once in addition to being heavyweight champion of the world.'

That championship was soon taken from Ali, but he never wavered from his cause. Speaking to a college audience, he proclaimed, 'I would like to say to those of you who think I've lost so much, I have gained everything. I have peace of heart; I have a clear, free conscience. And I'm proud. I wake up happy. I go to bed happy. And if I go to jail, I'll go to jail happy. Boys go to war and die for what they believe, so I don't see why the world is so shook up over me suffering for what I believe. What's so unusual about that?'

'It really impressed me that Ali gave up his title,' says former heavyweight champion Larry Holmes, who understands Ali's sacrifice as well as anyone. 'Once you have it, you never want to lose it; because once you lose it, it's hard to get it back.'

But by the late 1960s, Ali was more than heavyweight champion. That had become almost a side issue. He was a living embodiment of the proposition that principles matter. And the most powerful thing about him was no longer his fists; it was his conscience and the composure with which he carried himself:

Kwame Turé [formerly known as Stokely Carmichael]: Muhammad Ali used himself as a perfect instrument to advance the struggle of humanity by demonstrating clearly that principles are more important than material wealth. It's not just what Ali did. The way he did it was just as important.

Wilbert McClure [Ali's room-mate and fellow gold medal winner at the Olympics]: He always carried himself with his head high and with grace and composure. And we can't say that about all of his detractors; some of them in political office, some of them in pulpits, some of them thought of as nice, upstanding citizens. No, we can't say that about all of them.

Charles Morgan [former Director of the ACLU Southern Office]: I remember thinking at the time, what kind of a foolish world am I living in where people want to put this man in jail.

Dave Kindred: He was one thing, always. He was always brave.

Ali was far from perfect, and it would do him a disservice not to acknowledge his flaws. It's hard to imagine a person so powerful yet at times so naïve; almost on the order of Forrest Gump. On occasion, Ali has acted irrationally. He cherishes honour and is an honourable person, but too often excuses dishonourable behaviour in others. His accommodation with dictators like Mobuto Sese Seko and Ferdinand Marcos and his willingness to fight in their countries stand in stark contrast to his love of freedom. There is nothing redeeming in one black person calling another black person a 'gorilla', which was the label that Ali affixed to Joe Frazier. Nor should one gloss over Ali's past belief in racial separatism and the profligate womanising of his younger days. But the things that Ali has done right in his life far outweigh the mistakes of his past. And the rough edges of his earlier years have been long since forgiven or forgotten.

What remains is a legacy of monumental proportions and a living reminder of what people can be. Muhammad Ali's influence on an entire nation, black and white, and a whole world of nations has been incalculable. He's not just a champion. A champion is someone who wins an athletic competition. Ali goes beyond that.

It was inevitable that someone would come along and do what Jackie Robinson did. Robinson did it in a glorious way that personified his own dignity and courage. But if Jackie Robinson hadn't been there, someone else – Roy Campanella, Willie Mays, Henry Aaron – would have stepped in with his own brand of excitement and grace and opened baseball's doors. With or without Jack Johnson, eventually a black man would have won the heavyweight championship of the world. And sooner or later, there would have been a black athlete who, like Joe Louis, was universally admired and loved.

But Ali carved out a place in history that was, and remains, uniquely his own. And it's unlikely that anyone other than Muhammad Ali could have created and fulfilled that role. Ali didn't just mirror his times. He wasn't a passive figure carried along by currents stronger than he was. He fought the current; he swam against the tide. He stood for something, stayed with it, and prevailed.

Muhammad Ali is an international treasure. More than anyone else of his generation, he belongs to the people of the world and is loved by them. No matter what happens in the years ahead, he has already made us better. He encouraged millions of people to believe in themselves, raise their aspirations and accomplish things that might not have been done without him. He wasn't just a standard-bearer for black Americans. He stood up for everyone.

And that's the importance of Muhammad Ali.

MUHAMMAD ALI
AND BOXING

(1996)

'You could spend twenty years studying Ali,' Dave Kindred once wrote, 'and still not know what he is or who he is. He's a wise man, and he's a child. I've never seen anyone who was so giving and, at the same time, so self-centred. He's either the most complex guy that I've ever been around or the most simple. And I still can't figure out which it is. I mean, I truly don't know. We were sure who Ali was only when he danced before us in the dazzle of the ring lights. Then he could hide nothing.'

And so it was that the world first came to know Muhammad Ali, not as a person, not as a social, political or religious figure, but as a fighter. His early professional bouts infuriated and entertained as much as they impressed. Cassius Clay held his hands too low. He backed away from punches, rather than bobbing and weaving out of danger, and lacked true knockout power. Purists cringed when he predicted the round in which he intended to knock out his opponent, and grimaced when he did so and bragged about each new conquest.

Then, at the age of 22, Clay challenged Sonny Liston for the world heavyweight crown. Liston was widely regarded as the most intimidating, ferocious, powerful fighter of his era. Clay was such a prohibitive underdog that Robert Lipsyte, who covered the bout for *The New York Times*, was instructed to 'find out the directions from the arena to the nearest hospital, so I wouldn't waste deadline time getting there after Clay was knocked out'. But as David Ben-Gurion once proclaimed, 'Anyone who doesn't believe in miracles is not a realist.' Cassius Clay knocked out Sonny Liston to become heavyweight champion of the world.

Officially, Ali's reign as champion was divided into three segments. And while he fought through the administrations of seven Presidents, his greatness as a fighter was most clearly on display in the three years after he first won the crown. During the course of 37 months, Ali fought ten times. No heavyweight in history has defended his title more frequently against more formidable opposition in more dominant fashion than Ali did in those years.

Boxing, in the first instance, is about not getting hit. 'And I can't be hit,' Ali told the world. 'It's impossible for me to lose because there's not a man on earth with the speed and ability to beat me.'

In his rematch with Liston, which ended in a first-round knockout, Ali was hit only twice. Victories over Floyd Patterson, George Chuvalo, Henry Cooper, Brian London and Karl Mildenberger followed. Then, on 14 November 1966, Ali did battle against Cleveland Williams. Over the course of three rounds, Ali landed more than one hundred punches, scored four knockdowns and was hit a total of three times. 'The hypocrites and phonies are all shook up because everything I said would come true did come true,' Ali chortled afterward. 'I said I was The Greatest, and they thought I was just acting the fool. Now, instead of admitting that I'm the best heavyweight in all history, they don't know what to do.'

Ali's triumph over Cleveland Williams was followed by victories over Ernie Terrell and Zora Folley. Then, after refusing induction into the United States Army, he was stripped of his title and forced out of boxing. 'If I never fight again, this is the last of the champions,' Ali said of his, and boxing's, plight. 'The next title is a political belt, a racial belt, an organisation belt. There's no more real world champion until I'm physically beat.'

In October 1970, Ali was allowed to return to boxing, but his skills were no longer the same. The legs that had allowed him to 'dance' for 15 rounds without stopping no longer carried him as surely around the ring. His reflexes, while still superb, were no longer lightning fast. Ali prevailed in his first two comeback fights, against Jerry Quarry and Oscar Bonavena. Then he challenged Joe Frazier, who was the 'organisation' champion by virtue of victories over Buster Mathis and Jimmy Ellis.

'Champion of the world? Ain't but one champion,' Ali said before his first bout against Frazier. 'How you gonna have two champions of the world? He's an alternate champion. The real champion is back now.' But Frazier thought otherwise. And on 8 March 1971, he bested Ali over 15 brutal rounds.

'He's not a great boxer,' Ali said afterward. 'But he's a great slugger, a great street fighter, a bull fighter. He takes a lot of punches, his eyes close and he just keeps coming. I figured he could take the punches. But one thing surprised me in this fight, and that's that he landed his left hook as regular as he did. Usually, I don't get hit over and over with the same punch, and he hit me solid a lot of times.'

Some fighters can't handle defeat. They fly so high when they're on top that a loss brings them irrevocably crashing down. 'What was interesting to me after the loss to Frazier,' says Ferdie Pacheco, 'was we'd seen this undefeatable guy. Now how was he going to handle defeat? Was he going to be a cry-baby? Was he going to be crushed? Well, what we found out was, this guy takes defeat like he takes victory. All he said was, "I'll beat him next time."'

What Ali said was plain and simple: 'I got to whup Joe Frazier because he beat me. Anybody would like to say, "I retired undefeated." I can't say that no more. But if I could say, "I got beat, but I came back and beat him," I'd feel better.'

Following his loss to Frazier, Ali won ten fights in a row; eight of them against world-class opponents. Then, in March 1973, he stumbled when a little-known fighter named Ken Norton broke his jaw in the second round en route to a 12-round upset decision.

'I knew something was strange,' Ali said after the bout, 'because, if a bone is broken, the whole internalness in your body, everything, is nauseating. I didn't know what it was, but I could feel my teeth moving around, and I had to hold my teeth extra tight to keep the bottom from moving. My trainers wanted me to stop. But I was thinking about those nineteen thousand people in the arena and *Wide World of Sports*, millions of people at home watching in 62 countries. So what I had to do was put up a good fight; go the distance and not get hit on the jaw again.'

Now Ali had a new target; a priority ahead of even Joe Frazier. 'After Ali got his jaw broke, he wanted Norton bad,' recalls Lloyd Wells, a long-time Ali confidant. 'Herbert Muhammad [Ali's manager] was trying to put him in another fight, and Ali kept saying, "No, get me Norton. I want Norton." Herbert was saying, but we got a big purse; we got this, and we got that. And Ali was saying, "No, just get me Norton. I don't want nobody but Norton."'

Ali got Norton – and beat him. Then, after an interim bout against Rudi Lubbers, he got Joe Frazier again – and beat him too. From a technical point of view, the second Ali–Frazier bout was probably Ali's best performance after his exile from boxing. He did what he wanted to do, showing flashes of what he'd once been as a fighter but never would be again. Then Ali journeyed to Zaïre to challenge George Foreman, who had dethroned Frazier to become heavyweight champion of the world.

'Foreman can punch but he can't fight,' Ali said of his next foe. But most observers thought that Foreman could do both. As was the case when Ali fought Sonny Liston, he entered the ring a heavy underdog. Still, studying his opponent's armour, Ali thought he detected a flaw. Foreman's punching power was awesome, but his stamina and will were suspect. Thus, the 'rope-a-dope' was born.

'The strategy on Ali's part was to cover up, because George was like a tornado,' former boxing great Archie Moore, who was one of Foreman's cornermen that night, recalls. 'And when you see a tornado coming, you run into the house and you cover up. You go into the basement and get out of the way of that strong wind, because you know that otherwise it's going to blow you away. That's what Ali did. He covered up and the storm was raging. But after a while, the storm blew itself out.'

Or phrased differently, 'Yeah, Ali let Foreman punch himself out,' says Jerry Izenberg. 'But the rope-a-dope wouldn't have worked against Foreman for anyone in the world except Ali, because on top of everything else, Ali was tougher than everyone else. No one in the world except Ali could have taken George Foreman's punches.'

Ali stopped Foreman in the eighth round to regain the heavyweight championship. Then, over the next thirty months at the peak of his popularity as champion, he fought nine times. Those bouts showed Ali to be a courageous fighter, but a fighter on the decline.

Like most ageing combatants, Ali did his best to put a positive spin on things. But viewed in realistic terms, 'I'm more experienced' translated into 'I'm getting older.' 'I'm stronger at this weight' meant 'I should lose a few pounds.' 'I'm more patient now' was a cover for 'I'm slower.'

Eight of Ali's first nine fights during his second reign as champion did little to enhance his legacy. But sandwiched in between matches against the likes of Jean-Pierre Coopman and Richard Dunn and mediocre showings against more legitimate adversaries, Ali won what might have been the greatest fight of all time.

On 1 October 1975, Ali and Joe Frazier met in the Philippines, six miles outside of Manila, to do battle for the third time.

'You have to understand the premise behind that fight,' Ferdie Pacheco recalls. 'The first fight was life and death, and Frazier won. Second fight: Ali figures him out; no problem, relatively

easy victory for Ali. Then Ali beats Foreman, and Frazier's sun
sets. And I don't care what anyone says now; all of us thought that
Joe Frazier was shot. We all thought that this was going to be an
easy fight. Ali comes out, dances around, and knocks him out in
eight or nine rounds. That's what we figured. And you know
what happened in that fight. Ali took a beating like you'd never
believe anyone could take. When he said afterward that it was the
closest thing he'd ever known to death – let me tell you something: if dying is that hard, I'd hate to see it coming. But Frazier
took the same beating. And in the fourteenth round, Ali just
about took his head off. I was cringing. The heat was awesome.
Both men were dehydrated. The place was like a time-bomb. I
thought we were close to a fatality. It was a terrible moment, and
then Joe Frazier's corner stopped it.'

'Ali–Frazier III was Ali–Frazier III,' says Jerry Izenberg. 'There's
nothing to compare it with. I've never witnessed anything like it.
And I'll tell you something else. Both fighters won that night,
and both fighters lost.'

Boxing is a tough business. The nature of the game is that
fighters get hit. Ali himself inflicted a lot of damage on ring
opponents during the course of his career. And in return: 'I've
been hit a lot,' he acknowledged, one month before the third
Frazier fight. 'I take punishment every day in training. I take
punishment in my fights. I take a lot of punishment; I just don't
show it.'

Still, as Ferdie Pacheco notes, 'The human brain wasn't meant
to get hit by a heavyweight punch. And the older you get, the
more susceptible you are to damage. When are you best? Between
fifteen and thirty. At that age, you're growing, you're strong,

you're developing. You can take punches and come back. But inevitably, if you keep fighting, you reach an age when every punch can cause damage. Nature begins giving you little bills and the amount keeps escalating, like when you owe money to the IRS and the government keeps adding and compounding the damage.'

In Manila, Joe Frazier landed 440 punches, many of them to Ali's head. After Manila would have been a good time for Ali to stop boxing, but too many people had a vested interest in his continuing to fight. Harold Conrad served for years as a publicist for Ali's bouts. 'You get a valuable piece of property like Ali,' Conrad said shortly before his death. 'How are you going to put it out of business? It's like shutting down a factory or closing down a big successful corporation. The people who are making money off the workers just don't want to do it.'

Thus, Ali fought on.

In 1977, he was hurt badly but came back to win a close decision over Earnie Shavers. 'In the second round, I had him in trouble,' Shavers remembers. 'I threw a right hand over Ali's jab, and I hurt him. He kind of wobbled. But Ali was so cunning, I didn't know if he was hurt or playing fox. I found out later that he was hurt. But he waved me in, so I took my time to be careful. I didn't want to go for the kill and get killed. And Ali was the kind of guy who, when you thought you had him hurt, he always seemed to come back. The guy seemed to pull off a miracle each time. I hit him a couple of good shots, but he recovered better than any other fighter I've known.'

Next up for Ali was Leon Spinks, a novice with an Olympic gold medal but only seven professional fights.

'Spinks was in awe of Ali,' Ron Borges of the *Boston Globe* recalls. 'The day before their first fight, I was having lunch in the coffee shop at Caesars Palace with Leon and [his trainer] Sam Solomon. No one knew who Leon was. Then Ali walked in, and everyone went crazy. "Look, there's Ali! Omigod, it's him!" And Leon was like everybody else. He got all excited. He was shouting, "Look, there he is! There's Ali!" In 24 hours, they'd be fighting each other, but right then, Leon was ready to carry Ali around the room on his shoulders.'

The next night, Spinks captured Ali's title with a relentless 15-round assault. Seven months later, Ali returned the favour, regaining the championship with a 15-round victory of his own. Then he retired from boxing, but two years later made an ill-advised comeback against Larry Holmes.

'Before the Holmes fight, you could clearly see the beginnings of Ali's physical deterioration,' remembers Barry Frank, who was representing Ali in various commercial endeavours on behalf of IMG. 'The huskiness had already come into his voice and he had a little bit of a balance problem. Sometimes he'd get up off a chair and, not stagger, but maybe take a half step to get his balance.'

Realistically speaking, it was obvious that Ali had no chance of beating Holmes. But there was always that kernel of doubt. Would beating Holmes be any more extraordinary than knocking out Sonny Liston and George Foreman? Ali himself fanned the flames. 'I'm so happy going into this fight,' he said shortly before the bout. 'I'm dedicating this fight to all the people who've been told, you can't do it. People who drop out of school because they're told they're dumb. People who go to crime because they don't think they can find jobs. I'm dedicating this fight to all of you people who have a Larry Holmes in your life. I'm gonna whup my Holmes, and I want you to whup your Holmes.'

But Holmes put it more succinctly. 'Ali is 38 years old. His mind is making a date that his body can't keep.'

Holmes was right. It was a horrible night. Old and seriously debilitated from the effects of an improperly prescribed drug called Thyrolar, Ali was a shell of his former self. He had no reflexes, no legs, no punch. Nothing, except his pride and the crowd chanting, 'Ali! Ali!'

'I really thought something bad might happen that night,' Jerry Izenberg recalls. 'And I was praying that it wouldn't be the something that we dread most in boxing. I've been at three fights where fighters died, and it sort of found a home in the back of my mind. I was saying, I don't want this man to get hurt. Whoever won the fight was irrelevant to me.'

It wasn't an athletic contest; just a brutal beating that went on and on. Later, some observers claimed that Holmes lay back because of his fondness for Ali. But Holmes was being cautious, not compassionate. 'I love the man,' he later acknowledged. 'But when the bell rung, I didn't even know his name.'

'By the ninth round, Ali had stopped fighting altogether,' Lloyd Wells remembers. 'He was just defending himself, and not doing a good job of that. Then, in the ninth round, Holmes hit him with a punch to the body, and Ali screamed. I never will forget that as long as I live. Ali screamed.'

The fight was stopped after 11 rounds. An era in boxing – and an entire historical era – was over. Now, years later, in addition to his more important social significance, Ali is widely recognised as the greatest fighter of all time. He was graced with almost unearthly physical skills and did everything that his body allowed him to do. In a sport that is often brutal and violent, he cast a long and graceful shadow.

How good was Ali?

'In the early days,' Ferdie Pacheco recalls, 'he fought as though he had a glass jaw and was afraid to get hit. He had the hyper reflexes of a frightened man. He was so fast that you had the feeling, "This guy is scared to death; he can't be that fast normally." Well, he wasn't scared. He was fast beyond belief and smart. Then he went into exile; and when he came back, he couldn't move like lightning any more. Everyone wondered, 'What happens now when he gets hit?' That's when we learned something else about him. That sissy-looking, soft-looking, beautiful-looking child-man was one of the toughest guys who ever lived.'

Ali didn't have one-punch knockout power. His most potent offensive weapon was speed; the speed of his jab and straight right hand. But when he sat down on his punches, as he did against Joe Frazier in Manila, he hit harder than most heavy-weights. And in addition to his other assets, he had superb foot-work, the ability to take a punch, and all of the intangibles that go into making a great fighter.

'Ali fought all wrong,' acknowledges Jerry Izenberg. 'Boxing people would say to me, "Any guy who can do this will beat him. Any guy who can do that will beat him." And after a while, I started saying back to them, "So you're telling me that any guy who can outjab the fastest jabber in the world can beat him. Any guy who can slip that jab, which is like lightning, not get hit with a hook off the jab, get inside, and pound on his ribs can beat him. Any guy. Well, you're asking for the greatest fighter who ever lived, so this kid must be pretty good."'

And on top of everything else, the world never saw Muhammad Ali at his peak as a fighter. When Ali was forced into exile in 1967, he was getting better with virtually every fight. The Ali who fought Cleveland Williams, Ernie Terrell and Zora Folley was bigger, stronger, more confident and more skilled than the 22-year-old who, three years earlier, had defeated Sonny Liston. But when Ali returned, his ring skills were diminished. He was markedly slower and his legs weren't the same.

'I was better when I was young,' Ali acknowledged later. 'I was more experienced when I was older; I was stronger; I had more belief in myself. Except for Sonny Liston, the men I fought when I was young weren't near the fighters that Joe Frazier and George Foreman were. But I had my speed when I was young. I was faster on my legs and my hands were faster.'

Thus, the world never saw what might have been. What it did see, though, in the second half of Ali's career, was an incredibly courageous fighter. Not only did Ali fight his heart out in the ring; he fought the most dangerous foes imaginable. Many champions avoid facing tough challengers. When Joe Louis was champion, he refused to fight certain black contenders. After Joe Frazier defeated Ali, his next defences were against Terry Daniels and Ron Stander. Once George Foreman won the title, his next bout was against José Roman. But Ali had a different creed. 'I fought the best, because if you want to be a true champion, you got to show people that you can whup everybody,' he proclaimed.

'I don't think there's a fighter in his right mind that wouldn't admire Ali,' says Earnie Shavers. 'We all dreamed about being just half the fighter that Ali was.'

And of course, each time Ali entered the ring, the pressure on him was palpable. 'It's not like making a movie where, if you mess up, you stop and reshoot,' he said shortly before Ali–Frazier III. 'When that bell rings and you're out there, the whole world is watching and it's real.'

But Ali was more than a great fighter. He was the standard-bearer for boxing's modern era. The 1960s promised athletes who were bigger and faster than their predecessors. Ali was the proto-type for that mould. Also, he was part and parcel of the changing economics of boxing. Ali arrived just in time for the advent of satellites and closed circuit television. He carried heavyweight championship boxing beyond the confines of the United States and popularised the sport around the globe.

Almost always, the public sees boxers as warriors without ever realising their soft, human side. But the whole world saw Ali's humanity. 'I was never a boxing fan until Ali came along,' is a refrain one frequently hears. And while 'the validity of boxing is always hanging by a thread,' Hugh McIlvanney, who coined that phrase, acknowledges, 'Ali was boxing's salvation.'

An Ali fight was always an event. Ali put that in perspective when he said, 'I truly believe I'm fighting for the betterment of people. I'm not fighting for diamonds or Rolls-Royces or mansions, but to help mankind. Before a fight, I get myself psyched up. It gives me more power, knowing there's so much involved and so many people are gonna be helped by my victory.' To which Gil Noble adds, 'When Ali got in the ring, there was a lot more at stake than the title. When that man got in the ring, he took all of us with him.'

Also, for virtually his entire career, being around Ali was fun. Commenting on young Cassius Clay, Don Elbaum remembers, 'I was the matchmaker for a show in Pittsburgh when he fought Charlie Powell. We were staying at a place called Carlton House. And two or three days before the fight, Cassius, which was his name then, decided to visit a black area of Pittsburgh. It was winter, real cold. But he went out, walking the streets, just talking to people. And I've never seen anything like it in my life. When he came back to the hotel around six o'clock, there were three hundred people following him. The Pied Piper couldn't have done any better. And the night of the fight, the weather was awful. There was a blizzard; the schools were shut down. Snow kept falling; it was windy. Conditions were absolutely horrible. And the fight sold out.'

Some athletes are engaging when they're young, but lose their charm as their celebrity status grows. But Michael Katz of the *New York Daily News* recalls the day when Ali, at the peak of his popularity, defended his title against Richard Dunn. 'On the day of the fight,' Katz remembers, 'Ali got bored so he decided to hold a press conference. Word got around. Ali came downstairs, and we went to a conference room in the hotel but it wasn't set up yet. So every member of the press followed him around. We were like mice, going from room to room, until finally the hotel management set us up someplace. And Ali proceeded to have us all in stitches. He imitated every opponent he'd ever fought, including Richard Dunn, who he hadn't fought yet. And he was marvellous. You'd have paid more money to see Muhammad Ali on stage at that point than you'd pay today for Robin Williams.'

And Ali retained his charm when he got old.

'The first Ali fight I ever covered,' says Ron Borges, 'was the one against Leon Spinks, where Ali said it made him look silly to talk up an opponent with only seven professional fights so he wasn't talking. And I said to myself, "Great. Here I am, a young reporter about to cover the most verbally gifted athlete in history, and the man's not talking." Anyway, I was at one of Ali's workouts. Ali finished sparring, picked up a microphone, and told us all what he'd said before: "I'm not talking." And then he went on for about ninety minutes. Typical Ali, the funniest monologue I've ever heard. And when he was done, he put the microphone down, smiled that incredible smile, and told us all, "But I'm not talking." I'll always remember the joy of being around Ali,' Borges says in closing. 'It was fun. And covering the heavyweights isn't much fun any more. Ali took that with him when he left, and things have been pretty ugly lately.'

Muhammad Ali did too much for boxing. And the sport isn't the same without him.

MUHAMMAD ALI AND CONGRESS REMEMBERED

(2000)

At long last, Congress has enacted the Muhammad Ali Boxing Reform Act. As a cure for what ails boxing, the proposed legislation leaves a lot to be desired. Still, it's a step in the right direction. Meanwhile, Senator Jim Bunning of Kentucky is sponsoring legislation that would authorise President Clinton to award Ali a Congressional Gold Medal (the highest civilian honour that Congress can bestow upon an individual). Thus, it's worth remembering what an earlier generation of Congressmen had to say about Muhammad Ali at the height of the war in Vietnam.

On 17 February 1966, Ali was reclassified 1-A by his draft board and uttered the immortal words, 'I ain't got no quarrel with them Vietcong.' One month later, Congressman Frank Clark of Pennsylvania rose in Congress and called upon the American public to boycott Ali's upcoming bout against George Chuvalo:

The heavyweight champion of the world turns my stomach. I am not a superpatriot. But I feel that each man, if he really is a man, owes to his country a willingness to protect it and serve it in time of need. From this standpoint, the heavyweight champion has been a complete and total disgrace. I urge the citizens of the nation as a whole to boycott any of his performances. To leave these theatre seats empty would be the finest tribute possible to that boy whose hearse may pass by the open doors of the theatre on Main Street USA.

In 1967, Ali refused induction into the United States Army, at which point he was stripped of his title and denied a licence to box in all fifty states. That same year, he was indicted, tried, convicted and sentenced to five years in prison. Then, in October 1969, while the appeal of his conviction was pending, ABC announced plans to have Ali serve as a TV commentator for an upcoming amateur boxing competition between the United States and the Soviet Union. Congressman Fletcher Thompson of Georgia objected:

I take the floor today to protest the network that has announced it will use Cassius Clay as a commentator for these contests. I consider this an affront to loyal Americans everywhere, although it will obviously receive much applause in some of the hippie circles. Maybe the American Broadcasting System feels that it needs to appeal more to the hippies and yippies of America than to loyal Americans.

In December 1969, there were reports that Governor Claude Kirk of Florida would grant Ali a licence to fight Joe Frazier in Tampa. Congressman Robert Michel of Illinois took to the podium of the United States House of Representatives to protest:

> Clay has been stripped of his heavyweight title for dodging the draft. And I consider it an insult to patriotic Americans everywhere to permit his re-entry into the respected ranks of boxing. It should be recalled that Mr Clay gave as one of his excuses for not wanting to be drafted that he is in reality a minister and that even boxing is antagonistic to his religion. But apparently, he is willing to fight anyone but the Vietcong.

Ultimately, the authorities in Florida refused to give Ali a licence to box. Then, in September 1970, it was announced that Ali would fight Jerry Quarry in Georgia. Once again, Congressman Michel had his say:

> I read with disgust today the article in the *Washington Post* concerning the upcoming fight of this country's most famous draft dodger, Cassius Clay. The article said that Mr Clay was out of shape, overweight and winded. No doubt, this comes from his desperate and concerted efforts to stay out of the military service while thousands of patriotic young men are fighting and dying in Vietnam. Apparently, Mr Clay feels himself entitled to the full protection of the law, yet does not feel he has to sacrifice anything to preserve the institutions that

protect him. Cassius Clay cannot hold a candle to the average American boy who is willing to defend his country in perilous times.

Ali fought Jerry Quarry in Atlanta on 26 October 1970. Then a federal district court decision paved the way for him to fight Oscar Bonavena on 7 December (the anniversary of Pearl Harbor) in New York. After that, he signed to fight Joe Frazier at Madison Square Garden. Each fighter was to receive the previously unheard-of sum of $2,500,000. That outraged Congressman John Rarick of Louisiana, who spoke to his colleagues:

> Veterans who have fought our nation's wars feel that any man unwilling to fight for his country is unworthy of making a profit or receiving public acclaim in it. Cassius Clay is a convicted draft dodger sentenced to a five-year prison term which he is not serving. What right has he to claim the privilege of appearing in a boxing match to be nationally televised? The Clay affair approaches a crisis in national indignation.

On 8 March 1971, Ali lost a hard-fought fifteen-round decision to Joe Frazier. Meanwhile, he remained free on bail while the United States Supreme Court considered the appeal of his criminal conviction. This was too much for Congressman George Andrews of Alabama, who spoke to his brethren and compared Ali to Lieutenant William Calley, who had been convicted of murder in the massacre of 22 South Vietnamese civilians at My Lai:

Last night, I was sickened and sad when I heard about that poor little fellow who went down to Fort Benning. He had barely graduated from high school. He volunteered and offered his life for his country. He was taught to kill. He was sent to Vietnam. And he wound up back at Fort Benning, where he was indicted and convicted for murder in the first degree for carrying out orders. I also thought about another young man about his age: one Cassius Clay, alias Muhammad Ali, who several years ago defied the United States government, thumbed his nose at the flag and is still walking the streets making millions of dollars fighting for pay, not for his country. That is an unequal distribution of justice.

On 28 June 1971, fifty months to the day after Ali had refused induction, the United States Supreme Court unanimously reversed his conviction. All criminal charges pending against him were dismissed. The next day, Congressman William Nichols of Alabama expressed his outrage:

The United States Supreme Court has given another black eye to the United States Armed Forces. The decision overturning the draft evasion conviction of Cassius Clay is a stinging rebuke to the 240,000 Americans still serving in Vietnam and the 50,000 Americans who lost their lives there. I wish the members of the Supreme Court would assist me when I try to explain to a father why his son must serve in

Vietnam or when I attempt to console a widow or the parents of a young man who has died in a war that Cassius Clay was exempted from.

Not to be outdone, Congressman Joe Waggonner of Louisiana echoed his fellow lawmaker's expression of contempt:

The United States Supreme Court has issued the edict that Cassius Clay does not have to be inducted because he does not believe in war. No draft-age young man believes in a war that he will have to fight, nor does any parent of a draft-age son believe in a war that their own flesh and blood will have to fight and possibly give his life in so doing. But our people have always heeded the call of their country when asked, not because they love war, but because their country has asked them to do so. And I feel strongly about this. If Cassius Clay does not have to be drafted because of questionable religious beliefs or punished for refusing induction simply because he is black or because he is a prizefighter – and I can see no other real justification for the Court's action – then all other young men who wish it should also be allowed a draft exemption. Cassius Clay is a phoney. He knows it, the Supreme Court knows it and everyone else knows it.

Times change.

THE ATHLETE OF THE CENTURY

(1999)

As 1999 moves towards its long-awaited close, there have been numerous attempts to designate 'The Athlete of the Century'. Whoever is accorded the honour will doubtless also be recognised as 'Athlete of the Millennium'.

The consensus list for number one has boiled down to three finalists: Babe Ruth, Muhammad Ali and Michael Jordan. There's no right or wrong answer; just points of view.

It's hard to imagine anyone being better in a sport than Michael Jordan was in basketball. His exploits are still fresh in the mind, so suffice it to say that the Chicago Bulls won six world championships during his reign and Jordan was named the series' Most Valuable Player on all six occasions. He led the NBA in scoring ten times, has the highest career scoring average in league history and was one of the best defensive players ever.

Babe Ruth had an unparalleled genius for the peculiarities of baseball. In 1919, the American League record for home runs in a season was 12. Ruth hit 29 homers that year and 54 the year after. In 1927, the year Ruth hit 60 home runs, no other *team* in the American League had as many. Indeed, in all of major league baseball, there were only 922 home runs hit that year. In other words, Babe Ruth hit 6.5 per cent of all the home runs hit in the entire season.

Ruth's lifetime batting average was .342. Two-thirds of a century after his career ended, he stands second in RBIs, second in runs scored and second in home runs. And these marks were established despite the fact that Ruth was a pitcher during the first five years of his career. In 1916, at age 21, he pitched nine shutouts en route to a 23 and 12 record and led the league with an earned run average of 1.75. From 1915 to 1919, he won 94 games, lost only 46, and compiled an earned-run average of 2.28. In other words, if Mark McGwire pitched 29-2/3 consecutive scoreless innings in the World Series (which Ruth once did; a record that stood for 43 years), you'd have a phenomenon approaching The Babe. And one thing more. Ruth was a winner. He was with the Boston Red Sox for five full seasons, and they won the World Series in three of them. Then he was traded to the Yankees, who had never won a World Series, and the Yankee dynasty began.

As for Ali, a strong argument can be made that he was the greatest fighter of all time. His lifetime record of 56 wins and 5 losses has been matched by others. But no heavyweight ever had the inquisitors that Ali had – George Foreman, Sonny Liston twice, and Joe Frazier three times. Ali in his prime was the most beautiful fighting machine ever assembled. Pound for pound, Sugar Ray Robinson might have been better. But that's like saying, if Jerry West had been six foot six, he would have been just as good as Jordan. You are what you are.

Ali fought the way Michael Jordan played basketball. Michael Jordan played basketball the way Ali fought. Unfortunately, Jordan didn't play baseball the way Ruth did. But then again, I doubt that Ruth would have been much of a basketball player. However, The Babe was known to punch out people rather effectively as a young man.

Thus, looking at Michael Jordan, Babe Ruth and Muhammad Ali from a purely athletic point of view, it's Jordan (three points for first place), Ruth (two points for second place) and Ali (one point for third place) in that order.

But is pure athletic ability the standard? If pure athleticism is the only test, men like Jim Thorpe, Jim Brown and Carl Lewis should also be finalists in the competition for 'Athlete of the Century'. The fact that they aren't stands testament to the view that something more than achievement on the playing field must be measured; that social impact is also relevant. That's a bit like saying maybe Ronald Reagan should be considered the greatest actor of the twentieth century because of his impact on society. But here goes.

Ruth, Ali and Jordan reflected the eras in which they were at their respective athletic peaks. Ruth personified 'The Roaring Twenties'. Ali was at the heart of the social and political turmoil of the 1960s. Michael Jordan speaks to 'The Nineties', with its booming stock market, heightened commercialism and athletes as computer-action-game heroes.

Jordan hasn't changed society. Babe Ruth brought sports into the mainstream of American culture and earned adulation unmatched in his time. Nor was The Babe's impact confined to the United States. During the Second World War, long after his playing days were over, Japanese soldiers sought to insult their American counterparts by shouting 'to hell with Babe Ruth' at Guadalcanal. Meanwhile, Ali (to use one of his favourite phrases) 'shook up the world' and served as an inspiration and beacon of hope, not just in the United States, but for oppressed people around the globe.

One can argue that Jack Johnson, Joe Louis and Jackie Robinson all had a greater societal impact than Ali. Arthur Ashe once opined, 'Within the United States, Jack Johnson had a larger impact than Ali because he was the first. Nothing that any African-American had done up until that time had the same impact as Jack Johnson's fight against James Jeffries.'

Joe Louis's hold on the American psyche was so great that the last words spoken by a young man choking to death in the gas chamber were, 'Save me, Joe Louis.' When The Brown Bomber knocked out Max Schmeling at Yankee Stadium in 1938 in a bout that was considered an allegory of good versus evil, it was the first time that most people had heard a black man referred to simply as 'The American'.

Meanwhile, Jackie Robinson opened doors for an entire generation of Americans. If there had never been a Jackie Robinson, baseball would in time have become integrated; and, eventually, other sports would have followed. But that's like saying, if there had been no Michelangelo, someone else would have painted the ceiling of the Sistine Chapel.

Still, Ali's reach, more than that of any of his competitors, was worldwide. So for impact on society, it's Ali (three points), Ruth (two points), and Jordan (one point). That means there's a four-four-four tie, and we go to tie-breakers.

Babe Ruth seemed larger than life. So do Muhammad Ali and Michael Jordan. Ruth and Ali had much-publicised personal weaknesses. Jordan has flaws although they're less well known. All three men have been idolised. Ali has been loved. It would be presumptuous to choose among them as human beings.

So where do we go from here?

Sixty-four years after Babe Ruth hit his last home run, a half-century after his death, men like Mark McGwire still compete against him. Without Ruth ever having been on SportsCenter or HBO, he is still in the hearts of most sports fans. Ali might enjoy that type of recognition fifty years from now. It's less likely that Michael Jordan will.

That brings us down to Babe Ruth and Muhammad Ali.

And the envelope please ...

WHY MUHAMMAD ALI
WENT TO IRAQ

(1990)

Last month [November 1990] in Baghdad, Muhammad Ali embraced Saddam Hussein and kissed him on the cheek. The moment was televised throughout the world and troubled many people. Ali isn't a diplomat. His actions aren't always wise. There was danger in the possibility that a visit from history's best-known fistic gladiator would feed Hussein's ego and stiffen his resolve. Regardless of what else happened, the meeting would be used for propaganda purposes in the Third World, where Ali is particularly loved.

Some of Ali's closest friends were also concerned that, in going to Iraq, he was being used for personal gain by one or more members of his entourage. Several of his associates, past and present, are the subject of a federal inquiry into alleged financial irregularities. While Ali was in Iraq, one of his attorneys was indicted on charges of conspiracy and tax fraud. And among those who accompanied Ali to Baghdad was Arthur Morrison, a self-described businessman who has traversed the United States leaving a trail of arrest warrants behind.

As Ali's trip progressed, it became increasingly difficult for the world outside to distinguish between what he really said and what was reported by the Iraqi News Agency. There were self-appointed spokesmen purporting to act on 'hand signals' from the former champion. Others said, falsely, that Ali was unable to speak. But none of this is new to Ali. He has often dealt with con men and crazies. The sideshow that accompanied him on his recent journey shouldn't be allowed to overshadow why Ali went to Iraq. It was an act of love in quest of peace. He hoped that his presence would promote dialogue and forestall war.

I've spent the past two years researching and writing about Muhammad Ali. For much of that time, I've lived with him, travelled with him and interviewed hundreds of his family members, associates and friends. I know him well. At least, I think I do. And one thing is certain. Even though Muhammad's voice is not as clear as it used to be, his mind is alert and his heart is pure.

I've seen Ali get on a plane and fly to India because the children in an orphanage wanted to meet him. I've sat in his living-room as he talked with sadness of hatred and racism in all of their virulent forms. He's a gentle man who will do almost anything to avoid hurting another person.

Ali was in Louisville visiting his mother who had suffered a stroke when he was asked to go to Iraq. He is on medication for Parkinson's syndrome. When he left that afternoon, he had enough medication with him to last for five days; yet he stayed in Iraq for two weeks. He quite literally endangered his health because he believed that what he was doing was right.

That has been a constant theme throughout Ali's life. He has always taken risks to uphold his principles. During the 1960s, he was stripped of his title and precluded from fighting for three and a half years because he acted upon his beliefs and refused induction into the US Army during the height of the war in Vietnam. He now believes that all war is wrong. Ali is, and since Vietnam has been, a true conscientious objector.

Ali knows what many of us sometimes seem to forget; that people are killed in wars. Every life is precious to him. He understands that each of us has only one life to live. Many Americans now favour war with Iraq, although I'm not sure how many would feel that way if they personally had to fight. Ali, plainly and simply, values every other person's life as dearly as his own, regardless of nationality, religion or race. He is a man who finds it impossible to go hunting, let alone tolerate the horrors of war.

It may be that war with Iraq will become inevitable. If so, it will be fought. But that shouldn't cause us to lose sight of what Muhammad Ali tried to accomplish last month. Any war is a human tragedy and we should always be thankful for the peacemakers among us. That's not a bad message for this holiday season or any other time of year. After all, it's not how loudly Ali speaks but what he says and does that counts.

THE OLYMPIC FLAME

(1993)

The Atlanta Olympics are three years in the future, but elaborate groundwork has already been laid. Budweiser has agreed to become a national sponsor for a sum that might otherwise be used to retire the national debt. On-site construction has begun and television planning is underway. Eventually, the Olympic torch will be transported to the United States. The triumphal procession that follows will lead to the highlight of the games' opening ceremonies – lighting the Olympic flame.

Traditionally, someone from the host country ignites the flame. At the 1984 Olympics in Los Angeles, Rafer Johnson received the torch and carried it up the Coliseum steps to rekindle the world's most celebrated fire. Last year in Barcelona, a Spanish archer shot an arrow into a cauldron, thereby reawakening the flame. The eyes of the world are always on this moment. One wonders who will be chosen to fulfil the honour in Atlanta.

The view here is that the choice is obvious. One man embodies the Olympic spirit to perfection. He's a true American in every sense of the word and the foremost citizen of the world. At age 18, he won a gold medal in Rome fighting under the name Cassius Clay. Since then, he has traversed the globe, spreading joy wherever he goes. Atlanta has special meaning for him. It was there, after three years of exile from boxing, that he returned to face Jerry Quarry in the ring. He loves the spotlight, and the spotlight loves him. Indeed, one can almost hear him saying, 'When I carry that Olympic torch, every person in the world will be watching. Babies in their mother's tummies will be kicking and hollering for the TV to be turned on. It will be bigger than Michael Jackson. Bigger than Elvis. Bigger than the Pyramids. Bigger than me fighting Sonny Liston, George Foreman and Joe Frazier all at the same time. Bigger than the Olympics –'

Wait a minute, Muhammad. This *is* the Olympics.

Anyway, you get the point. So I have a simple proposal to make. I'd like the International Olympic Committee to announce that, as its gift to the world, Muhammad Ali has been chosen to light the Olympic flame in Atlanta. Muhammad has already given us one memorable Olympic moment as Cassius Clay. Now let him share another with the world as Muhammad Ali. That way, the 26th Olympiad will truly be 'the greatest'.

ALI AS DIPLOMAT: 'NO! NO! NO! DON'T!'

(2001)

In 1980, in response to the Soviet Union's invasion of Afghanistan, the Carter Administration sought to organise a boycott of the Moscow Olympics. As part of that effort, it sent Muhammad Ali to five African nations to gather support for America's position.

Ali's trip was a disaster. *Time* magazine later called it 'the most bizarre diplomatic mission in recent US history'. Some African officials viewed Ali's presence as a racial insult. 'Would the United States send Chris Evert to negotiate with London?' one Tanzanian diplomat demanded. Ali himself seemed confused regarding the facts underlying his role and was unable to explain why African nations should boycott the Moscow Olympics when, four years earlier, the United States had refused to join twenty-nine African countries in boycotting the Montreal Olympics over South Africa's place in the sporting world.

'Maybe I'm being used to do something that ain't right,' Ali conceded at one point. In Kenya, he announced that Jimmy Carter had put him 'on the spot' and sent him 'around the world to take the whupping over American policies' and said that, if he'd known the 'whole history of America and South Africa', he 'probably wouldn't have made the trip'.

That bit of history is relevant now because Jack Valenti (president of the Motion Picture Association of America) has unveiled tentative plans for a one-minute public service announcement featuring Ali that will be broadcast throughout the Muslim world. The thrust of the message is that America's war on terrorism is not a war against Islam. The public service spot would be prepared by Hollywood 9/11 – a group that was formed after movie industry executives met on 11 November with Karl Rove (a senior political advisor to George Bush). In Valenti's words, Ali would be held out as 'the spokesman for Muslims in America'.

The proposed public service announcement might be good publicity for the movie industry, but it's dangerous politics.

Ali is universally respected and loved, but he isn't a diplomat. He doesn't understand the complexities of geopolitics. His heart is pure, but his judgements and actions are at times unwise. An example of this occurred on 19 December 2001, at a fund-raising event for the proposed Muhammad Ali Center in Louisville – which is intended to be an educational facility designed to promote tolerance and understanding among all people. At the fund-raiser, Ali rose to tell several jokes.

'No! No! No! Don't,' his wife Lonnie cried.

Despite her plea, Ali proceeded. 'What's the difference between a Jew and a canoe?' he asked. Then he supplied the answer: 'A canoe tips.' That was followed by: 'A black, a Puerto Rican and a Mexican are in a car. Who's driving?' The answer: 'The police.'

Afterwards, Sue Carls (a spokesperson for the Ali Center) sought to minimise the damage, explaining, 'These are not new jokes. Muhammad tells them all the time because he likes to make people laugh and he shocks people to make a point.' Two days later, Lonnie Ali added, 'Even the Greatest can tell bad jokes.'

The problem is, this is a situation where misjudgements and bad jokes can cost lives.

Ali is not a bigot. He tells far more 'nigger' jokes than jokes about Hispanics and Jews. But Ali sometimes speaks and acts without considering the implications of his words and conduct. And he can be swayed by rhetoric; particularly when the speaker is a Muslim cleric with a following in some portion of the world.

What happens if, six months from now, Ali makes an intemperate statement about Israel? What happens if Ali calls for a halt to all American military action against terrorism in the heartfelt belief that a halt will save innocent lives? Will he then still be 'the spokesman for Muslims in America'?

Muhammad Ali leads best when he leads by example and by broad statements in support of tolerance and understanding among all people. To ask more of him in the current incendiary situation is looking for trouble.

GHOSTS OF MANILA

(2001)

Albert Einstein once remarked, 'Nature, to be sure, distributes her gifts unevenly among her children. But it strikes me as unfair, and even in bad taste, to select a few of them for boundless admiration, attributing superhuman powers of mind and character to them.'

But society did just that with Muhammad Ali. Few people have ever received accolades equal to those that have been showered upon him. Indeed, Wilfrid Sheed, who himself was sceptical of Ali's merit as a social figure, once observed that boxing's eras would be forever known as BC (before Clay) and AD (Ali Domini).

Enter Mark Kram. Kram is a very good writer. How else can one describe a man who refers to Chuck Wepner as having a face that looks as though it has been 'embroidered by a tipsy church lady', and likens Joe Frazier's visage after Ali–Frazier I to 'a frieze of a lab experiment that was a disaster'.

Kram covered boxing for *Sports Illustrated* for eleven years. Now, a quarter of a century later, he has written *Ghosts of Manila:*

The Fateful Blood Feud Between Muhammad Ali and Joe Frazier. The book, in the first instance, is the story of two men whose rivalry was ugly, glorious, brutal and enthralling. And secondarily, Kram declares, 'This book is intended to be a corrective to the years of stenography that have produced the Ali legend. Cheap myth corruscates the man. The wire scheme for his sculpture is too big.'

Thus Kram seeks to raise Joe Frazier to a level virtually equal to that of Ali in the ring and perhaps above him in terms of character. In so doing, he portrays what he believes to be the dark side of Ali.

Ghosts of Manila is divided into four parts. They cover, in order, (1) Ali and Frazier in retirement; (2) the emergence of both men as fighters and in the public consciousness; (3) their three fights; and (4) the two men, again, in retirement.

Kram concedes Ali's ring greatness. 'As a fighter,' Kram writes, 'he was the surface of a shield, unmalleable, made for mace and chain, flaring with light.' Describing Ali in the ring moments before Ali–Frazier I, he acknowledges, 'Whatever you might think of him, you were forced to look at him with honest lingering eyes, for there might never be his like again. Assessed by ring demands – punch, size, speed, intelligence, command and imagination – he was an action poet, the equal of the best painting you could find.'

As for Frazier, Kram calls him 'the most skilful devastating inside puncher in boxing history', and goes so far as to rank him among the top five heavyweights of all time. That seems a bit silly. Joe was a great fighter and every bit as noble a warrior as Ali. But there's a time-honoured axiom in boxing that styles make fights.

And the list of fighters with the style to beat Joe Frazier numbers far more than five.

Kram is on more solid ground when he catalogues Frazier's hatred for Ali. The story of how Muhammad branded Joe an 'Uncle Tom' before their first fight, 'ignorant' before Ali–Frazier II and a 'gorilla' before Ali–Frazier III is well known, but *Ghosts of Manila* makes it fresh and compelling. Thus, Kram writes, 'Muhammad Ali swam inside Joe Frazier like a determined bacillus … Ali has sat in Frazier's gut like a broken bottle.' And he quotes Frazier's one-time associate Bert Watson as saying, 'You don't do to a man what Ali did to Joe. Ali robbed him of who he is. To a lot of people, Joe is still ignorant, slow-speaking, dumb and ugly. That tag never leaves him. People have only seen one Joe; the one created by Ali. If you're a man, that's going to get to you in a big way.' And Kram quotes Frazier as saying of Ali, 'When a man gets in your blood like that, you can't never let go. Yesterday is today for me. He never die for me … If we were twins in the belly of our mama, I'd reach over and strangle him … I'll outlive him.'

Kram writes with grace and constructs his case against Ali's supervening greatness in a largely intelligent way. But his work is flawed.

First, there are factual inaccuracies. For example, Kram is simply wrong when he discusses Ali's military draft reclassification and states, 'Had he not become a Muslim, chances are he would have remained unfit for duty.'

That's not the case. In truth, Ali had been declared unfit for military duty by virtue of his scoring in the 16th percentile on an Army intelligence test. That left him well below the requirement of 30. But two years after that, with the war in Vietnam expanding, the mental-aptitude percentile required by the military was lowered from 30 to 15. The change impacted upon hundreds of thousands of young men across the country. To suggest that Ali was somehow singled out and the standard changed because of his religion is ridiculous.

Also, there are times when Kram is overly mean-spirited. For example, Bryant Gumbel (who aroused Kram's ire with negative commentary on Joe Frazier) is referred to as 'a mediocre writer and thinker' with 'a shallow, hard-worked ultra-sophistication and ego that not even a mother could love'. Ali in his current condition is labelled 'a billboard in decline', of whom Kram says uncharitably, 'Physical disaster of his own making has kept his fame intact. He would have become the bore dodged at the party. The future promised that there would be no more clothes with which to dress him up.' Indeed, Kram goes so far as to call the younger Ali 'a useful idiot' and 'near the moronic level'.

Kram's failure to distinguish fully between Nation of Islam doctrine and orthodox Islamic beliefs is also troubling. During what might have been the most important 14 years of Ali's life, he adhered to the teachings of the Nation of Islam; a doctrine that Arthur Ashe later condemned as 'a racist ideology; a sort of American apartheid'. Yet reading *Ghosts of Manila*, one might come away with the impression that Nation of Islam doctrine was, and still is, Islam as practised by more than one billion people around the world today. That's because Kram has the annoying habit of referring to Ali's early mentors as 'the Muslims', which is like lumping Billy Graham and the Ku Klux Klan together and calling them 'the Christians'.

Then there's the matter of Kram's sources; most notably, his reliance on two women named Aaisha Ali and Khaliah Ali.

Muhammad met Aaisha Ali in 1973 when he was 31 years old and she was a 17-year-old named Wanda Bolton. To his discredit, they had sexual relations and she became pregnant. Kram makes much of the fact that Wanda was 'on her way to becoming a doctor'. Given the fact that she was a high school junior at the time, that's rather speculative. Regardless, Ms Bolton subsequently claimed that she and Ali had been 'Islamically married' and changed her name to Aaisha Ali. Muhammad acknowledged paternity and accepted financial responsibility for their daughter, Khaliah.

Kram describes Aaisha several times as 'a mystery woman', which is a cheap theatrical trick. Her presence in Ali's past has been known and written about for years. More significantly, Kram uses Aaisha and Khaliah as his primary sources to trash Ali's current wife Lonnie (who Kram calls Ali's 'new boss'). Indeed, after describing Ali as 'a careless fighter who had his brain cells irradiated', Kram quotes Lonnie as telling Khaliah, 'I am Muhammad Ali now.' Then, after referring to 'Lonnie and her tight circle of pushers', he quotes Khaliah as saying of her father, 'It's about money. He's a substance, an item.' After that, Kram recounts a scene when Ali and Lonnie were in a Louisville hospital visiting Ali's mother, who was being kept alive on a respirator. The final days of Odessa Clay's life were the saddest ever for Ali. Yet again, relying wholly on Khaliah, Kram quotes Lonnie as saying, 'We can't afford this, Muhammad.'

The problem is, there are a lot of people who think that Aaisha Ali and Khaliah Ali aren't particularly reliable sources. I happen

to have been present at one of the incidents regarding which
Kram quotes Khaliah. It involved a championship belt that was
given to Ali at a dinner commemorating the 20th anniversary of
the first Ali–Frazier fight. The dinner took place on the night of
14 April 1991, although Kram mistakenly reports it as occurring
on an unspecified date five years later. Khaliah left Ali's hotel
room that night with the belt. I experienced the incident very
differently from the way Kram recounts it.

However, my biggest concern regarding *Ghosts of Manila* is its
thesis that Ali's influence lay entirely in the sporting arena. Kram
acknowledges that Ali 'did lead the way for black athletes out of
the frustrating silence that Jackie Robinson had to endure'.
However, even that concession is tempered by the claim that,
'Ali's influence in games today can be seen in the blaring unend-
ing marketing of self, the cheap acting out of performers, and the
crassness of player interactions. His was an overwhelming presence that, if you care about such things, came at a high cost.'

Then Kram goes on to say, 'What was laughable, if you knew
anything about Ali at all, was that the literati was certain that he
was a serious voice, that he knew what he was doing. He didn't
have a clue … Seldom has a public figure of such superficial
depth been more wrongly perceived.'

'Ali,' Kram says flatly, 'was not a social force.' And woe to those
who say he was, because their utterances are dismissed as 'heavy
breathing' from 'know-nothings' and 'trendy tasters of faux
revolution'.

Apparently, I'm one of those heavy breathers. Kram refers to
me as 'a lawyer-Boswell who seems intent of making the public
believe that, next to Martin Luther King, Ali is the most impor-

tant black figure in the last half-century'. And in case anyone misses his point, Kram adds, 'Current hagiographers have tied themselves in knots trying to elevate Ali into a heroic defiant catalyst of the anti-war movement, a beacon of black independence. It's a legacy that evolves from the intellectually loose sixties, from those who were in school then and now write romance history.'

Actually, Kram has misquoted me. I believe he's referring to a statement in *Muhammad Ali: His Life and Times* in which I wrote, 'With the exception of Martin Luther King, no black man in America had more influence than Ali during the years when Ali was in his prime.' I still believe that to be true.

Was Ali as important as Nelson Mandela? No. Was Ali in the late 1960s more important than any other black person in America except for Dr King? I believe so. Indeed, Nelson Mandela himself said recently, 'Ali's refusal to go to Vietnam and the reasons he gave made him an international hero. The news could not be shut out even by prison walls. He became a real legend to us in prison.'

Kram's remarkable gift for words notwithstanding, Muhammad Ali in the 1960s stood as a beacon of hope for oppressed people all over the world. Every time he looked in the mirror and uttered the phrase, 'I'm so pretty,' he was saying 'black is beautiful' before it became fashionable. When he refused induction into the US Army, regardless of his motives, he stood up to armies around the globe in support of the proposition that, unless you have a very good reason for killing people, war is wrong.

Dick Gregory once said, 'If you wanted to do a movie to depict Ali, it would just be a small light getting bigger and bigger and bigger and bigger. That was Ali in a sea of darkness.' One can imagine Kram gagging at imagery like that. But the truth is, Muhammad Ali found his way into the world's psyche.

Perhaps Reggie Jackson put it in perspective best. 'Do you have any idea what Ali meant to black people?' Jackson said to me once. 'He was the leader of a nation; the leader of black America. As a young black, at times I was ashamed of my colour; I was ashamed of my hair. And Ali made me proud. I'm just as happy being black now as somebody else is being white, and Ali was part of that growing process. Think about it! Do you understand what it did for black Americans to know that the most physically gifted, possibly the most handsome, and one of the most charismatic men in the world was black? Ali helped raise black people in this country out of mental slavery. The entire experience of being black changed for millions of people because of Ali.'

In sum, Muhammad Ali might not have meant much to Mark Kram. But he meant a great deal to a lot of people. He made an enormous difference.

REDISCOVERING JOE FRAZIER THROUGH DAVE WOLF'S EYES

(2009)

Muhammad Ali and Joe Frazier fought three fights that are the pyramids of boxing. Dave Wolf was in the Frazier camp for each of them.

Dave was a gifted writer who later gained recognition as the manager of Ray Mancini and Donny Lalonde. He died in December 2008. Three months later, his daughter and brother gave me a carton filled with file folders containing handwritten notes that detail Dave's years in the Frazier camp.

The notes are fragments: a phrase here, a sentence there. I've reviewed some of them and joined Dave's words together to form an impressionistic portrait.

Everything that follows flowed from Dave's pen. Joe Frazier is often referenced as 'JF' because that's how Dave's notes refer to him. For the same reason, Muhammad Ali is frequently referred to as 'Clay'. As explained in the notes, 'JF calls him "Clay". Knows his name is "Ali". Called him "Ali" until he heard what Clay was saying about him. Now calls him "Clay" out of disrespect.'

In several instances, I've added an explanatory note to clarify a point. These clarifications are contained in brackets.

I don't agree with everything in Dave's notes. Some of it runs counter to views I've expressed in *Muhammad Ali: His Life and Times* and other works I've written. What I can vouch for is that this article is faithful to Dave's contemporaneous recording of the relationship between Muhammad Ali and Joe Frazier as seen through Joe's eyes.

Born in Beaufort, South Carolina, on 12 January 1944 ... Grew up rural poor. Quit school in ninth grade ... Married Florence Smith at age 16 ... Lived in Brooklyn and Philadelphia ... Worked in slaughterhouse; took home $125 a week.

Frustrated by poverty ... Starts boxing in 1962 ... 1964 Olympic gold medal.

Post-Olympic problems ... Hand operation ... No help from Olympic committee ... Cold Christmas ... Father dies.

Turns pro on own ... Modest goals. Some material things. Wanted to be important. Believed he'd become somebody.

Others doubt his potential ... Not a natural athlete ... Small compared to past heavyweight champs.

Likes to fight … Fighting style like his personality … Hit often but doesn't mind. Doesn't feel most punches. High pain threshold. Accepts punishment as part of job.

Formation of Cloverlay to back him … Embarrassed at times by lack of education. Problems with public speaking. Called Cloverlay a 'co-operation' at first press conference.

Has been a drinker in past. Knows little about drugs.

Inspires loyalty.

Spartan training camp regardless of fight … Roadwork at 4.00am … Brutal training routine. Punishes body.

JF: 'I love to work.'

Can't understand sparring partners' lack of desire … Eats and lives with them. Pushes them hard. Only the tough last.

Gambling with sparring partners as diversion; mostly loses. Doesn't understand odds. Fleeced by crooked dice.

Yank Durham is great manager and friend. Yank succeeds because he wins JF's complete unquestioning dedication and trust.

JF: 'I still remember the look on Florence's face [Joe's wife] when I told her about no sex before fights. Imagine the look on my face when Yank told me.'

JF liked Clay at first. Understands how others like him.

JF: 'I liked his humour and style. Till I got to know him, I admired him a lot; so it's not hard for me to see why others do.'

When Clay first switched to Muslims, JF thought he was sincere. Knew little about the religion. Shared many racial feelings.

JF: 'You feel more comfortable when you're around your own people. I don't care who you are. That's the life you know. When you're around them, you can say little bad words. You can call each other niggers and everything else. You can talk that talk. When you're around a mixed crowd of people, white and black, you got to be careful.'

Always, JF ambition was to beat Clay. From first pro fight, training for him ... Watched Clay's fights on TV with Yank. Imagined self in ring. Always felt he would win.

Upset by Clay's treatment of Patterson ... JF: 'I feel like, why take advantage of a great champ? Once, he was a great champion. And if you're gonna knock the man out, go ahead and knock him out. You don't suffer people, especially a good athlete. After seeing him playing around with Patterson, I felt like I could straighten that out. Why pick on somebody like that? Try me.'

Watched Clay–Mildenberger. Not impressed.

Watched Clay–Williams in theatre. Felt sorry for Williams … JF: 'Why was that fight allowed?'

Yank moved and matched JF perfectly. Protected him from too much pressure.

First Bonavena fight a problem. JF disdainfully over-confident; forced fight but careless. Floored lunging in by sneaky right. Floored again; in danger of losing by three knockdowns. Still aggressive. Split decision. Most writers had JF a clear winner. JF thought he'd lost fight. Most impressive: ability to get off the canvas. Durham furious. JF held hands low and didn't bob and slip. JF realises things had gotten too complacent; thought he couldn't be hurt.

Doug Jones fight. Left hook in sixth, Jones hanging on ropes. JF might have killed him but held up punch. Jones fell, unconscious for two minutes.

George Chuvalo fight … JF: 'Joe Louis picked against me. I was a little upset when I heard. But Yank said, "You got to realise, they brought him in for publicity. The Garden tells him who to pick. They pay him. He needs the work." I was surprised why a man like him go through these scenes. Seems like a man could stand up for what he believe and not have to choose who somebody else say. I always thought, if I could be like Joe Louis, I'd have it made. Thinking about it was depressing.'

JF [on being shaken by George Chuvalo before knocking him out]: 'It's a feeling that, if you get up in the morning and raise up out of the bed; you not fully awake and you not giving your blood time enough to circulate through your body; everything is not quite together yet and you fall back on the bed, tired. It's not pain; it's just that everything isn't quite focused. It's a little hazy or something. It's like a TV where the thing is a little out of focus and you think you ought to mess with the focus dial a little bit.'

JF [on the party after the Chuvalo fight]: 'I got to the party and my mom was there. I came over and hugged her. She was smiling but I could see she looked uneasy.

JF: 'How'd you like that?'

Mother: 'I was yelling at the referee to stop my son from killing that man.'

JF: 'Mom, that's the fighting game.'

Mother: 'The man was bleeding. You could have killed him.'

JF: 'Mom, you should have been hollering for me, not him.'

Mother: 'Well, I seen you was all right.'

JF: 'I felt a little sad that she wasn't happy like I felt. It would have been better if she'd just come to visit without seeing the fight. She'd never seen me act like that before. I felt she must be thinking, "My son has become a killer." I got the feeling she wouldn't want to see too many more fights.'

First meeting with Clay. In Madison Square Garden basement. Clay sparring for Folley fight. Joe in ring for picture session. Clay condescending; mocks Joe's suspenders.

JF disappointed when Clay was stripped of title for refusing induction. Wanted to win title from him. Had worked three years for shot at Clay. Felt Clay shouldn't lose title except in ring. Didn't want to capitalise on Clay's misfortune.

Respected Clay's draft stand. Believed a man should stand up for his religious beliefs ... While most press and even many blacks attacked Clay early, Joe often defended Clay in street arguments. Argued with Yank about him.

WBA sanctions eight-man tournament for championship ... Durham convinces Cloverlay to pass up tournament. Didn't like fixed money: $50,000–$75,000–$125,000 for three fights. Doesn't want so many risky fights. Frazier angered by Yank's decision. Later sees it was correct.

WBA dropped Frazier from 2 to 9 in rankings. Jimmy Ellis won WBA title.

Joe knocks out Buster Mathis to win New York State championship at Madison Square Garden.

JF: 'I knew I'd never feel like the champ till I beat Clay in the ring.'

Clay moved to Philadelphia ... JF met doing roadwork ... Clay seemed down and out. Said he had financial problems. Unable to leave US to fight. Unable to get licence to fight in US. Buried by legal fees and alimony problems ... Muslims wouldn't loan him money. Told Joe his friends and supporters had abandoned him. Very depressed.

Beginning of strange relationship that existed during next few years ... JF felt sorry for Clay. Wanted to help Clay because black brother ... Once joined Clay at mosque.

Contact during next few years mostly by phone. Got to know Clay better.

One time, JF teased Clay about car. Felt bad when Clay seemed embarrassed.

Phone conversation: Clay said he wished he'd gone in Army. Said he'd been misled; lawyers told him he'd get off easy.

JF began to wonder about Clay's relationship with Muslims ... Clay seemed trapped ... Joe convinced Muslims are phoney. Learned hypocrisy of leaders ... No longer respected Nation of Islam. Impressed they are anti-drug and for black business. Respects their pride in blackness. But feels they are hypocrites. Their ministers don't practise what they preach. Leaders live in luxury; followers are poor. They are violent, even against each other. They use the black movement and the little man as a front.

Clay asked JF for publicity ... 'Don't leave me out here alone' ... Said he didn't care what name JF used. Joe originally used 'Ali' and 'Clay' interchangeably. Joe asked what name he wanted: 'I don't care. Call me nigger.'

Chance meeting. Joe doing roadwork in Fairmont Park. Clay suggested mock fight. Joe rejected: 'I don't go for crap.'

Yank and Clay press Joe to knock Clay. Joe reluctant. Really, nothing against each other ... Clay encourages ... Joe doesn't like it but goes along. Inner suspicion Clay will turn on him and 'use this stuff on me' ... But dismisses idea: 'He's a brother and a religious man.' Assumes Clay will eventually defuse phoney feud.

JF calls Clay 'un-American' ... Not true feelings. Believed much Clay said was valid. Joe opposed Vietnam war ... 'It does no good' ... He opposed killing. People assumed opposite because he was Clay's rival ... Didn't speak out against war because he knows little and doesn't presume to tell others.

JF agrees to series of staged confrontations with Clay.

PAL 23rd Street Gym in Philadelphia. Joe got angry at 'real champ' taunts. Police called.

Mike Douglas taping, next day. Clay friendly in private. Joe asks him before show to 'cool it' ... On set, Clay whispers 'hold me' and starts scene. Joe angry.

Cheetah in New York City, next night. Joe invited Clay into dressing-room ... 'But cut the shit' ... Clay beats on and breaks door. Joe angry. Disliked surprise scenes.

Joe tiring of Clay's act … 'He's like a little kid that can't stop' … Dislikes role that has so many blacks down on him. Frustrated that people, especially blacks, appear to be against him and for Clay … Complained to Yank: 'It's making us look bad' … Yank dismissed: 'Don't worry; there's no harm' … Yank saw big money down the road.

Frazier reputation growing. Perceived as legitimate opponent for Clay.

Regardless of rivalry, Yank not convinced Joe is ready. Bruce Wright [Frazier's attorney] told Joe he could avoid Clay: 'You don't have to fight him. He won't get a licence if you say you won't fight him. Clay is finished if you say "no".'

Joe always said 'yes'. When promoters or writers called about Clay, Joe said he would fight him. At banquets, told [New York State Athletic Commission chairman] Dooley and [Pennsylvania State Athletic Commission chairman] Wildman that he wanted them to license Clay.

JF victories over Manuel Ramos, Oscar Bonavena [rematch] and Dave Zyglewicz.

June 1969: Joe training for Quarry fight … Yank told Bruce Wright, 'Joe's ready for Clay.'

Movement to get Clay–Frazier … Yank had kept contact and had good relationship with Herbert Muhammad [Ali's manager]. Yank and Herbert agreed to 50–50 split.

Series of false alarms … Murray Woroner offer, $1.2 million [for Ali–Frazier fight] in Tampa or Orlando. Vigorous political and veterans opposition … Astrodome offer. Roy Hofheinz promises governor will license. Contracts sent to Texas. Hofheinz admits governor wouldn't go along. Deal killed by Texas politics … Joe met with Detroit promoters at Yank's house. Clay parties at meeting. Contract signed. Nothing happens.

Joe began to doubt fight would take place. Yank pessimistic. Convinced Clay going to jail. Bruce Wright to Harry Markson [president of Madison Square Garden boxing]: 'Get Ellis.'

Eddie Futch comes in to help train JF for Ellis fight. Much to Yank's credit, he accepted Futch. Delicate situation. Futch importance grows. Works well with Yank. Futch did the fine-tuning.

JF destroys Jimmy Ellis, KO 5.

Prospects for Ali fight brightened as mood of nation changed … Campaigns of Bobby Kennedy and Eugene McCarthy … Cambodia, Kent State … Feelings grew against war … Much draft resistance. Ali stayed while others fled … Ali an athlete whose battle to avoid military service transformed him into a kind of folk hero.

Clay licence for Atlanta … Boxes exhibition … Fights Quarry in Atlanta. Treated like conquering hero … Clay licensed in New York … Beats Bonavena. Frazier unimpressed, feared Clay might lose.

Now JF knows Clay fight inevitable if Clay doesn't go to jail first … Wanted Clay bad … People bugged him on street, reporters' questions.

Negotiations for fight, simmering for several months, boil. Ante rising fast. Clearly headed for richest purse in history … Garden offered $1.3 million; Astrodome offered $1.3 million … Yank, Herbert and Arum pushing for Houston. Bruce Wright suspicious; felt offer too low. Frazier not aware of specific negotiations.

Series of meetings in Arum's office. Jesse Jackson roughly rebutted. Christmas coming when Bruce Wright calls Joe and says it looks like something about to happen … Jerry Perenchio offer: $2.5 million for each fighter. Fight set for Madison Square Garden.

Nation polarising … Ali becoming hero of left and Frazier hero of right … Clay escalates feud to unsettle Frazier for fight … JF: 'It got out of control.'

JF hurt by Clay's better ability to communicate to white press … JF becomes symbol of Ali's oppression. Clay trying to make him appear enemy of black people.

JF becoming aware of unpopularity with blacks. Began to find self perceived as 'Uncle Tom'. Unfair but inevitable.

JF: 'Clay is a phoney. He never worked. He never had a job. He don't know nothing about life for most black people. He talks out both sides of his mouth. Doesn't act as he preaches. Lies to the public. Gets people riled up. Exploits race problems and real black pride. No real minister would act that way.'

Clay issues more inflammatory quotes. JF hurt and surprised when he intensifies insults. Real dislike growing.

JF often teased in street … Reaction to being called ugly.

JF: 'Black people are ashamed of me. They don't know what I'm really like.'

JF thought Clay liked him … JF: 'He never did. He wants to be bigger than everyone else, so he tries to make them small. Even when we signed to fight, he still looked down on me as nothing. I'm his black brother, but he used me.'

Night before the fight. Joe tense, didn't sleep … Believes he'll win, but will feel no shame if he loses.

In dressing-room before fight, Futch is calm centre of storm.

Joe beats Clay in the most famous fight of all time. Knockdown, unanimous decision, little press disagreement. JF says afterwards, 'He's the greatest I ever fought.'

Traditionally, fighters who achieve great victory allowed to enjoy acclaim that goes with it. Loser treats winner with respect of fellow athlete, even if momentary controversy or rivalry very intense.

JF victory tarnished … Ali attacks Frazier after fight: 'I didn't lose the fight. The white people said I lost it' … Spends next two years trying to diminish JF victory. Occasionally admitted he lost. But most often, in public, claimed he had won; that fight was 'stolen' for 'political reasons'.

Period of title not as pleasant for JF as might have been. Clay attacks make victory appear suspect. JF not fully appreciated as a fighter or a man.

JF: 'Clay was responsible for my time as champion not being as happy as it could have been.'

What it's like to be champ: People awed. Everyone recognises you, feels it's an honour to be in your presence. JF visits Nixon at White House. Invited to speak before South Carolina legislature. Requests to appear on major TV shows. Marvels at how far he has come.

JF setting stage for losing title. Too involved with being champ. Demands on time.

Relationship with Yank changed. Not together as often. Joe more assertive.

JF much too involved with music group, Joe Frazier and the Knockouts. Argued with Yank over music. Yank caved … Bad reviews for group. European tour bombs.

Yank privately hurt by Joe. But Yank had changed also. Much more abrasive and self-important. Decided secretly that Joe should avoid tough fights. Didn't tell Joe, who thought no contender would fight him.

For twenty-two months, no tough fights … Two over-matched opponents, Terry Daniels and Ron Stander … JF didn't work as hard. Overweight for both fights. Put less pressure on opponents, not doubling up. Wins came too easily.

Eddie Futch saw changes in Joe. Tried to tell him. Can't when still winning. JF feeling invincible.

JF: 'I lay my hands on and they fall.'

JF: 'Nobody can knock me out.'

Joe decides he wants to fight George Foreman … Loses in two rounds.

Dealing with defeat … 'The former heavyweight champion of the world.'

Back to the drawing board ... JF gives up most outside activity. Draws closer to Yank. Happy in training ... Decision over Joe Bugner in London.

August 1973: Yank dies.

Eddie Futch takes over.

Negotiations for Clay II ... Fight made.

JF feelings about Clay had mellowed ... Thought attacks were over ... Clay escalates feud, stirs racial issue again.

Joe cries in back of car ... Still not accepted or understood by many blacks ... Many painful incidents ... Hassled by people in street.

JF: 'We'll never get along. I got the best of him in ring, but he caused a lot of my own people to turn on me.'

Bombardment continues.

Joe bothered by lack of formal schooling. Can't read.

JF: 'Clay goes out of his way to mock my education. Makes this image of me that I'm dumb and ugly. I don't think this guy have any kind of feeling for anybody. Maybe his wife and his kids. But general people, I don't think so.'

Problems in training … Joe misses Yank … Inconsistent and unimpressive in gym. Up too high, taking too many rights … Complaining about sore shoulder and other aches, lingering cold.

Studio brawl when Clay calls Joe 'ignorant'.

Joe increasingly paranoid, restless … Self-doubts without Yank … Futch admits JF uptight too soon [before the fight]; fears JF losing confidence in him.

On fight night, dressing-room too chaotic … Confusion on exit time. JF warms up twice.

First fight without Yank … Clay wins unanimous decision.

Clay beats Foreman to regain championship.

JF: 'I admire him regaining the title. He KO'd the man who KO'd me.'

Ali–Frazier III in Manila.

Pre-fight, Ali labels Joe a gorilla.

JF: 'Every once in a while, the ugliness that's behind that cocky smile sees the sunshine … Clay is a phoney and a hypocrite who uses people, mostly his own people … He must be bigger than anyone else or he tries to make them smaller.'

Wanted to actually kill Clay in ring, hated him so much.

[Ali–Frazier III was contested on the outskirts of Manila at 10.45 a.m. on 1 October 1975.]

Evening of 29 September … Joe on king-sized bed, watching TV, running fingers over guitar strings … 'One day, I'm gonna learn how to play this thing.'

Ali on TV, predicting, 'The first combination, he will fall.'

JF: He's still trying to make himself believe. But it's too late, way too late. I got the noose around that cat's neck.'

TV coverage of Ali workout … JF hand tightens around handle of guitar when Ali jokes, 'Joe's so ugly, when he was a baby and cried, the tears turned around and ran back up his face into his eyes.'

Commentator in ring with Ali says, 'He calls you "Clay" because he can't spell "Muhammad".' … JF face clouds and he shakes his head silently … 'Shut it off.'

30 September … JF up at 3.30 a.m. Walks one mile … Back in room, pulls off boots, strips to underwear, pours alcohol on chest, lets it run down … Discusses letters he's getting from Christians.

JF: 'They say don't worry about the fight. God will take care of everything … That's cool. When the bell ring, I'll just sit on the stool and say, "Okay, God; take over" … Maybe I better not take no chances. I'll do a little fighting too.'

Takes a nap. Sleeps till 10.30 a.m. … Stays in room playing black-jack most of afternoon … Face grim.

Lies on bed, watches TV … *The Flying Nun* and *Porky Pig* … Chewing gum, cracking it.

At 5.30 p.m., JF eats fried fish, peas and rice.

Florence comes into room and sits by bed … Florence sacrifices. JF doesn't always appreciate her … JF and Florence have long quiet talk … Florence leaves.

JF: 'Florence been sacrificing for years to make things happen for me. When we got married, we was so poor, she needed her sister's ring. Now she's got her own Cadillac.'

8.10 p.m.: JF shuts off light, goes to sleep.

1 October 1975 … Joe leaves room at 7.15 a.m. … Wearing green shirt, beige slacks, brown suspenders … Siren wailing … Arrives at arena … Sits on red couch.

7.45a.m.: Ali–Frazier III in three hours … JF lays back with head on red pillow, closes eyes and sleeps.

A HOLIDAY SEASON FANTASY

(2004)

In the 1960s and 70s, Muhammad Ali's most important contribution was to force an understanding of the divisions between black and white in American society and, ultimately, to help bridge that gap. Now there's a more threatening chasm; the horrible hatred that exists between the Islamic and non-Islamic world.

Ali is only one man. But he might be the most recognised and most loved person on the planet. He has a reservoir of goodwill that draws upon the love and good feeling that he has earned from all races, all nationalities and all religions.

More than a decade ago, Ali told me, 'I got a plan. Someday I'm gonna hitchhike from New York to California with no money, no clothes except what I'm wearing, nothing. Then I'm going from California over to Asia, and from Asia to Europe and Africa and South America. I'm going all around the world with just my face to see how people greet me and take care of me. I could go just about any place in the world, knock on any door, and people would know me and let me in. I might even march on foot through Egypt, Israel, Lebanon, all them countries, and tell people to stop fighting and agree on a peace that's fair to everyone. Some people say that might be dangerous, but you gotta take risks. Columbus discovered America by sailing around the world when people thought he'd fall off. We got men on the moon by risking their lives.'

It's only a fantasy. But what if Muhammad Ali were to walk through the troubled regions of the world today on a year-long journey to promote tolerance and understanding among all people?

It would be a dream-like quest. But Ali is a dreamer, as were Mahatma Gandhi and Nelson Mandela when they began their journeys.

Would it be dangerous? Absolutely. But Ali was one of the most reviled people in America in the 1960s. It was a decade of assassinations in the United States. John F. Kennedy, Robert Kennedy and Malcolm X were all shot down. How did Muhammad respond to the threat?

'I'm an easy target,' Ali said in 1965. 'I'm everywhere; everybody knows me. I walk the streets daily and nobody's guarding me. I have no guns, no police. So if someone's gonna get me, tell them to come on and get it over with; if they can get past God, because God is controlling the bullet.'

If Ali undertook a walk for peace, it would be the modern equivalent of the wanderings described in the holy books of the world.

The journey could begin with a statement: 'I'm embarking on this undertaking as a way of speaking out against the hatred and violence that imperil the world. I'm not going to talk about political issues. I'm not going to take sides. I'm going to embrace every person I meet regardless of that person's religion, colour or ideology. My presence will speak for itself. My message is simple. Killing is wrong. Hating is wrong. Every person is deserving of love. Whatever happens to me on this journey, I want no blood shed or prejudice voiced at any time ever in my name.'

To be successful, Ali's journey would have to be independent of governments and any other entity, religious or otherwise, no matter how well-intentioned that group might be. There would be no spin-masters; no spokespeople; no pre-arranged meetings with selected groups. It would be one man walking where he chose to walk; speaking without words; telling every person he met by virtue of his presence that hate has to be cleansed from people's hearts one person at a time.

In his inaugural speech, John F. Kennedy declared, 'Let us go forth to lead the land we love, asking His blessing and His help, but knowing that, here on Earth, God's work must truly be our own.'

Were Ali to undertake the journey described above, he would truly be doing 'God's work'. He would be a prophet of peace.

But it's just a fantasy.

MUHAMMAD ALI:
A CLASSIC HERO

(2013)

Let us celebrate Muhammad Ali.

We live in an age when people pay homage to celebrities, superstars and champions.

Ali is something more. He is a hero.

Our record of heroes begins with *The Iliad*, the oldest known work in Western literature.

The Iliad was fashioned by a series of story-tellers represented by the Greek poet, Homer. The telling began around 800 BC and was codified over hundreds of years. In final form, it recounts a period of several weeks during the last year of the siege of Troy.

The ancient Greeks revered heroes as a class of men who occupied a position midway between common mortals and gods. Heroes were worshipped by communities as protecting spirits. The failure to pay homage to them was often seen as responsible for misfortune such as poor crops and pestilence.

Achilles is *The Iliad's* greatest hero warrior. Neither his death nor his heel is referenced in the epic poem. It wasn't until the first century AD that the Roman poet Statius advanced the idea that Achilles' mother, Thetis, sought to make her son invulnerable by dipping him in the River Styx as she held him by the heel. Indeed, Book 21 of *The Iliad* recounts Achilles being wounded by a spear thrown by Asteropaeus that draws blood from his elbow.

The Iliad also contains the first telling of a boxing match in Western literature: the confrontation between Epeios and Euryalos at the funeral games for Patroclus. The winner is to receive an unbroken horse; the loser, a two-handled goblet.

Prior to the contest, Epeios declares, 'I say no other of the Achaeans will beat me at boxing. I will mash his skin apart and break his bones. Let those who care for him wait nearby to carry him out after my fists have beaten him under.'

Thereafter, 'The two men strode to the middle of the circle and faced each other and put up their huge hands at the same time. Great Epeios came in and hit Euryalos on the cheek as he peered out from his guard, and he could no longer keep his feet.'

Victory was followed by compassion.

'Great-hearted Epeios took Euryalos in his arms and set him upright, and his true companions stood about him and led him out of the circle, feet dragging as he spat up thick blood and rolled his head over on one side.'

When Homer's tales were first woven together, the world known to those who listened to them was very small. No one could have imagined Muhammad Ali.

Ali, once known as Cassius Marcellus Clay Jr, burst upon the scene as a gold medal winner at the 1960 Rome Olympics. In the decades that followed, he brought unprecedented grace to boxing and changed for ever what we expect a champion to be.

Ali's accomplishments in the ring were grist for the milling of legends. There were two fights against Sonny Liston, when he proclaimed himself 'The Greatest' and proved that he was; three epic wars against Joe Frazier; and a stunning victory over George Foreman, when Ali travelled to Africa and reclaimed the crown that had been unfairly taken from him.

In ancient Greece, hundreds of people gathered around fires to hear of Achilles' battle against Hector. Three millennia later, hundreds of millions of people waited for word of Ali's exploits on battlefields as far flung as Kinshasa and Manila.

Ali is a hero for modern times. His personal magnetism, good looks and charisma made him ideal for the age of television. But beyond that, he meets the criteria for classic heroism.

A hero must achieve something substantial. Heroes can be presidents, military leaders, sports champions or quite average (such as a teenager who leaps into a rushing river to save a drowning child). But a hero must do something that most people can't do or haven't done.

A hero overcomes substantial odds.

There must be an element of risk that has been met head-on.

Heroes often 'do it alone'.

Ali's ring exploits are in line with the above. But true heroism requires something more. A hero places principles and loyalty above personal gain, a higher good ahead of self-interest.

Ali's devotion to principle inspired the world.

Initially, Ali stood as a beacon of hope for oppressed people around the globe. Every time he looked in the mirror and said, 'I'm so pretty,' he was saying 'Black is beautiful' before that became fashionable. He demanded equality for himself and others. Then he refused induction into the US Army at the height of the war in Vietnam, was stripped of his championship and threatened with imprisonment. He became a symbol of the belief that, unless there's a very good reason for killing people, war is wrong.

Sadly, Ali's ring career tracked the arc of a classic Greek tragedy.

In that genre, a hero is endowed with *arete*: excellence, the attributes that make him great.

Ali had preternatural physical gifts: strength, speed, stamina and a seeming imperviousness to pain.

Then the hero gives in to *hubris*: a mixture of overconfidence and pride leading to the belief that he's invincible and immune to the pitfalls that destroy other men.

Hear Ali's words: 'I'm young, I'm handsome, I'm fast. I can't possibly be beat. I am The Greatest.'

A *nemesis* is sent by the gods to threaten the hero's destruction.

Achilles versus Hector … Ali versus Joe Frazier.

Even if the hero triumphs over his nemesis, the seeds of his destruction have been sown.

Finally, there is *ate*: the demise, the inability to see one's own fate until it is too late.

In 1996, at the 26th Summer Olympiad in Atlanta, the world watched as Muhammad Ali lit a cauldron with a torch carrying the Olympic flame. Ali was in less than good health by then. It was a difficult physical task. More than one billion people around the world were watching.

The people who witnessed Ali's struggle that night were united in love and caring for one man. More than a billion people, if only for a moment, had all the hate and prejudice removed from their hearts.

Ali prevailed. The flame moved from torch to cauldron. It was the perfect benediction for a hero's life devoted in large measure to helping others.

Ali today enjoys a status that is bestowed upon few men in their lifetime: the knowledge that he is immortal.

ELVIS AND ALI

(2011)

I saw Elvis Presley perform in 1971.

One month earlier, I'd finished a stint as a law clerk for a United States district judge. Five years as a litigator at a large Wall Street law firm would follow. I was taking three months off between jobs to travel cross-country and explore America.

I stopped in great cities and small towns; staying with friends, camping out at night, checking into cheap motels and spending several days at a commune in Wolf Creek, Oregon. I visited steel mills, Disneyland and the Grand Canyon. I passed through corn-fields in Iowa, fields of wheat in Nebraska and potatoes in Idaho. There were times when I drove too fast because I was young and foolish and didn't consider what the consequences of an unseen pothole along the open highway might be. I walked the streets of Selma, Alabama, at a time when the term 'nigger' was commonly used, and retraced the route that John Kennedy travelled in Dallas on 22 November 1963.

On the night of 14 August, I was at the International Hilton in Las Vegas.

Two years earlier, Presley had signed a five-year contract that called for him to perform at the International for eight weeks each year. During his run, there were two shows nightly, at 8.00 p.m. and midnight. The ballroom seated 2,200. Elvis was Las Vegas's signature act. All 826 of his shows, which continued until his death in 1977, sold out.

I arrived at the Hilton at 7.45 p.m., knowing that no tickets were available. I just wanted to feel the mood. Hundreds of people were standing in line outside the ballroom. They had tickets for the midnight show and were queuing up because they wanted to sit as close to the stage as possible. The audience for the 8.00 p.m. performance had long since been seated.

As unlikely as it sounds, there was only one security man at the main door and he was looking away. I simply walked in.

The ballroom was jammed, but I found an open seat at a table with a group of women. The show began with a set from Elvis's back-up group, the Sweet Inspirations. A comedian was up next.

Then the sound of *Thus Spake Zarathustra* (popularly referenced as the theme from Stanley Kubrick's *2001*) pulsated through the ballroom. Elvis strode onto the stage wearing a white fringed suit accessorised with a purple scarf. The audience roared its approval.

It was an off night for Elvis. By mid-performance, he was letting the orchestra carry the tune while he wandered around the stage, mopping his brow. There were flashes of greatness but not much more. I didn't appreciate what I was seeing then as much as I do now.

Thirty-one years later, when I was in Memphis to cover the heavyweight championship fight between Lennox Lewis and Mike Tyson, I visited Graceland.

Elvis lived there from 1957 until his death at the age of 42. The mansion reflected his tastes. Some of the décor is garish. Many of the furnishings are what one might find in a typical middle-class home. There are the obligatory Elvis artefacts: gold records, movie posters, outfits that Elvis wore onstage. And a 'jungle room' with an indoor waterfall.

After I returned home, I found myself listening to Elvis's music more than before.

I met Muhammad Ali in 1967. I was a senior at Columbia University, hosting a weekly radio show called *Personalities in Sports* for the student-run station. Ali was in his prime, preparing to fight Zora Folley at Madison Square Garden. It would be his seventh championship defence in less than a year.

Ali told me to turn on my tape recorder. We talked about Nation of Islam doctrine, with some questions about the military draft and boxing thrown in. Ten minutes after we began, Muhammad announced, 'That's all I'm gonna do,' and the interview was over.

In 1988, through a twist of fate, I became Ali's biographer. Over the course of a decade, we spent countless hours together in his home and mine. I experienced the joy of travelling around the world with him.

I've been thinking a lot lately about the parallels between Elvis and Ali. They grew out of the same soil, the segregated American south; one black and one white. Each had a magnetic personality. They were remarkably good-looking, albeit in different ways;

instinctive showmen with an energy about them. They weren't deep thinkers; they did what they did. Ali fought intuitively. Elvis sang intuitively. It was genius on each man's part. They were craftsman with remarkable natural gifts who honed their gifts in marvellous ways.

Elvis and Ali were curiosities, human-interest stories for a slow day in the newsroom, before they evolved into something more.

Then they became counterculture symbols; feared as Pied Pipers, who would lead their followers (young people for Elvis, black people for Ali) in rebellion against the establishment and the status quo.

They weren't trying to change the culture. They were simply doing what they wanted to do.

Over time, they became 'safe' – benevolent monarchs in all their glory, sharing the bond of almost incomprehensible fame. Elvis was a global superstar unlike any who had come before him. Ali followed suit, rising to iconic status in his lifetime.

Finally, they got old and their dissolution made them even safer. Neither let his disability keep him out of the public eye.

I'm recognised as an authority on Muhammad Ali. I'm not an Elvis Presley scholar. But I lived through Elvis's rise and fall and grew up in a culture that was shaped in part by his music and persona. I decided recently that I wanted to write about Elvis.

Elvis Aaron Presley was born in Tupelo, Mississippi, on 8 January 1935. Franklin Roosevelt's 'New Deal' was just coming into being. Social Security had not yet been enacted.

Elvis was an only child. His twin brother was stillborn. The family often found it difficult to make ends meet. 'Poor we were,'

Vernon Presley (Elvis's father) acknowledged years later. 'I'll never deny that. But trash, we weren't. We always had compassion for people. We never had any prejudice. We never put anybody down. Neither did Elvis.'

Elvis's first love was gospel music. At the age of ten, he entered a singing contest at the Mississippi-Alabama Fair and Dairy Show. At 12, he performed on a local radio show.

In 1948, the Presleys moved to Memphis, Tennessee. Elvis graduated from Humes High School in 1953. Classmates later described him as a loner. He wasn't about fitting in. He dressed and styled his hair differently from the other students. He was obsessed with music.

After graduation, Elvis took a job driving a truck and began studying to be an electrician. In August 1953, he went to a Memphis recording studio and, for four dollars, cut a two-sided record of 'My Happiness' and 'That's When Your Heartaches Begin' as a birthday present for his mother. The only accompaniment was his own primitive acoustic guitar playing. He returned in January 1954 to cut another record. This time, Sam Phillips (owner of the studio and a record producer) was there.

In some ways, America's airwaves in 1954 were as segregated as other closed institutions. Mainstream radio stations wouldn't play 'race music' by black recording artists. Phillips had once said, 'If I could find a white man who had the Negro sound and the Negro feel, I could make a billion dollars.'

Now he had found him.

Six months later, Phillips called Presley back to the studio and matched him with guitarist Scotty Moore and bass player Bill

Black. Soon, Elvis's records were being played locally. Then they rippled through the south.

In the mid-1950s, the youth market in the United States was exploding as a separate economic entity. Families no longer sat around the living-room listening to the radio together. Adolescents had their own radio in their own room and their own money to spend on records. Music was a common denominator among the young and a primary lifeline for the new youth culture.

Before long, the spirit of Elvis Presley was wafting through America.

In November 1955, Sam Phillips sold Presley's contract to RCA for the then generous sum of $40,000. RCA released 'Heartbreak Hotel' in January 1956. It was Elvis's first number one hit. That was followed by an 'LP album' entitled *Elvis Presley*. Soon after, a record that paired 'Don't Be Cruel' and 'Hound Dog' rose to the top of the charts and stayed there for 11 weeks – a mark that would not be surpassed for 36 years.

At the same time, Elvis began performing outside the south; most notably, on a 15-city Midwest tour. More significantly, he was discovered by the exploding medium of television.

Elvis's first national TV exposure came on CBS's *Stage Show* in early 1956. That was followed by two appearances on *The Milton Berle Show* and one with Steve Allen. By mid-1956, he was receiving ten thousand fan letters a week.

Elvis had soulful eyes and a sensual voice. He wore his hair in a pompadour style that looked as though it had been made for him. At times, he curled his lip into a sneer, but always with a twinkle in his eye. The sneer was akin to a secret smile; good-natured, not mean; part sexual come-on, part flouting of authority.

There had been popular music stars before Elvis; most notably Rudy Vallee, Bing Crosby and Frank Sinatra. But their performances had been highly stylised and controlled. Yes, women screamed when the young Sinatra sang. But he'd been cloaked in the elegance and glamour of the Tommy Dorsey band.

Popular music wasn't sexy before Elvis.

Elvis put sex (not love, sex) in the music. Sinatra whispered in your ear in the wee small hours of the morning. Elvis grabbed at your body with the lights on.

Before Elvis, singers were heard. Elvis was heard and seen. Gyrating, thrusting his hips. If he'd come along a decade later, his long hair and gyrations might have seemed unremarkable. But audiences in 1955 were accustomed to seeing some guy wearing a suit and tie sing, 'M-o-o-o-n over Miami …'

Elvis onstage was like a force of nature. He was spontaneous. He let it all hang out. His music resonated. He never explained intellectually what he did or why. He just did it.

'You have to put on a show for the people,' he said of his performing style. 'People can buy your records and hear you sing. They don't have to come out and hear you. If I just stood out there and sang and never moved a muscle, the people would say, "My goodness; I can stay home and listen to his records."'

But it was more than that.

'I don't know where I picked up my style,' Elvis acknowledged. 'I just started out doing what I'm doing now. I do whatever I feel onstage. It's like a surge of electricity going through me. It's almost like making love, but it's even stronger than that. Sometimes I think my heart is going to explode.'

The message in Elvis's music was simple. Express your emotions; do what you want; feel good about yourself; the world is yours.

'Presley, more than anyone else,' it was later written, 'gave the young a belief in themselves as a distinct and unified generation.'

Adolescence is a time when boys and girls are developing their own artistic tastes and finding new dimensions within themselves. Before Elvis, there had been a hint of teen rebellion in the culture, personified by James Dean in *Rebel Without a Cause*. To young men and women who came of age in the mid-1950s, Elvis was something more.

At a certain age, liking the music is about being part of a group. Elvis was the group leader, brimming with promise and doing things that simply weren't allowed.

Sex is the most mysterious and exciting of unknowns for adolescent girls. Elvis was an adolescent girl's fantasy machine. He was a bad boy with an innocence about him; handsome, exciting and safe at the same time. When the powers that be refused to show him from the waist down on television, the imagination kicked in. There's nothing more enticing to a girl entering puberty than forbidden fruit that her parents don't want her to see.

Girls dreamed about Elvis, literally. Boys thought he was cool. And identifying with Elvis was a good way for them to impress girls. They grew sideburns and let their hair grow long.

The first article about Elvis in a national magazine ran in April 1956 in *Life* (the USA's premier general interest magazine at the time). It referenced him as a 'howling hillbilly' and likened his gyrations to burlesque. That was in keeping with the view that his music was vulgar and had the potential to lead young people into sexually wanton conduct.

In May 1956, after Elvis performed in La Crosse, Wisconsin, the local Catholic diocese newspaper sent an 'urgent' letter to FBI director J. Edgar Hoover, warning, 'Presley is a definite danger to the security of the United States. His actions and motions were such as to rouse the sexual passions of teenaged youth.'

Three months later, when Elvis performed in Florida, Reverend Robert Gray told the congregation at Trinity Baptist Church in Jacksonville, 'Elvis Presley has achieved a new low in spiritual degeneracy.'

A local judge ordered Elvis to tone down his act. He responded by forsaking gyrations during the show but wiggling his little finger suggestively throughout.

However, sex wasn't the only perceived threat that Elvis posed. There was another theme, more ominous to some, lurking in the background.

Elvis was becoming the dominant symbol of a new form of music: rock and roll. Rock and roll, especially the way he sang it, played into issues of race.

There were no black entertainment icons in America in the mid-1950s. Elvis fused black and white music in his art, blending country music, gospel and rhythm-and-blues. He was a white man who 'sang black', creating his own form of expression and bringing it into the mainstream of American culture.

He was blurring the lines between the races, and also opening a door that would allow black men and women to become crossover stars.

'Elvis was a blessing,' Richard Penniman (better known as Little Richard) said years later. 'They wouldn't let black music through. He opened the door for black music.'

Then Elvis got bigger.

Within the entertainment industry, *The Ed Sullivan Show* was the most influential television programme in America. Sullivan was stung by the fact that, for the first time ever, rival Steve Allen had drawn a higher rating than he had. Allen's featured attraction that night had been Elvis Presley.

In response, Sullivan booked Presley for three appearances. The first, on 9 September 1956, was seen by sixty million viewers; a mind-boggling 82.6 per cent of the television-viewing audience. Performances on 28 October 1956 and 21 January 1957 drew comparable numbers.

Millions of Americans who were young at the time still remember where they were when Elvis appeared on *The Ed Sullivan Show*. It had been decreed that camera angles would be such that the most provocative of his gyrations would not be shown. He also toned his act down for the shows. At the close of his third appearance, Sullivan assured the country that this was 'a real decent fine boy'.

Elvis's appearances on *The Ed Sullivan Show* boosted his celebrity status to unprecedented proportions. He was a tidal wave washing over American culture. There had never been a phenomenon like him. Then he added Hollywood to his credits, appearing in a feature film entitled *Love Me Tender*.

Ironically, in many ways, Elvis represented conservative American values. He revered his mother. He was a Southern Baptist. All he wanted to do, really, was sing, buy a car and make money.

Press conferences were awkward affairs. Offstage, Elvis was polite and a bit shy. When called upon to speak publicly, he struggled with his words and never knew quite what to say apart from platitudes about loving whatever city he was in and appreciating the opportunity to perform before a live audience.

'I don't like to be called "Elvis the Pelvis",' he told a radio interviewer in Florida. 'It's one of the most childish expressions I've ever heard coming from an adult. But if they want to call me that, there's nothing I can do about it.'

Asked about rock and roll, he replied, 'Rock and roll has been in for about five years. I'm not going to say that it's gonna last, because I don't know. All I can say is, it's good; the people like it; it's selling; and I enjoy doing it.'

Then Elvis's world was turned upside down. He was drafted and, on 24 March 1958, inducted into the US Army. The haircut he received at the start of basic training was as symbolic as any shearing ever. The old culture had asserted itself.

A more debilitating blow followed. In August 1958, Elvis's mother fell gravely ill. He was granted an emergency leave to visit her. Two days after he arrived in Memphis, Gladys Presley died. She was 46 years old.

Elvis lost his centre when his mother died. As she lay in an open coffin at Graceland, he stroked her face again and again, saying, 'Wake up, mama. Wake up, baby, and talk to Elvis.' He had to be restrained from climbing on top of her coffin when she was laid in the grave. He came close to a complete emotional breakdown. There was inconsolable extended grieving.

'He changed completely,' Lillian Mann Smith (Elvis's aunt) said years later. 'He didn't seem like Elvis ever again.'

For most of his time in the military, Presley was stationed with the 3rd Armored Division in West Germany. He was honourably discharged on 5 March 1960. Two months later, he was on a television variety show again; this time as the featured guest on *The Frank Sinatra Timex Special.*

Several years earlier, Sinatra had belittled Elvis as utterly lacking in talent. Now the two men, each wearing a tuxedo, stood side by side. Sinatra (looking uncomfortable) sang 'Love Me Tender'. Elvis (without sideburns) sang 'Witchcraft', one of his host's signature songs.

Two-thirds of Americans watching television that night watched *The Frank Sinatra Timex Special.* Elvis was back. But the rebellious rock-and-roll figure had died.

On 17 January 1942, six years before the Presleys moved to Memphis, Cassius Marcellus Clay Jr was born in Louisville, Kentucky.

Kentucky was a Jim Crow state. Segregated facilities were mandated by law. In parts of the country at that time, blacks were denied the right to vote and it was a crime punishable by ten years in prison for a black and a white to intermarry. Major league baseball ('America's national pastime') had yet to open its doors to Jackie Robinson.

In some respects, Cassius Clay was very much like Elvis. He adored his mother. He was a Southern Baptist, who said 'yes, sir' and 'no, sir'. He wanted to make money and own a red Cadillac convertible. He was remarkably telegenic, photogenic and charismatic. One can argue that he and Elvis had two of the prettiest smiles ever.

Elvis's art was singing. Clay's was fighting. Each was an entertainer. Elvis's performances were scripted and safe. Clay's world was more brutal. He put his physical wellbeing on the line every time he entered the ring.

Like Elvis, Cassius was obsessed with his art when he was young and had a rhythm all his own.

Older generations had condemned Elvis, saying, 'He wouldn't have to jump around and shake his hips like that if he could sing.' Older generations condemned Clay's ring style, saying, 'He wouldn't have to dance around like that if he could fight.'

On 22 November 1963, John F. Kennedy was assassinated in Dallas. On 9 February 1964, the Beatles made their American television debut on *The Ed Sullivan Show* (drawing 73 million viewers). Sixteen days after that, Cassius Clay knocked out Sonny Liston to claim the most coveted title in sport, the heavyweight championship of the world.

'The Sixties' had begun.

Two days after defeating Liston, Clay announced that he had accepted the teachings of a black separatist religion known as the Nation of Islam. On 6 March 1964, he took the name 'Muhammad Ali', which was given to him by his spiritual mentor, Elijah Muhammad. On 17 February 1966, he was reclassified 1-A (eligible for the military draft) by the Selective Service System and uttered the now immortal words, 'I ain't got no quarrel with them Vietcong.'

Elvis's followers had expected him to go into the military. He would have lost their love and respect if he hadn't.

The Nation of Islam had different expectations with regard to Ali. On 28 April 1967, citing his religious beliefs, he refused induction into the US Army.

Elvis had set music free in America, and, in doing so, asked the question, 'What would it be like to be free of my parents' rules?'

Like Elvis, Ali was about personal freedom. But he was meeting issues of racism head-on and asking, 'What would it be like to be free of society's rules?'

Ali was perceived by the establishment as being even more dangerous than Elvis had been.

Meanwhile, popular culture was passing Elvis by. By the time he was discharged from the Army, rock and roll was in full bloom and evolving at the speed of sound. By 1964, the Beatles were dominating pop culture the way that Elvis had a mere eight years earlier. Mick Jagger did everything onstage that Elvis had done (and more). Bob Dylan freed music with lyrics that were as different and daring as Elvis's gyrations had been. Elvis's music, which had been socially relevant in the 1950s, wasn't any more.

Elvis's manager, Colonel Tom Parker (as he liked to be called), contributed to the decline. Parker (who had been born in Holland and whose real name was Andreas Cornelis van Kuijk) had an overbearing manner and managed to extract an exorbitant percentage of Elvis's earnings for himself.

As soon as Elvis was discharged from the Army, Parker locked him into a series of Hollywood movie contracts that lasted for the better part of a decade. During that time, Elvis starred in 27 films in which, whatever the role, the character he played was always a thinly veiled version of himself.

James Dean had been one of Elvis's boyhood heroes. Elvis wanted to be a serious actor. With good training and better roles, he might have become one. Instead, he was mired in a string of low-budget musicals that were profitable but critically panned. The soundtracks had a formulaic assembly-line quality. The Beatles were conquering the world, and he was in films like *Tickle Me* and *Harum Scarum*.

Ali would lose three years of his ring career because of his refusal to accept induction into the US Army. Elvis wasted a decade of his life making bad Hollywood movies.

'I'd like to make better films than the films I made before,' he said ruefully when the run was over. 'I didn't have final approval of the script, which means I couldn't say, "This is not good for me." I don't think anyone was consciously trying to harm me. It was just, Hollywood's image of me was wrong, and I knew it and I couldn't do anything about it. The pictures got very similar. Something was successful and they'd try to recreate it the next time around. I'd read the first four or five pages, and I'd know it was just a different name with 12 new songs in it. It worried me sick. I didn't know what to do. I was obligated a lot of times very heavily to things I didn't believe in, and it was very difficult. I had thought they would get a property for me and give me a chance to show some acting ability, but it did not change. I became very discouraged. I would have liked to have something more challenging instead of Hollywood's image of what they thought I was.'

Then Elvis's world turned again; this time for the better.

In 1968, America was in turmoil. Martin Luther King Jr and Robert Kennedy were assassinated. The anti-war movement was in full bloom. Mayor Daley's police rioted at the Democratic National Convention in Chicago. A new drug culture was sweeping the country.

On 3 December 1968, NBC aired its highest-rated show of the year. It's now known as 'The Comeback Special'. At the time, it was titled *Elvis*.

The show mixed a handful of elaborately produced studio numbers with songs performed in an intimate setting before a small live audience. Elvis wore black leather, looked good and sang well. It was his first 'live' performance since 1961. A whole new generation took notice and said, 'Hey! This guy is pretty cool.' And for those who had been young in the 1950s, Elvis was back.

Five months after Elvis's comeback special, the International Hotel (soon to be acquired by Hilton) announced that it had signed him to perform 57 shows over a four-week period in Las Vegas for the then astronomical sum of $500,000.

Thirteen years earlier, in April 1956, a young Elvis Presley had unsuccessfully played the New Frontier Hotel in Las Vegas. The audience had been unimpressed. A reviewer for the *Las Vegas Sun* wrote at the time, 'For the teenagers, the long, tall Memphis lad is a whiz. For the average Vegas spender or showgoer, a bore. His musical sound with a combo of three is uncouth, matching to a great extent the lyric content of his nonsensical songs.'

Times change.

Elvis opened at the International on 31 July 1969. The next day, the hotel extended his contract to provide for eight weeks of performances annually (in February and August) over a five-year period. His salary would be one million dollars a year.

Elvis and Ali met twice in Las Vegas. The first time, Muhammad saw him onstage and they chatted briefly afterward. 'All my life, I admired Elvis,' Ali said years later. 'It was a thrill to meet him.'

Their second meeting, in February 1973, was more consequential.

Ali was less threatening to the establishment by then. He'd been stripped of his championship and denied a licence to box after refusing induction into the United States Army. After three years in exile, he was allowed by court order to fight again, but had lost to Joe Frazier in 'The Fight of the Century'. His rematches with Frazier and triumphant battle against George Foreman in Zaïre to reclaim the heavyweight crown were yet to come. Ali's adversaries had exploited his vulnerabilities and seemed to have beaten him down.

From time to time, Elvis's life had intersected with the sweet science. He tried out for his high school boxing team, but quit the first day after suffering a bloody nose. Later, in the 1962 movie *Kid Galahad*, he'd played a professional fighter.

On 14 February 1973, Ali fought Joe Bugner at the Las Vegas Convention Center. Prior to the bout, he and Elvis met in a hotel suite and Elvis presented him with with a faux-jewel-studded robe emblazoned with the words 'The People's Choice'. Ali wore the robe that night and beat Bugner.

The Las Vegas years are an important part of Elvis's legacy. The city's dream machine revived him and gave him new life as a superstar. Soon, he was performing around the country again.

'The most important thing is the inspiration I get from a live audience,' Elvis said in Houston before a 1970 engagement at the Astrodome. 'I was missing that.'

Time and again, he elaborated on that theme: 'A live concert to me is exciting because of all the electricity that's generated in the crowd and onstage. It's my favourite part of the business … I missed the closeness of a live audience. So as soon as I got out of the movie contract, I decided to play live concerts again … It's a good feeling. There's a new audience each time. What's interesting about music and all the people here [his back-up musicians] is, they find new sounds and they do things differently themselves; so it's like a new experience every day.'

Elvis was appearing onstage more often now than ever before. In 1973, there were 168 concert performances; the most notable of them at the Honolulu International Center in Hawaii.

Aloha Hawaii was taped in January and aired in the United States on 4 April 1973, capturing 57 per cent of the viewing audience. More significantly, it was transmitted by satellite to 36 countries around the world.

Meanwhile, Ali was experiencing a rebirth of his own. In 1974, he dethroned George Foreman to regain the heavyweight championship of the world. Then he abandoned the separatist teachings of the Nation of Islam and, while still a devout Muslim, embraced the philosophy that hearts and souls know no colour.

Ali's kingdom was now the world. And Elvis had become a symbol larger than himself; the quintessential larger-than-life celebrity rock star. He was an Elvis; the only one of its kind.

Only a select few people have ever experienced what Elvis and Ali came to experience in the mid-1970s. They were icons of the highest order, universal royalty, instantly recognisable around the globe.

Ali loved being king. But Elvis couldn't ride the wave and seemed burdened by the crown.

There are people the spotlight never turns away from. Wherever they go, they can never be anonymous. These people either give in to their fame and embrace it (in the manner of Ali); manage their fame by setting strict boundaries; or it devours them.

Ali embraced his fame, gave himself completely to the public and mingled joyously with them. People who met Ali one-on-one loved him more afterwards. If Ali was feeling low, he could walk down the street and cause a traffic jam by hugging people and signing autographs to lift his spirits.

For Elvis, that was the stuff of nightmares. Fame was a trap that he couldn't escape. He was oppressed by it. He cut himself off from the public and lived largely in seclusion.

'I felt sorry for Elvis,' Ali said a decade after Presley's death. 'He didn't enjoy life the way he should. He stayed indoors all the time. I told him he should go out and see people. He said he couldn't because, everywhere he went, they mobbed him. He didn't understand. No one wanted to hurt him. All they wanted was to be friendly and tell him how much they loved him.'

In many ways, fame is a stronger test of character than adversity. People act obsequiously and pay homage to the famous. Ali had the fact that he was black and people were throwing punches at him to remind him of life's harsh realities. Also, Ali had something much larger than himself – his religion – to flow into.

Elvis had music, which was his means of expression. But it wasn't enough. His fantasies had come to fruition when he was

21 years old. After that, what was left? In his orbit, everything was about him. He was surrounded by a tight coterie of enablers who indulged his every whim, never held him to the standards of accountability that apply to most men and women, and lived off him. But he had a fragile psyche and never found a calm centre. He grew older but not wiser. He lost his way.

Ali was more comfortable with who he was than Elvis was. He was at peace with himself. And he was stronger at his core.

Where Elvis's 'real-life' interaction with women is concerned, one can speculate that the happiest relationship he enjoyed was with Ann-Margret (his co-star in the 1963 film *Viva Las Vegas*).

He married once.

Elvis and Priscilla Beaulieu met in 1959. Her father was a US Air Force officer serving in Germany. Elvis was 24 years old; she was 14. They were married eight years later. On 1 February 1968, nine months to the day after their wedding, their only child (Lisa Marie) was born.

Elvis pushed Priscilla away sexually after the birth of their daughter. That and his profligate womanising led to an affair on her part. Soon after Christmas 1971, she told him that she wanted a divorce. Their marriage was formally dissolved on 9 October 1973.

One can speculate from anecdotal evidence that Elvis was an unsophisticated lover. He was more comfortable cuddling and kissing than he was making love. After Priscilla left him, the women who stayed in his life for any length of time moved quickly from sexual object to caretaker.

As the 1970s progressed, things got worse. Elvis had looked like he was having so much fun when he was young, particularly onstage. Then the fun came to an end and it seemed as though life was an ordeal.

After the *Aloha Hawaii* special, his weight burgeoned out of control. Worse, he became increasingly dependent on prescription drugs.

Elvis had begun self-medicating heavily long before his marriage ended. The drug use increased after he and Priscilla separated. He took pills and over-ate because he was depressed. He took pills and over-ate because he was bored. He took pills and over-ate because he was nervous. He took pills to help him sleep at night, to start his day (which often began in mid-afternoon), to raise his energy level to perform and to calm down afterwards.

In October 1973, Elvis was hospitalised in semi-comatose condition after receiving excessive injections of Demerol. He was nursed back to health, then relapsed. In 1974, he added cocaine to his drug habits.

It had always been hard to imagine Elvis Presley doing anything normally. During the last few years of his life, his mood swings became more and more pronounced and he was increasingly out of control.

He was reclusive but, at the same time, afraid to be left completely alone.

He acted petulantly towards those around him; then sought to regain their affection by lavishing gifts upon them. On a single day (27 July 1975), he bought and gave away 13 Cadillacs.

The drugs interfered with his sex life.

He shot at television sets and fired his gun into ceilings and walls.

There were times when he fell asleep with his mouth full of food.

He was still surrounded by enablers, who gave him whatever was necessary to maintain their favoured position. But like Humpty Dumpty, Elvis had suffered a great fall. There was no way that all the king's horses and all the king's men could put him back together again.

He had lost his dignity and self-respect. He was dangerously depressed. Each day when he woke up and looked in the mirror, he was reminded of what he'd become. His famous hair had begun to thin. He underwent cosmetic surgery around his eyes in an effort to conceal the ravages of drug abuse. There was an emptiness inside that he couldn't fill. He needed an emotional centre to stabilise his life, and it wasn't there.

Yet, through it all, Elvis kept performing. He needed the adulation that he received from his adoring fans. He wanted to give of himself and make them happy. And he still loved music. It was the only anchor that he had in his life. Without music, he was nothing.

For the most part, the reviewers were kind. But a few of them incorporated hard truths in their critiques.

After Elvis returned to the International Hilton in August 1973, the *Hollywood Reporter* declared, 'It's Elvis at his most indifferent, uninterested and unappealing. He's not just a little out of shape, not just a little chubbier than usual. The Living Legend is fat and ludicrously aping his former self. His voice was thin, uncertain and strained. His personality was lost in one of the most ill-prepared, unsteady, most disheartening performances of his Las Vegas career. It is a tragedy and absolutely depressing to see Elvis in such diminishing stature.'

That was followed by a two-week engagement in Lake Tahoe. A review in *Variety* noted that Elvis was 'thirty pounds over-weight' (a kind estimate) and observed, 'He's puffy, white-faced and blinking against the light. The voice sounds weak; delivery is flabby. Attempts to perpetuate his mystique of sex and power end in weak self-parody.'

The last four days of the Lake Tahoe engagement were cancelled.

Elvis onstage in the 1950s had been uninhibited. Elvis onstage in the 1970s was increasingly out of control. There were times when he seemed like an Elvis impersonator; lumbering around, engaging in rambling monologues that were all but impossible to understand. Sometimes he forgot the words to songs he'd sung a thousand times. There were moments when he seemed peril-ously close to having a psychiatric breakdown in front of his audience. Or maybe he was having one.

Yet he remained a viable ticket-seller, performing before over-flow crowds in huge arenas until the end. He was obese and drugged out. He was a heart attack waiting to happen. But he was still Elvis Presley, and still capable of isolated moments of extraordinary performance art.

Elvis had a beautiful voice and had learned to use it well. In some respects, his celebrity status overshadowed his talent. Throughout his career, he captured the emotional import of his songs. He understood intuitively what worked musically and what didn't. He was passionate about his music and sang from the heart.

When he was young, his music was characterised by sexual energy and excitement. As he aged, it was more about showing off the range of his voice and how long he could hold a note. But his singing also became more powerful. He could sell a ballad. He began to tell stories – often about sadness and regret – and give deeper meaning to the lyrics. He could sing anything.

But by June 1977, when his final tour began, Elvis could barely perform. There was nothing left in him any more. He died at Graceland on 16 August 1977. Fourteen drugs were found in his system; ten of them in significant quantities. The assumption is that 'polypharmacy' was the primary cause of death.

He was an old 42 when he died.

As Elvis was sliding towards the precipice, Ali was also in decline. Like Elvis, he was in a profession where it's hard to age gracefully. But if Ali had a bad night, he paid for it with a beating.

The damage to Elvis's health had been self-administered. The damage to Ali was inflicted by others. The punishment he took began to mount. Against Joe Frazier in Manila in 1975; at Madison Square Garden against Earnie Shavers seven weeks after Elvis died; in Las Vegas in 1980 at the hands of Larry Holmes.

Elvis had paid an emotional price for his greatness. For Ali, the cost was physical. The ravages of Parkinsonism turned his face into a mask and restricted his movements as surely as Elvis had been diminished.

Time goes by. Thirty-four years have passed since Elvis died. He's still a cultural force. His music remains popular. Thousands of entertainers around the globe dress up as Elvis impersonators and groom themselves in a certain way in an effort to imitate his performances. No other star, past or present, has that sort of following.

The entertainment conglomerate CKX now controls Elvis's name, likeness and image for commercial purposes. It also manages Graceland. Six hundred thousand fans make the pilgrimage to the mansion on Elvis Presley Boulevard in Memphis each year.

CKX has also acquired a controlling interest in Ali's name, likeness and image for commercial purposes. But to date, Elvis has been a more profitable marketing venture.

Elvis and Ali were passionate men who inspired passion in others. They grew up in humble surroundings and dreamed of being more than it was thought they could possibly be.

Each man impacted most significantly on society when he was young. Elvis, before he went in the Army; Ali, before his exile from boxing.

Elvis in the Las Vegas years gave pleasure to the people who saw him sing, but he was no longer an important social force. The acceptance of Ali as a beloved monarch marked an important turn for American society. But he was no longer setting the world ablaze.

Neither man set out to be the leader of a movement. They were just doing their thing. But each was an agent of change.

Elvis was a precursor of the sexual revolution and a transitional figure who brought black music into the mainstream of American culture. He was the standard-bearer for, and one of the founding fathers of, rock and roll. Like Frank Sinatra, he defined his genre.

Elvis's legacy is as an entertainer. He was about the music. He shied away from political issues. When asked to comment on anti-war protests at the height of the war in Vietnam, he responded, 'I'd just as soon keep my own personal views about that to myself. I'm just an entertainer.'

'Do you think other entertainers should keep their views to themselves too?' the questioner pressed.

'No, I can't say that,' Elvis answered.

By contrast, Ali has two legacies: as an athlete and as a moral force. Elvis was a superstar. Ali was a superstar and a hero, who fit into the two great moral crusades of the 1960s (the civil rights and anti-war movements). For most of his adult life, he sought to use his fame to make the world a better place. He wanted to advance the cause of racial justice and world peace. His work had social, political and religious implications.

The day after beating Sonny Liston, Cassius Clay told the media (and by extension, the American power structure), 'I don't have to be what you want me to be. I'm free to be what I want.'

Elvis exploded on the national scene in the same manner. But while Ali stayed true to that creed, Elvis didn't. Ali's greatness in and out of the ring sprang from personal courage. That quality was less evident in Elvis's life. In the end, he seemed intent on trying to be what his fans wanted him to be.

That said, singing is no less real than fighting. Ali earned universal recognition as a great fighter. Elvis was an amazing talent who brought joy to a lot of people and, like Ali, changed the way his art was practised. They didn't just mirror the culture they lived in. They helped shape it.

And they were so good when they were young.

PART II

PERSONAL MEMORIES

THE DAY I MET MUHAMMAD ALI

(2004)

In September 1964, when I was a sophomore at Columbia University, I began hosting a radio show called *Personalities in Sports* for the student-run radio station. For an 18-year-old sports fan, it was heady stuff. Each week, I'd take a bulky reel-to-reel tape recorder into the field and interview the biggest names I could get. I reached nirvana one afternoon when I found myself in the New York Yankees dugout as the Bronx Bombers readied to nail down their 14th pennant in 16 years. The first interview I conducted was with Tom Tresh. Whitey Ford was next. Then Mickey Mantle entered the dugout and, gathering my courage, I approached him.

'Mr Mantle. My name is Tom Hauser, and I wonder if I could interview you for WKCR.'

'Fuck.'

That was all Mantle said. Not even 'fuck you'. Just 'fuck', which I assumed meant 'no', since he then turned and walked away.

Recovering from the rebuff, I moved on to Elston Howard, Jim Bouton and Johnny Keane. My final interview was with Ralph Terry. I asked who he was planning to vote for in the upcoming presidential election between Lyndon Johnson and Barry Goldwater. Terry told me that his political views were none of my business, and the interview ended on that note.

The following week, I had similar success with New York Mets pitcher Tracy Stallard. Three years earlier, while on the mound for the Boston Red Sox, Stallard had earned a place in baseball history by throwing home run number 61 to Roger Maris. I suggested to Stallard that he tell WKCR's listeners all about it, and he responded, 'I think you know all about it, and your listeners know all about it, and I don't want to talk about it.'

Regardless, over the next thirty months, I taped dozens of interviews. New York Knicks centre Walter Bellamy gave me the first great quote I ever got from an athlete when I asked about reports that he'd had a bad attitude while playing for the Baltimore Bullets. 'I've never known an attitude to go up and dunk a basketball,' Bellamy told me.

Joe Namath, who'd just signed a three-year contract with the New York Jets for the unheard-of sum of $427,000, talked at length about the transition from college to pro football. Pete Rozelle and Joe Foss (commissioners of the warring National and American football leagues) gave of their time. Wills Reed, Barry Kramer, Eddie Donovan, Tom Gola, Matt Snell, Weeb Eubank. The list went on …

With one particularly memorable moment.

In March 1967, Muhammad Ali was preparing to fight Zora Folley at the 'old' Madison Square Garden; that is, the arena on

Eighth Avenue between 49th and 50th Streets. The bout was scheduled for 22 March; 44 days after Ali's brutalisation of Ernie Terrell. At that point in his career, Ali was virtually unbeatable. This would be his seventh championship defence in less than a year. Folley was a decent human being and a respected journey-man, who'd been a professional fighter for 15 years.

John Condon, the director of publicity for Madison Square Garden, arranged the interview for me. Ali–Folley would be the last heavyweight championship fight at the old Garden and also Ali's final bout before a three-and-a-half-year exile from boxing. The war in Vietnam was at its peak. The National Selective Service Presidential Appeal Board had voted unanimously to maintain Muhammad's 1-A classification, and he'd been ordered to report for induction in April. The assumption was that he would refuse induction. Ali himself had hinted as much when he said, 'Why should they ask me to put on a uniform and go ten thousand miles from home and drop bombs and bullets on brown people in Vietnam, while so-called Negro people in Louisville are treated like dogs?'

At the Garden, I watched Ali go through a series of exercises. Then I stood at the edge of the ring as he sparred with Jimmy Ellis. When that was done, he went into his dressing-room and I followed. John Condon introduced us. Ali was wearing a white terrycloth robe. I wasn't from the *New York Times* or any other news organisation of note, but that didn't seem to matter. Ali told me to turn on my tape recorder. We talked mostly about Nation of Islam doctrine, with some questions about the military draft, Zora Folley and boxing in general thrown in. It's a sign of the times that both of us used the word 'Negro'. Ten minutes after

we began, Ali announced, 'That's all I'm gonna do,' and the interview was over.

But I had one more request. An autograph. Not for me, but for
my younger brother, who loved sports every bit as much as I did.
Earlier in the year, he'd given me a copy of a book entitled *Black
Is Best: The Riddle of Cassius Clay*. Now, I wanted to give the book
back to him. As I looked on, Ali inscribed the title page:

> To Jim Hauser
> From Muhammad Ali
> World Heavyweight Champion
> Good luck
> 1967

I still remember the look on Jim's face when I gave it to him.

While Ali took a shower, I taped an interview with Angelo
Dundee. Then I returned to the ring, where Zora Folley was
finishing his sparring session. Folley told me how he planned to
exploit the fact that Ali held his hands too low and backed away
from punches instead of slipping them. The interviews aired on
the night of the fight. For the first time ever, the *New York Times*
listings for radio programmes of interest cited *Personalities in
Sports* and yours truly by name.

Years later, I would come in contact with John Condon again.
In 1984, I was researching a book entitled *The Black Lights: Inside
the World of Professional Boxing*. Condon had become president of
Madison Square Garden Boxing. With characteristic generosity,
he opened doors on my behalf. Our final meeting came in 1989.
As fate would have it, Ali and I had also moved full circle. I'd

been chosen to be his official biographer and was in the process of writing *Muhammad Ali: His Life and Times*. Condon was one of two hundred people I wanted to interview for the project. He was dying of cancer and knew it. At the close of our interview, John gave me a copy of *Black Is Best: The Riddle of Cassius Clay* that had been on a shelf in his office for more than twenty years. 'Keep it,' he told me. 'I won't be needing it any longer.' That night, I listened to the tape of my WKCR radio interview with Ali for the first time in more than two decades.

Eventually, of course, I played the tape for Ali. One night when he was at my apartment for dinner, I took my old reel-to-reel tape recorder out of the closet and turned it on.

About a minute into the interview, Muhammad reached into the formidable sack of one-liners that he carries with him at all times. 'I remember that afternoon,' he said. 'You were wearing a blue shirt.'

'And you were wearing a white terrycloth robe.'

We listened to the rest of the tape in silence. Then Ali asked, 'Was I really wearing a white terrycloth robe?'

'Yes. Was I really wearing a blue shirt?'

Ali laughed. 'You're crazy,' he said.

TRANSCRIPT OF MARCH 1967 RADIO INTERVIEW CONDUCTED BY THOMAS HAUSER WITH MUHAMMAD ALI

Q: Your outlook on life is different from that of a great many other people. It's based on your religion. Could you give us some idea of what it is?

ALI: As far as my outlook is concerned, I'd say that 90 per cent of the American public feels just the way I do as far as racial issues are concerned; as far as intermarriage is concerned; forced integration and total integration such as many Negro civil rights groups are trying to accomplish today. We who follow the Honorable Elijah Muhammad don't believe that this is the solution to our problem. Unity among self, respect for self, doing for self is what we believe. And this don't make me no different from whites, because the masses of them believe and have been practising this ever since we've been in America. So my outlook on life is really the same as 90 per cent of the whites in America. They're just shocked and surprised to see that we the Negro who have accepted the teachings of Elijah Muhammad now want to be with ourselves and live among ourselves and don't want to force integrate, and that's such a surprise to the whites, which makes us controversial and different but really we're not different. We're just different from the Negro who's striving for forced integration. But as a whole, the whites believe like we do and have been believing like we do all the time.

Q: Would you like to see a world some day where the white man and Negro can live together and call each other friends?

ALI: I'm not the one to say. I would like to see peace on earth. If separation will bring it, I say let's separate. If integration will bring it, I say let's integrate. But let's not just stand still, where one man holds another in bondage and deprives him of freedom, justice and equality, neither integrating or letting him go to self.

I don't like that. But I like seeing peace, whatever means will bring it.

Q: Do you think the Negro is better than the white man or just different? Are we the same underneath the skin?

ALI: Nobody on earth is made the same. Some are born blind; some crippled; some are yellow; some are red; some are black; some are white. No men are really equal or the same. As far as going into the differences and why they're different, I couldn't say. But the man that we follow for all of our spiritual teachings, who gives us knowledge and understanding, is Elijah Muhammad. And I'm sure that, if you have him on your radio show, he can tell you why we are not alike and dig into the depths of why we're different. But it's not my job to know who's who and who's different, because I'm not that wise. That's up to Elijah Muhammad, our leader.

Q: You've had an outstanding boxing career; perhaps the most outstanding of anyone in the ring today. Who's the toughest opponent you've had to face?

ALI: The toughest opponent I've had to face is Sonny Liston.

Q: What about Floyd Patterson?

ALI: He was easy.

Q: You've said that, in the ring, you tried to humiliate Floyd Patterson and Ernie Terrell. Is that true?

ALI: Yes.

Q: Why?

ALI: Because they talked about me and my religion; mocked my leader and teacher and advisers; and didn't want to respect me as Muhammad Ali, which is my name now. So they're lucky they got off as easy as they did.

Q: Do you think that two wrongs make a right? Was it right to humiliate them like that?

ALI: Is it right to go to war? Is it right that we're in a war now, killing people? I have my beliefs, and I'll defend them.

Q: One of the things that people are interested in now is your status with the draft. What will you do if your final appeals fall through and you're drafted? Will you then resist going into the Army?

ALI: I don't think it would be respectful to the draft board or the government or the Justice Department to make a decision now. That's a hypothetical question. I haven't been drafted yet. My appeals haven't run out. It's in the hands of my lawyer; he's handling it. So it wouldn't be respectful to make a decision or say anything on this radio show. But the world knows that I am a

Muslim. The world knows that I'm a sincere follower to death of Elijah Muhammad. And we say five times a day in our prayers, 'My prayers, my sacrifices, my life and my death are all for Allah.' I repeat, 'My prayers, my sacrifices, my life and my death are all for Allah.' This is what I sincerely believe. I've upheld my faith through the past years. I gave up one of the prettiest Negro women in the country; cost me one hundred seventy thousand dollars in alimony. This was all controversy and publicity before the draft started. The white businessmen of Louisville, Kentucky, will tell you that I've turned down eight million dollars in movie contracts, recordings, promotions and advertisements because of my faith. So I don't see why I should break the rules of my faith now.

Q: There seems to be an opinion circulating that Zora Folley is just here for a pay-day for himself and for you and to keep you in shape. Do you think that Folley represents a genuine threat?

ALI: These are just the hypocrites and the phonies, the newspaper writers that are shook up because everything that I said would come true did come true. I said that I was the greatest. They thought I was just acting the fool. Now instead of admitting that I'm the greatest and admitting that I'm the best heavyweight in all history, they'd rather belittle the contenders and say it's just a pushover. They were complaining because Patterson didn't fight but once a year. They were complaining because Liston didn't fight but once a year. They were complaining because Johansson didn't fight but once a year. The game was dead. Now I revive it, fighting every two months. And what more can I do but fight the number one contender? Zora Folley is the number one man on earth next to me. So they can call him a bum. They can call him an old man. All I say is, 'If he's a bum, if he's an old man; then why do the boxing authorities in this country rank him number one?' So they're just looking for fault, and they don't know what to do. They're all shook up. They said Terrell would be tough; they built him up to be tough. He was nothing. They said Patterson would be tough. He was nothing. They said Cleveland Williams would be a big test. He was nothing. They said Chuvalo would be nothing. He was tough. So don't pay attention to the critics in the press. They don't know nothing about boxing. They never trained a day in their life. They can't throw a left jab. All they can do is talk. They've been wrong, and I've been right. I look for Zora Folley to be tougher than Ernie Terrell.

Q: Who among the young fighters such as Joe Frazier, Buster Mathis and Jerry Quarry do you look for to give you the most trouble in the years ahead?

ALI: I'd say Joe Frazier.

Q: What does he have that would make him tougher than the others?

ALI: He's strong; he hits hard. I've never really seen none of them fight. But from what I hear, he'd be the toughest.

Q: Have you given any thought to retirement?

ALI: Not really. I believe I'll just stay here and keep whupping them until they find somebody who can whup me.

Q: What sort of long-range plans do you have for when you finish up in the ring?

ALI: I want to be a minister for the Islamic faith as taught by the Honorable Elijah Muhammad. That's all I want to be is a minister.

I WAS AT ALI–FRAZIER I

(2004)

I was an ardent sports fan when I was young. I played a lot of baseball, football and basketball. Those were also my favourite sports to watch. I followed boxing but without the intense interest in the sweet science that I have today.

Like many Americans, I became aware of Cassius Marcellus Clay Jr at the 1960 Rome Olympics. I found him charming and followed his career as he rose to conquer Sonny Liston. Then, like a lot of people, I was turned off by his adherence to Nation of Islam ideology. The lure of Muhammad Ali's personality was strong, and I had no problem with his message of empowerment for black Americans. But I took issue with the notion that white people were devils who had been created 6,600 years ago by an evil scientist named Mr Yakub and that apartheid was a preferred way of life. Regardless, in 1967, Ali won me over again when he refused induction into the US Army during the height of the war in Vietnam.

In 1970, I graduated from Columbia Law School and began clerking for a federal judge prior to a five-year stint as a litigator on Wall Street. The United States Supreme Court had yet to rule on Ali's appeal of his conviction for refusing induction and he was facing five years in prison.

Then, in early 1971, I read that Ali and Joe Frazier had signed to fight at Madison Square Garden. Obviously, it would be a memorable athletic competition. Two great fighters, each one undefeated with a legitimate claim to the heavyweight championship of the world. But just as clearly, it was going to be an event that transcended sports.

The tumultuous decade just passed had been marked by assassinations, men landing on the moon and the rise of a new drug culture. But its most important markers were Black America rising to assert itself and opposition to the war in Vietnam. Ali symbolised both of those markers.

Joe Frazier, by contrast, was perceived as a symbol of the ruling order. Fairly or unfairly, as Bryant Gumbel later wrote, 'Frazier became an instrument of the oppressors. The blackest man in the ring was cast as the villain to blacks across the land and was called hero and saviour by the most bigoted of white men.'

Tickets for Ali–Frazier I were priced from $20 to $150. The day they went on sale, I bought two mezzanine seats at $20 apiece. On fight night, scalpers were getting ten times those numbers.

I went to the fight with a friend. Entering the Garden, I bought an 'official programme'. It was a generic publication with a LeRoy Neiman painting of Ali and Frazier on the cover and a 16-page insert on 'The Fight'.

I'd been to Madison Square Garden for boxing once before, but this night was different from its predecessor. Early in Ali's career, Budd Schulberg wrote, 'Cassius Marcellus Clay is doing for fistic glamour what Marilyn Monroe did for sex.' Now the Garden was glamour personified.

The arena was jammed. There was electricity in the air. Major superstars who were used to sitting on camera in the first row were 15 rows from ringside and happy to be in the Garden at all. Frank Sinatra wangled a press credential by agreeing to photograph the fight for *Life Magazine*. Thousands of fans stood outside the arena just to be there and watch the celebrities come in.

None of the preliminary fights was slated for more than six rounds. The most notable undercard bout featured Ali's brother, Rahaman, against Danny McAlinden.

Rahaman had fought on the undercard of both Ali–Liston fights and Ali versus Oscar Bonavena. His record stood at 7 wins and 0 losses with 2 knockouts. McAlinden was a heavyweight from Ireland via England. His record was 14-1-2 with 13 KOs, and he had never fought off the sceptred isle before.

Fights in New York were scored at that time on a round-by-round basis; not on points. McAlinden won a majority decision: 4-2, 3-2-1, 3-3.

As the night wore on, the tension grew.

Then, finally, it was time.

'I've covered sports for a half-century,' Jerry Izenberg later reminisced. 'I've been to every kind of championship and seen every great athlete of the past fifty years. No moment I've ever seen had the electricity of Muhammad Ali and Joe Frazier coming down the aisle and entering the ring that night.'

People forget how young Ali and Frazier were at the time. Muhammad was 29 and Joe only 27. But even though some of Ali's greatest ring triumphs lay in the future, as a fighter he was already growing old.

The fight was even in the early rounds. The crowd was evenly divided. But as the night wore on, Frazier partisans had more reason to cheer.

I remember Ali going to the ropes, beckoning Frazier in. I remember round eleven, when Joe wobbled Muhammad with a big left hook. And most painfully, I remember the fifteenth round, when Joe hit Muhammad as hard as a man can be hit and Ali went down. At that point, the fight was lost and my hope was that Muhammad would be able to finish on his feet. He did, although the judges ruled against him: 11-4, 9-6, and 8-6-1.

Ali had been defeated in his first 'superfight'. Against Sonny Liston in 1964, Cassius Clay had been widely perceived as nothing more than a kid coming to get beaten up. Ali–Liston II drew only two thousand paying fans. Now, when it mattered most and the world truly cared, 'The Greatest' had failed.

I left Madison Square Garden that night feeling depressed but knowing that I had witnessed something historic.

REFLECTIONS ON TIME SPENT WITH MUHAMMAD ALI

(COMBINED PIECES WRITTEN FROM 1991 TO 1997)

My personal relationship with Muhammad Ali began in 1988, when we met in New York to explore the possibility of my writing the book that ultimately became *Muhammad Ali: His Life and Times*.

The idea originated with Muhammad's wife Lonnie, who wanted a book which would place Muhammad in context, not just as a fighter but also as a social, political and religious figure. I was approached because I had previously written a book about professional boxing entitled *The Black Lights*, as well as books about race relations, public education, United States foreign policy and a number of other subjects of concern to Muhammad.

On paper, the fit between us seemed good. I was 42 years old, only four years younger than Ali, so I'd experienced his era, from the civil rights movement to the rock music he loves. I'd spent five years as a lawyer on Wall Street, and thus was able to work my way through the financial entanglements of Muhammad's life and the complex litigation that followed his refusal to accept induction into the US Army. And while I was determined to maintain my objectivity in writing, I was a lifelong Ali fan.

Writing a biography about a living subject is an extremely personal endeavour, and I wanted to make sure that, if the project went ahead, Muhammad and I would get along. I also wanted to make sure that I could capture Muhammad's voice. At the time, Mike Tyson was the undefeated undisputed heavyweight champion of the world. Some experts were going so far as to proclaim that Tyson was better than Ali in his prime. Thus, before I met with Muhammad and Lonnie, I spent an afternoon writing a piece entitled 'I'm Coming Back to Whup Mike Tyson's Butt'. Then, when we got together, I read the piece aloud and presented it to Muhammad. His response was to take a pen from his pocket and write across the front page, 'To Tom Hauser from Muhammad Ali – This is what I can still do to Tyson right now.'

But there was another threshold issue to confront. Like millions of admirers, I'd seen Muhammad on television. Sometimes he'd looked well. Other times, though, the light seemed all but gone from his eyes. I didn't want to involve myself with the project unless Muhammad was capable of making a significant contribution to it. Also, I didn't want to spend several years working on a book that would be a source of depression instead of joy.

To resolve those issues, after meeting initially with Muhammad and his wife, I accepted their invitation to spend five days at their home in Berrien Springs, Michigan. My first two days there, I was intimidated by Ali's presence. I found it hard to make eye contact with him. Other than John F. Kennedy, who was my boyhood hero, I don't think there's a person on the planet who would have affected me in that manner and certainly not to that extent. Then, on the third morning, I went downstairs to the kitchen. Muhammad was sitting at the breakfast table, finishing his cereal and toast. He looked up and asked if I wanted corn-flakes or granola. In that moment, I realised that any distance between us was my own fault. Muhammad didn't want to be put on a pedestal. He wanted me to relate to him the same way I'd relate to anyone else.

I also realised over time that, despite Ali's speech difficulties, his health is better than most people think it is. Muhammad suffers from Parkinson's syndrome, which refers to a series of symptoms, the most noticeable of which are slurred speech, stiffness in walk-ing and an occasional facial 'mask'. The most common cause of Parkinson's syndrome is Parkinson's disease. In Ali's case, the symptoms were brought on by repeated blows to the head; blows that destroyed cells in his brain stem which produce a substance called dopamine. But the condition is not life-threatening. And more important, it's a motor-skills problem. There are no intel-lectual deficits. Muhammad's wit is sharp and his thought processes are clear. Indeed, when we signed our contract for me to write the book, I couldn't resist saying, 'Muhammad, stick with me and I'll make you famous.' Ali countered, 'More famous than Elvis Presley?'

In short, Muhammad doesn't feel sorry for himself because of his physical condition, and there's no reason for anyone else to feel sorry for him. He loves being Muhammad Ali, and he's as happy with each day as anybody I know.

As for the process of researching Ali's life, I proceeded on several levels. First, there were Muhammad's personal papers, medical records, newspapers, magazines, tapes, and cartons of

legal and financial documents. After that, I interviewed approximately two hundred people – members of Ali's family, friends,
former wives, ring opponents, business associates, doctors, world
leaders and others who have known him best. And of course,
there were countless days spent with Muhammad. I travelled
with him around the world, spent weeks in his home and entertained him in mine.

One of my memories is of waking up one morning in the Ali's
home in Berrien Springs and hearing Lonnie cry out, 'Oh my
God! Muhammad! What have you done?'

Naturally, I was curious. So I put on my clothes, went downstairs, and found Lonnie standing in the living-room amid piles
of clothes, boxes and other belongings. Apparently, during the
night, Muhammad had been unable to sleep. As he often does
under those circumstances, he'd gone downstairs to read the
Qur'an. Then, for reasons known only to him, he'd grown curious as to what was in the closets. The easiest way to satisfy that
curiosity was to empty all of them out onto the living-room
floor. Suffice it to say that Lonnie assumed it was Muhammad
(and not me) who had done the deed.

Unlike Ali's earlier biographers, I enjoyed total access to
Muhammad and to virtually all of the key people in his life. My
questions were answered with candour by almost everyone. And
I enjoyed the advantage of perspective, since I was writing at a
time when Ali's ring career and the tumultuous era of American
history that went with it had come to an end.

Inevitably, writing the book involved revisiting my own youth.
It led me to recall watching the 1960 Olympics on television and
reading newspapers in high school for reports of Cassius Clay's

early fights. I re-experienced listening to the radio as a 17-year-old college freshman the night Clay beat Sonny Liston for the heavyweight championship. The war in Vietnam; assassinations; riots in Newark, Harlem and Watts. In one way or another, so many of the key events in American history that I remembered were intertwined with Ali's life. And I relived sitting in a New York theatre on 2 October 1980, turning my face away from the screen to avoid watching the brutalisation of an ageing Ali at the hands of Larry Holmes.

In some ways, Ali is a very simple man. In others, he's quite complex. But first and foremost, Muhammad is deeply religious and spiritual. There was a time when he moulded his religious beliefs to accommodate what he wanted to do. Now it's the other way around. I don't think I've met anybody ever who is more sincere about his religious principles than Muhammad. God is the main factor in his life. At the end of each day, Ali asks himself, 'If God were to judge me based just on what I did today, would I go to heaven or hell?' And he lives his life accordingly. 'I'm not afraid of dying,' Ali told me once. 'I have faith; I do everything I can to live my life right; and I believe that dying will bring me closer to God.'

Yet Muhammad has never sought to impose his religious beliefs on other people. Indeed, once when I accompanied him to services at a mosque to share that part of his life, he told me, 'When we say our Islamic prayers, you can say your Jewish prayers. Only don't say them out loud because it might offend someone.'

I also recall another moment between us that turned on Muhammad's religious beliefs. One day we were discussing Ali's

1976 'autobiography'. The book contains numerous allegorical tales, including the claim that young Cassius Clay threw his Olympic gold medal into the Ohio River after being denied service at a segregated restaurant.

'You didn't really do that, did you?' I queried.

'Yes, I did.'

'Swear to Allah.'

There was no response.

'Swear to Allah,' I pressed.

'Someone stole it,' Ali admitted. 'Or I lost it.'

Ali is a kind man, who speaks often of his dreams and never of his troubles. Those who meet him are virtually never disappointed. He has an endurance and tolerance for others that's extraordinary. He's forgiving, perhaps to a fault. There are people who have stolen literally millions of dollars from him. He knows they've done it, yet he refuses to say one word against them. To some, that means he's a soft touch. To others, he has a tender heart. Ali himself says only, 'God is merciful and forgiving, so I should be too.' Also, he once told me, in a reflective moment, 'Maybe I should say more about certain things. Sometimes I don't say what I feel, because God gave me so much power that I'm afraid, if I yell at someone, it will hurt them too much.' That might be Ali's way of avoiding personal confrontations, an avoidance he too often seeks. But it's also a mark of character.

Ali sometimes makes mistakes. There's an irrational side to his personality. At times he's manipulated and easily led. But his heart is pure; he loves people. And that love manifests itself every day; if not on a world stage, then in his private life. In November 1990, against the advice of some of his closest friends, Muhammad journeyed to Iraq to meet with Saddam Hussein in the hope that his presence would forestall war in the Persian Gulf. Afterwards, I asked if he thought it was wise to have gone. Ali answered, 'People risk their lives for war all the time. Why shouldn't I risk mine for peace?' Meanwhile, three months later, away from the glare of publicity, Muhammad and Lonnie Ali quietly adopted a six-week-old boy.

'That's a very lucky little boy,' I told him. 'You've changed the course of his entire life.'

'We're lucky too,' Muhammad answered. 'It's a good baby.'

There are so many memories I have of Ali that conjure up a smile. Once, when Muhammad and I got in his car to do some errands, he told me, 'You get in back; I'll drive; and it will be like *Driving Miss Daisy.*'

On another occasion, when Ali and his wife were coming to my apartment for dinner, I invited one of his favourite rock stars – Chubby Checker, who lives in Philadelphia – to join us. Chubby drove ninety miles to New York. When Ali saw him, he started jumping up and down, shouting, 'It's Chubby Checker! It's Chubby Checker!' But what touched me most about that evening was an exchange that came after dinner. We were sitting in the living-room. Muhammad looked at Chubby and asked, 'Did you drive all the way from Philadelphia just to see me?' Chubby said yes. And Ali responded, shaking his head, 'I can't believe it. I'm honoured.'

I researched and wrote *Muhammad Ali: His Life and Times* for two years. Finally, in September 1990, I journeyed again to Berrien Springs to meet with Muhammad, Lonnie and Howard Bingham. For ten days, we read every word of my manuscript aloud. By agreement, there was to be no censorship. The purpose of our reading was to ensure that the book would be factually accurate.

There were portions of the manuscript that troubled Muhammad, because they reflected negatively on persons other than himself. Also, it was important to him that the book be accurate with regard to all facets of Islam. As for his first concern, ultimately he understood that it was important for the story of his life to be told honestly and completely. With respect to the latter, a careful reading of the manuscript by Dr Ibrahim Oweiss, a leading Islamic scholar, put Ali's worries to rest.

One moment that I remember well from our sessions in Berrien Springs came when Lonnie was reading a quotation from television boxing analyst Alex Wallau. Wallau had expressed the view that, even if Ali had been given foreknowledge of how boxing would affect his physical condition, 'If he had it to do all over, he'd live his life the same way; he'd still choose to be a fighter.'

As soon as Lonnie read those words, Muhammad sat up straight in his chair and said, 'You bet I would.'

Muhammad Ali: His Life and Times was published in 1991. Muhammad helped promote the book and, among other things, attended book signings at Barnes & Noble and Waldenbooks stores in New York. Each signing was enormously successful. Both stores reported that Ali sold more books in a single session than any previous subject or author.

The final promotional event in New York was Ali's attendance at the annual Boxing Writers Association of America dinner. Muhammad spoke briefly, and told the audience about a slave named Omar. It was a parable that preached the message of humility and was met by sustained applause. Then Ali sat down. The programme resumed. HBO's Jim Lampley was speaking, when suddenly Muhammad returned to the podium and announced, 'I forgot to tell you. I had two book signings this week, and I broke the all-time record at both stores.'

That left Lampley to wonder aloud, 'Muhammad, would Omar the slave brag about his book signings?'

'He would if he sold a thousand books,' Muhammad countered.

Eventually, *Muhammad Ali: His Life and Times* was published in Great Britain, and we journeyed to England for a book tour. One afternoon, I was sitting next to Ali at a book signing in London, when a woman in her forties passed through the line. She looked at Muhammad, then at me, and in a thick Irish accent asked, 'Excuse me, are you Ali's son?'

'No, ma'am,' I replied.

'Oh,' she said with obvious disappointment. 'You look just like him.'

My initial reaction was to dismiss her as daft. After all, I'm white and only four years younger than Muhammad. But then it occurred to me that this was one more example of how, when it comes to Ali, people are colour-blind. And of course, it's a compliment of the highest order to be told that you look just like Muhammad Ali.

As our tour of England continued, there were also poignant moments. Late one afternoon, we found ourselves in Nottingham. It had been a long day. That morning, we'd been in Leeds, where Muhammad had signed nine hundred books, posed for photographs, kissed babies and shaken hands with literally thousands of admirers. Now that scene was being repeated with five hundred more people who had waited in line for hours for their hero to arrive.

Ali was tired. He'd been awake since 5.00 a.m., when he'd risen to pray and read from the Qur'an. His voice, already weak from the ravages of Parkinson's syndrome, was flagging. The facial 'mask' which accompanies his medical condition was more pronounced than usual.

Most of the people in line were joyful. But one of them, a middle-aged woman with a kind face, wasn't. Muhammad's condition grieved her and, as she approached him, she burst into tears.

Ali leaned over, kissed her on the cheek, and told her, 'Don't feel bad. God has blessed me. I've had a good life, and it's still good. I'm having fun now.'

The woman walked away smiling. For the rest of her life, she would remember meeting Ali. Moments later, she turned to look back at him, but Muhammad's attention was already focused on the next person in line, a tall handsome black man. 'You're uglier than Joe Frazier,' Ali told him.

That brings us again to Joe. Of all Muhammad's ring opponents, the only one who still holds a grudge against him is Frazier. Joe makes no secret of his dislike for Muhammad, and sometimes his antipathy extends to Muhammad's friends. In recent years, Joe and I have gotten along fairly well. He's been a guest in my home and he's cordial when we meet. But it wasn't always that way.

In 1991, I was in Atlantic City for a WBO heavyweight championship bout between Ray Mercer and Tommy Morrison.

Frazier was in attendance, and I introduced him to a friend of mine named Neil Ragin.

Joe's response was a resounding, 'Grhummpf!'

'It's nothing against you,' I explained to Neil. 'Joe doesn't talk to me a whole lot.'

Which gave Neil a chance to ingratiate himself to Joe and keep the conversation going. 'Of course, Joe doesn't talk with you. You're Ali's man. Everybody knows you're Ali's man. Right, Joe?'

Whereupon Joe said simply, 'Right! And I ain't talking to you either, 'cause you the friend of Ali's man.'

Muhammad told me once, 'If Joe Frazier wants to forgive and forget, I'll be friends. And if he wants to fight, I'm still whuppin' him.' Then, on a more serious note, he added, 'Joe Frazier is a good man. I couldn't have done what I did without him, and he couldn't have done what he did without me. If God ever calls me to a holy war, I want Joe Frazier fighting beside me.'

Still, I have to say, even today, if Ali and Frazier were together and Joe had a balloon, Muhammad would want to pop it. And when it comes to Joe, Muhammad still gives as good as he gets. Once, I was with them at a ceremony at the United Nations. Ali's son, Asaad, who was a year old at the time, was also there. Joe was looking for trouble. Smiling at Asaad, he told onlookers, 'Hmmm, that boy looks just like me.'

Ali didn't miss a beat. 'Don't call my boy ugly,' he said.

During the time I spent with Ali, he was constantly creating new memories and generating 'new material'. For example, we were in Seattle to attend a dinner where Muhammad was honoured as 'The Fighter of the Century'. The festivities included a fight card at The Kingdome. And meeting Ali, the undercard fighters were in awe. One of them, a lightweight with a losing record in a handful of professional bouts, went so far as to confess, 'Mr Ali, I just want you to know, when I'm going to the ring for a fight, I get real nervous, so I say to myself, "I'm Muhammad Ali, I'm the greatest fighter of all time and no one can beat me."'

Ali leaned towards the fighter and whispered, 'When I was boxing and got nervous before a fight, I said the same thing.'

'If you do roadwork in the snow, it makes you tough,' another young fighter told Muhammad.

'If you do roadwork in the snow, it makes you sick,' Ali countered.

Once, Muhammad reflected on a $100,000 fee he received for attending two promotional screenings of a made-for-television documentary and told me, 'Ain't life amazing. Twenty-five years ago, they wouldn't let me fight to earn a living. And now they're paying me $100,000 to go to the movies.'

Another time, Ali stopped to shake hands with an elderly white man who had a deep Southern accent.

'How old are you?' Muhammad queried.

'Eighty-one.'

'Where are you from?'

'Mississippi.'

'Did you ever call anyone a nigger?'

'Oh, no. Not me.'

After the man left, Muhammad turned to me, laughing. 'Do you believe that? An 81-year-old white man from Mississippi, never called anyone a nigger.'

Shortly thereafter, we attended a tribute to Muhammad at the Smithsonian Institution in Washington, DC. I made some opening remarks and referred to an incident that had occurred years earlier when Ali took a shuttle flight from Washington to New York. As the flight crew readied for take-off, an attendant instructed him: 'Mr Ali, please buckle your seatbelt.'

'Superman don't need no seatbelt,' Ali informed her.

'Mr Ali,' the flight attendant said sweetly. 'Superman don't need no plane.'

When I retold that story, Muhammad's face lit up and he laughed as hard as anyone in the audience. Ali's ability to laugh at himself also surfaced when we authorised Easton Press to publish 3,500 copies of a leather-bound edition of *Muhammad Ali: His Life and Times*. Pursuant to contract, we each agreed to sign 3,500 signature pages for insertion in the book. I was to receive three dollars per signature; Ali considerably more.

'This is fantastic,' I told myself. 'If I do ten signatures a minute, that's 600 signatures an hour … Divide 3,500 by 600 … Wow! I'll get $10,500 for six hours' work.'

Except when I started signing, I found that I couldn't sign more than a few hundred pages at a time. 'Any more than that,' I confided in Muhammad, 'and I can't connect the letters properly. Something starts misfiring in my brain.'

'Now you know,' Ali told me, referring to his own physical condition. 'It wasn't boxing. It was the autographs.'

Spending time together also rekindled memories for Muhammad. In 1996, we were on a media bus in Atlanta. Several video monitors were showing a tape of Cassius Clay's antics prior to his first fight against Sonny Liston.

'It's sad Sonny Liston is dead,' Muhammad told me. 'I'd like to be able to sit down with him. Two old men, just sitting around, talking about old times.'

'What would you say to him?'

Ali's eyes grew wide. 'I'd tell him, "Man, you scared me."'

Then 'The Rumble in the Jungle' came on the screen, and Ali's eyes grew wistful.

'So many people come up to me and tell me they remember where they were when I whupped George Foreman. I remember where I was too.'

'What were you thinking when you looked down at Foreman on the canvas?'

'It felt good.'

'But what was going through your mind?' I pressed.

'I didn't think. Things just happened.'

The perfect metaphor for Ali's life, if ever there was one.

That same year, Muhammad and I travelled around the United States to speak with students about the need for tolerance and understanding. One person who was particularly supportive of our efforts was Roy Jones, who attended several gatherings with us including one at Locke High School in Los Angeles.

When Muhammad was introduced in Los Angeles, he received his usual roar of acclamation. But Roy got something extra. When his name was mentioned, a substantial number of the girls screamed the kind of scream reserved over the decades for Elvis Presley, the Beatles and other heart-throbs. Muhammad didn't miss a beat. Feigning jealousy, he stood up from his chair, smacked his fist into the palm of his hand and challenged Roy to fight.

Roy responded. And for thirty seconds, two great fighters sparred for an adoring crowd.

Muhammad and Roy were having fun. But as fighters, they were also measuring each other.

'He's good,' Muhammad said afterwards. 'He has good moves, and he's fast.'

'I was surprised at how well Ali moved,' Roy acknowledged. 'He's got a lot more left than most people realise.'

But as usual, Muhammad had the last word. 'Take my advice,' he told Roy when it was over. 'Get a gun.'

I also remember the year that Muhammad telephoned to wish me a Merry Christmas. 'Think about it,' I suggested. 'A Muslim calling a Jew to wish him well on a Christian holiday. There's a message in that for anyone who's listening.'

'We're all trying to get to the same place,' Muhammad told me.

And the Ali magic remains. It always will. A while back, Muhammad was at a party, surrounded by the usual chaos that accompanies his presence. Men who would rarely think of hugging another man fell into his embrace. Women were asking for kisses. There were requests for autographs and photographs when, amid it all, a mother brought her four-year-old daughter over to Ali.

'Do you know who this is?' she asked her child.

The four-year-old nodded reverentially and told her mother, 'It's the Easter Bunny.'

'I'M COMING BACK TO WHUP MIKE TYSON'S BUTT'

(1988)

Author's note: This is the piece referenced above that I wrote for Ali prior to our meeting in October 1988. Muhammad had respect for Mike Tyson as a fighter, but considered him beatable. It was his view that Iron Mike would have knocked out Joe Frazier, but that George Foreman would have KO'd Tyson. Even when Mike was undefeated, Ali told me, 'Tyson is predictable, the way he moves his head. He has fast hands, but he's slow on his feet and my hands were faster than his. The way to beat Tyson is with a fast jab, a hard right hand; and if he hits you, you have to be able to take a punch.'

Still, many commentators saw things differently. And I sensed that Muhammad was a bit miffed by the view that Iron Mike would have beaten him. Thus, I wasn't surprised when my telephone rang on the night of 11 February 1990, moments after James 'Buster' Douglas dethroned Mike Tyson in Tokyo. 'What do you think people will say now when someone asks them who was greater, Mike Tyson or me?' Muhammad asked rhetorically. 'Buster Douglas saved me the trouble of coming back and whupping Mike Tyson myself.'

★ ★ ★

People are weeping and crying all the time these days, because Mike Tyson is heavyweight champion of the world. He's a bully, and no one can beat him. But that don't mean nuthin'. They said Sonny Liston was unbeatable, and I beat him. They said George Foreman was unbeatable, and I beat him. They say Tyson is unbeatable, but I'm coming back. I got a time machine, and I'm coming back to whup Mike Tyson.

Mike Tyson is too ugly to be champion. He's got gold teeth. He's got bald spots all over his head. I used to call Joe Frazier 'The Gorilla', but next to Tyson, Joe Frazier was like a beautiful woman. Everyone I fought, I had names for. Sonny Liston was 'The Bear'. George Chuvalo was 'The Washer Woman'. Floyd Patterson was 'The Rabbit'. George Foreman was 'The Mummy'. Mike Tyson is ugly; he's ugly like King Kong, so I'm calling him 'Kong'.

And Tyson is nuthin'. He never fought no one. He fought Larry Holmes when Holmes was an old man. He fought Trevor Berbick, and Berbick was a crazy old man. He fought Tyrell Biggs, and Biggs was an amateur. Michael Spinks was a light-heavyweight. Tony Tubbs; he was an embarrassment. Bonecrusher Smith; he lost the first nine rounds against Frank Bruno. Tyson never fought Sonny Liston; he never fought Joe Frazier; he never fought George Foreman; like I did, fighting all of them in their prime.

So I'm coming back to whup Mike Tyson. It's the biggest fight in the history of time. Bigger than David against Goliath; bigger than Napoleon against England and Russia. Too big for home television. Too big for closed-circuit. They're putting this fight on special 3-D closed-circuit with cameras and lenses like you ain't never seen before.

And the whole world is holding its breath. Everyone's rooting for me, but they're saying, Muhammad Ali, he's just a man and now he's fighting Kong. They're saying Mike Tyson is too strong, too mean. He hits too hard.

Here's how it goes.

Round One: It'll be all over in one; that's what they're saying. And Tyson comes out for the kill. Ali's dancing, jabbing. Pop-pop-pop-pop. Tyson swings – WHOOSH – hits nuthin' but air.

Pop-pop-pop-pop.

WHOOSH. Tyson hits nuthin' but air again.

Pop-pop-pop-pop. At the end of the round, the television people are adding up their punch stats, and they can't believe it. Muhammad Ali: 107 jabs, 92 landed. Mike Tyson: 40 punches, and he didn't land one.

Round Two: It's just like round one.

Pop-pop-pop-pop.

WHOOSH.

Pop-pop-pop-pop.

WHOOSH.

Ali is pretty. The crowd's going wild. *Ali! Ali!*

Tyson lands a punch, but it don't do no harm.

Round Three: Ali's landing right hands. It's early in the fight, and already Tyson's left eye is starting to close. Women and children are holding their breath. Ali looks good. He's better than good. Muhammad Ali is the greatest, but there's nine more rounds to go, and Tyson is getting dirty now. He's butting and thumbing, throwing elbows and hitting low.

Round Four: Pop-pop-pop-pop. Ali is still dancing. Floats like a butterfly, but he stings like a bee. Pop-pop-pop-pop. Tyson is bleeding: the left eye. He's cut and the blood is flowing down. The experts is shaking their heads. Muhammad Ali is making Tyson look like a child.

Round Five: Tyson is taking a bad whuppin'. The crowd's going wild. Ali! Ali! Tyson's getting tired. Ali's talking to him, asking, 'Who's the greatest?' Tyson won't answer, so Ali hits him four-five-six right hands.

Round Six: It's the Ali Shuffle. Two billion people round the world, they're jumping up and down, hugging each other, weeping with joy. It's the real Ali. Not the Ali who lost to Larry Holmes; not the Ali you thought was old. This is Muhammad Ali, who destroyed Zora Folley; Muhammad Ali, who done in Cleveland Williams. Ali! Ali!

Round Seven: Tyson's gold teeth get knocked out into the crowd, and you can see his mother-in-law running after them. The crowd's in a state of histomania. Ali's punching so fast now, no one can hear the pops. It's p–p–p–p–p–p–p–p. Ali winds up for a bolo punch. The crowd is praying. They're pleading, don't take no chances; don't get careless with Tyson. But Ali's still winding up for the bolo, and Tyson's moving closer. Tyson is getting ready. He's gonna kill Ali. The crowd holds its breath. Tyson leaps with a left hook. But Muhammad Ali throws a right hand. It's faster than a speeding bullet. Faster than the punch that knocked down Sonny Liston. The eye can't see it, except with a super slo-mo replay camera.

TYSON IS DOWN ! ! !

Tyson gets up at seven.

Ding! There's the bell.

And now Tyson is mad. He's embarrassed. He's been humili-

MUHAMMAD ALI
AT NOTRE DAME:
A NIGHT TO REMEMBER

(1998)

Notre Dame versus Michigan, 1990. The first game of the season for two of college football's most fabled institutions. Notre Dame was the top-ranked team in the country. Michigan was rated as high as number two, depending on which poll you followed. The game had been sold out for months and was the hottest ticket in the nation.

Meanwhile, Howard Bingham and I were tired. Howard is Muhammad Ali's best friend. I was Ali's biographer. It was the day before the game, and we'd been reading aloud for five days. More specifically, we'd been reading the manuscript for *Muhammad Ali: His Life and Times* – all one thousand pages – with Muhammad and his wife Lonnie. I'd just finished the first draft of the book and wanted to make sure it was factually accurate. Also, I knew that reading it aloud would be the best way to elicit further thoughts from Muhammad.

Howard and I are sports fans. And since Notre Dame is only a 20-minute drive from the Ali's home, we thought it would be ated. He's coming out for the next round, determined to put Muhammad Ali down.

Round Eight: Tyson charges out of his corner, throwing punches like wild. He's spitting blood. There's fire in his eyes. He's doing everything he can. And … OH NO ! Ali is tired. Ali has stopped dancing. After seven rounds with Kong, Ali's legs is gone. Ali's moving back. Tyson comes in for the kill. Ali's in a corner – he's in trouble. Tyson is ugly. He's a monster that has to be fed, and Muhammad Ali is the monster's meal.

Tyson with a left. Tyson with a right. The whole world is covering its eyes.

Wait a minute ! ! !

IT'S THE ROPE-A-DOPE ! ! !

Muhammad Ali tricked the monster, and now Ali is coming back strong.

Ali with a left. Ali with a right. It's Muhammad Ali; the greatest fighter of all time.

AND TYSON IS DOWN ! ! !

The count is one, two …

Tyson's eyes is closed!

Three, four …

He's not moving!

Five, six …

We have a brand new champion!

Seven, eight …

This is the greatest moment of all time!

Nine, ten …

It's all over! It's all over! The tyrant is dead! Long live the true King!

fun to go to the game. Ali doesn't care a whole lot about football. But his presence opens doors; he likes big events; and he's a sweetheart when it comes to doing things for friends. Thus, my call to the Notre Dame Athletic Department: 'Would it be possible for Muhammad Ali to buy three tickets for tomorrow night's game?'

There was a long pause on the other end of the line. 'Let me call you back,' the woman said. Five minutes later, the telephone rang. 'How do we know the tickets are really for Mr Ali?'

'That's easy,' I told her. 'He'll pick them up in person.'

'All right; come by the Athletic Department today before five o'clock.'

'Do you want Muhammad to bring his driver's licence for identification?'

'That's not necessary. I think we'll recognise him.'

Shortly before noon, we drove to Notre Dame to pick up the tickets. The Athletic Department wanted to give them to us, but we insisted on paying; a small gesture given their open-market value. Then we went home, read *Muhammad Ali: His Life and Times* for another five hours; read some more on Saturday; and drove back to Notre Dame.

The game was scheduled for 8.00 p.m. Central Standard Time. We arrived around six o'clock. The weather was perfect and the scene surrounding the stadium was quintessential bigtime college football. Tens of thousands of fans had set up grills and were barbecueing everything from hamburgers to shrimp. Many of them didn't even have tickets to the game. They just wanted to be near the action, and their reaction to Muhammad was as expected. As we walked around, we heard a lot of 'Omigod! It's

Muhammad Ali.' And Muhammad has certain opportunities that aren't available to the rest of us. For example, he can walk around a tailgate party until he finds something that looks particularly good to eat, and what he invariably hears is, 'Muhammad Ali! Please join us.'

In other words, we ate quite well thanks to the generosity of strangers. Then we went inside the stadium to our seats, which happened to be on the 50-yard line. That was nice for us and, I suspect, also good for Notre Dame recruiting since the folks around us were suitably impressed by Ali's presence.

Muhammad sat between Howard and myself. Notre Dame was coached by Lou Holtz. Its brightest star was Raghib Ismail, who was joined in the backfield by Rick Mirer, Tony Brooks, Ricky Watters and Rodney Culverhouse. Michigan was in its first year under new head coach Gary Moeller, who had the unenviable task of succeeding Bo Schembechler. But his job was made easier by the presence of Elvis Grbac, Jarrod Bunch, Jon Vaughn and Greg Skrepenak.

It was a great game. Notre Dame surged to a 14–3 lead, and it seemed as though everyone on earth was singing, 'Cheer, cheer for old Notre Dame.' Then Michigan began to roll and scored three unanswered touchdowns, whereupon 'Hail to the victors valiant' was very much in vogue.

Meanwhile, as the game progressed, I began to talk with an elderly woman sitting to my left. She was Ellen Stonebreaker, grandmother of the Notre Dame co-captain and middle-line-backer, Mike Stonebreaker. If I had to guess, I'd say she was about 80. She was charming. And when Notre Dame was on defence, her eyes never left the field. Even Ali noticed the intensity with which she was watching. 'Look at that old lady,' he told me. 'She's like a hawk.'

Notre Dame won. Down ten points going into the fourth quarter, they rallied for two late touchdowns capped by an 18-yard scoring pass from Mirer to Adrian Jarrell with 1:40 left to play. But one moment stands out in my mind.

It came in the second half. Ellen Stonebreaker had been sneaking glances at Muhammad for some time. Finally she said to me, 'You know something; that boxer is a good-looking fellow.'

'Tell her I don't fool around with white women,' Muhammad advised me. Which I duly reported to Mrs Stonebreaker, who seemed more bemused than disappointed. However, she did have one request.

'I haven't done this since I was a young girl,' she acknowledged. 'But could you get me that fellow's autograph?'

I asked how she'd like her name written. She said she'd prefer it if Muhammad used her maiden name. She spelled it for him. He wrote it out, drew a little heart, and signed 'Love, Muhammad Ali.'

Then he kissed her.

It was just another day for Muhammad; one that I'm sure he's long since forgotten. But as is often the case, whenever and wherever he travels, it was a memorable night for everyone around him.

MUHAMMAD ALI: THANKSGIVING 1996 – 'I'VE GOT A LOT TO BE THANKFUL FOR'

(1996)

As is his custom, Muhammad Ali awoke shortly after 5.00 a.m. on Thanksgiving Day. He was in Los Angeles to pursue his latest mission: teaching people how to love. *HEALING* is a cause that Ali can wrap himself around.

After washing himself with clear running water, Ali put on clean clothes and said the first of five daily prayers. Then he moved behind his hotel-room desk and began signing bookplates that would be distributed to fans who attended one of several book signings in the days ahead.

Ali's weight has been over 250 pounds for several years, and he recently decided to get down to 220. Accordingly, he skipped breakfast as part of his personalised brand of dieting and announced, 'This is my third day of not eating, except for one meal a day.' However, as the day progressed, Ali ate pears, apples and oranges from a large basket of fruit that had been sent to his room by the hotel management.

'And maybe a muffin,' Ali admitted.

Correct that. Several muffins. And chocolate chip cookies, cheese and crackers; all before his 'one meal of the day' – a large Thanksgiving dinner.

'I'm losing weight because I'm planning a comeback,' Ali said. 'On my 55th birthday, I think I'll fight the top three heavy-weights in the world, one round each, at Madison Square Garden.'

'You'd better get in shape fast,' Muhammad was cautioned. 'Your 55th birthday is in seven weeks.'

'Seven weeks? Maybe I'll do it when I'm 60 instead.'

At 9.00 a.m. Pacific Coast time, Ali turned on the television to accommodate yours truly who wanted to watch the Kansas City Chiefs versus the Detroit Lions. 'In my whole life,' he admitted, 'I've never watched a football game on television from beginning to end. Sometimes I go to the Super Bowl because the people around me want to go, and because of me, they can get in. But the only sports I'm interested in now are big fights. I like watching big fights to see how I'd do if I was in them.'

On the TV screen, Detroit's Barry Sanders was seen making a particularly shifty move. Muhammad's eyes widened. 'How old is he?'

'Twenty-eight.'

'When I fought Sonny Liston, that man wasn't even born.'

The Detroit Lions scored a touchdown, and the obligatory end zone dance followed.

'You started that,' I told Ali. 'All the dancing and celebrating and showing off started with you.'

'I started the big salaries too. Big salaries started when me and Joe Frazier got $2,500,000 each the first time we fought.'

The Chiefs vanquished the Lions 28–24, at which point the Dallas Cowboys took the field against the Washington Redskins. Meanwhile, Ali had begun turning the pages of a Bible, pointing out contradictions.

'Look at Exodus 33:11 [And the Lord spake unto Moses face to face, as a man speaketh unto his friend]. Now look at Exodus 33:20 [And the Lord said, 'Thou canst not see my face, for there shall be no man see me and live']. Some people think the Bible is the word of God,' Ali continued. 'But in one part of Exodus, it says Moses saw God's face. And in another part, it says no man can see God and live. How can the word of God be two different things? Here's another contradiction. John 5:31 [Jesus said, 'If I bear witness of myself, my witness is not true.'] Now read John 8:14 [Jesus answered and said unto them, 'Though I bear record of myself, yet my record is true']. You're educated. You tell me, is Jesus' witness true or not true? Heavy, ain't it?'

Shortly after 2.00 p.m., Ali left the hotel to travel to the home of Connye Richardson, a long-time family friend. Richardson lives in Hancock Park; the section of Los Angeles that Ali lived in during his marriage to Veronica Porche.

Ali has mixed feelings about his years in Los Angeles. The period encompassed some of his greatest glories, but it was in Hancock Park that his fortunes began to turn. He was living there when he lost to Leon Spinks, Larry Holmes and Trevor Berbick. It was in Hancock Park that his health began to fail, his family life [now on a solid foundation again] began to unravel, and he felt himself growing old.

Connye Richardson's home was spacious and comfortable. During the course of the day, twenty family members and friends dropped by. Ali was wearing tan slacks and a white short-sleeved shirt, his still-powerful forearms visible. Thanks to new medication [a combination of Artane and Medapar] his voice was clearer and his face more animated than they have been for several years.

As he often does when he feels at home in someone else's living-room, Muhammad turned on the television. A movie about Vietnam starring Gene Hackman was showing. The last twenty minutes were unremitting violence and gore.

'I made a wise decision when I didn't go to Vietnam,' Ali told one of the other guests. 'All that killing was wrong.'

Then he switched to CNN, which had a brief feature on a presidential pardon given by Bill Clinton to a 45-pound turkey. Instead of winding up on someone's dinner table, the turkey would spend the rest of its years on a petting farm in Virginia.

Ali was asked if he thinks it's right for people to kill animals to eat when other types of food are available. He considered the issue and responded, 'Everything that God made, he made for a purpose. I don't believe in hunting just to kill an animal. That bothers me. But I think it's all right to eat animals like turkeys and fish and cows.'

Connye Richardson had been cooking for days, and it seemed as though every one of God's foods was served. If Muhammad is truly planning to fight again in Madison Square Garden, this wasn't the place to slim down. But it was a good Thanksgiving. Ali was both happy and in a reflective mood as the day drew to a close.

'God has been good to me,' Muhammad said in the car going back to the hotel. 'I'm thankful I've got a good wife and nine healthy children. I'm thankful I was three-time heavyweight champion of the world. I'm thankful I live in a country like America. I'm thankful I've been able to travel and meet people all over the world. I'm thankful that, even though I haven't fought for 15 years, people still remember me. I have a good life. I've got a lot to be thankful for.'

As noted earlier in this volume, I spent part of 1996 and 1997 travelling around the country with Muhammad Ali, speaking to students about tolerance and understanding. On 27 February 1997, our travels took us to Pensacola, Florida. The plan called for Muhammad and myself to address 7,600 students at the Pensacola Civic Center on the subject of HEALING. But a group of Christian fundamentalists threatened legal action to halt the event, claiming that our appearance was a plot between a Muslim and a Jew to teach heresy to their children. For several weeks, a controversy raged. Then, inexorably, the community came together in support of our visit. Florida Governor Lawton Chiles attended the assembly and praised its purpose. The event was an enormous success. My own remarks to the students of Pensacola follow.

PENSACOLA, FLORIDA: 27 FEBRUARY 1997

1997

As most of you know, Muhammad Ali and I have co-authored a book about bigotry and prejudice. Early in the book, there's a statement by Muhammad that has led to some controversy in Pensacola, and I'd like to discuss that quotation with you. Muhammad's words were as follows:

My mother was a Baptist. She believed Jesus was the son of God, and I don't believe that. But even though my mother had a religion different from me, I believe that on Judgement Day my mother will be in Heaven. There are Jewish people who lead good lives; and when they die, I believe they're going to heaven. If you're a good Muslim, if you're a good Christian, if you're a good Jew; it doesn't matter what religion you are, if you're a good person, you'll receive God's blessing.

The words I just read to you reflect Muhammad's belief that all people serve the same God; we just serve Him in different ways. Obviously, there are people who disagree with Muhammad's view. They believe that the only way a person can go to Heaven is to embrace Jesus Christ as his, or her, Saviour. That belief is their right. But some people in this community have carried their beliefs a step further by trying to halt this assembly.

I got a telephone call recently from one of these people. She didn't give her name. Instead, she began by demanding, 'How dare you question the word of God?' I told her, 'I'm not questioning the word of God. I'm questioning your ability to interpret the word of God for me, because I believe in a loving God, who bestows His blessings upon all people.' That was the end of the conversation, because she hung up.

I want to make it as clear as I possibly can that no one on this stage today is here to challenge what any of you believe insofar as it relates to your own personal religious convictions. I hope you like your religion and are fully satisfied with it. Muhammad and I like our respective religions too. All we ask is that you keep in mind that we all have the same Creator, and all of us have to work to get along. Our message is simple. Let's understand each other and be tolerant of our differences, whether those differences relate to our religion, the colour of our skin, the language we speak, the country we come from or any of the other sources of diversity that sometimes divide us.

As you go through life, you will find that your education, your jobs, your personal relationships and your government are all dependent in varying degree upon the will of others. That's the nature of living. No one goes through this world on their own. But there's one area where each of you will have total control over your own destiny. Each and every one of you has complete control over your own moral fibre. That means you can be as bigoted and prejudiced and hateful – or as tolerant and understanding – as you want to be. Hate is ugly. It's ugly when it's shouted out on the street. And it's ugly – it will eat you up and destroy you – when it lies in your heart. So if you hate, let go of it.

It's unlikely that any of you will ever become as good a fighter as Muhammad Ali or have the same impact on history as Muhammad Ali. But in your own way, each of you can become as good a person as Muhammad Ali. All you have to do is take the best qualities that people like Muhammad have to offer and make them part of your own individual personalities. But don't stop with famous people. There's a horrible misconception in our society that just because someone is famous or a big celebrity, that person is a hero or a good role model. And that's not necessarily the case. Some celebrities are lousy role models.

But if you look around, you'll find people in your everyday lives who are wonderful role models. I'm sure there are teachers in your schools who care about you and work hard to give you the best education they possibly can. Those teachers are wonderful role models. I would hope that all of you have one or more relatives who love you and provide for you and do everything they can to give you good values. Those relatives are wonderful role models. And whether you know it or not, each of you is a role model. There are kids in grade school who look up to you and want to be like you. Many of you have younger brothers and sisters who feel the same way. And as role models, you young men and women have a responsibility to be the best people you can possibly be.

Focus on what's best in yourselves. Learn to treat other people with dignity and respect. Learn how to love.

Thank you.

A DAY OF REMEMBRANCE

(1997)

On 24 June 1997, Muhammad Ali awoke in the nation's capital at 5.00 a.m. He said his prayers, ate a light breakfast and read quietly from the Qur'an. Then, accompanied by his wife Lonnie and several friends, he left the Hay Adams Hotel and drove to a unique destination – the United States Holocaust Memorial Museum.

The museum was not yet open to the public when Ali arrived at 7.45 a.m. He had come early because he feared his presence during normal visiting hours would cause a commotion unsuited to the decorum of his surroundings. Several staff members greeted Muhammad and his party when they arrived. There were introductions and the tour began.

The mission of the United States Holocaust Memorial Museum is to inform, honour and inspire. More specifically, it is designed to present the history of the persecution and murder of six million Jews and millions of other victims of Nazi tyranny; to commemorate those who died; and to encourage visitors to contemplate the moral implications of their own civic responsibilities.

Ali began by assimilating facts as he walked through the museum … One-and-a-half million children were exterminated in the Holocaust … It wasn't just Jews … Gypsies, the physically disabled, mentally handicapped and other 'undesirables' were also victims … Books were burned, synagogues destroyed …

As the tour progressed, Muhammad began to draw parallels between the Holocaust and the slavery that his own ancestors endured. Ali has spoken often about how black Americans were robbed of their African names and given slave names instead. Now he learned of people whose Jewish names were replaced by numbers tattooed on their forearms. Standing in a boxcar used to transport Jews to death camps in Poland, he imagined himself in the cargo hold of a slave ship two centuries earlier.

Midway through the tour, Ali came to a glass wall bearing the names of thousands of communities eradicated during the Holocaust.

'Each of these names is a whole town?' Muhammad asked incredulously.

'Yes.'

'I never knew it was that bad.'

The tour went on … A pile of shoes taken from the dead at Majdanek … Bales of hair cut from the heads of concentration camp victims … A crude metal table where bodies were placed and gold teeth extracted with pliers … Grainy films of nude bodies piled high being bulldozed into trenches.

Ninety minutes after the tour began, Ali stopped to read a quotation in silver letters on a grey wall:

First they came for the socialists.

And I did not speak out because I was not a socialist.

Then they came for the trade unionists.

And I did not speak out because I was not a trade unionist.

Then they came for the Jews.

And I did not speak out because I was not a Jew.

Then they came for me.

And there was no one left to speak for me.

Finally, Ali entered the Hall of Remembrance and placed a white rose beside the museum's eternal flame.

During the course of his life, Muhammad Ali has taken many courageous stands. But his presence at the United States Holocaust Memorial Museum on 24 June 1997 is among his most important statements of principle.

The victims' faces on this particular morning were Jewish. But they could just as easily have been faces from Cambodia, Bosnia or Rwanda. By virtue of his presence, Ali demonstrated once again his solidarity with all victims of persecution. And he joined his spirit with millions of Holocaust victims and with the survivors who remember them.

REMEMBERING
JOE FRAZIER

(2012)

I've been thinking a lot lately about Joe Frazier, who died one
year ago, on 7 November 2011.

I met Joe at the Sahara Hotel in Las Vegas on 1 December
1988. I'd just signed a contract to become Muhammad Ali's official biographer. Two days of taping were underway for a documentary entitled *Champions Forever* that featured Ali, Frazier,
George Foreman, Ken Norton and Larry Holmes. I was there to
conduct interviews for my book.

On the first morning, I sat at length with Foreman; the pre-
lean-mean-grilling-machine model. George was twenty months
into a comeback that was widely regarded as a joke. Six more
years would pass before he knocked out Michael Moorer to
regain the heavyweight throne.

'There was a time in my life when I was sort of unfriendly,'
George told me. 'Zaïre was part of that period. I was going to
knock Ali's block off, and the thought of doing it didn't bother
me at all. After the fight, for a while I was bitter. I had all sorts of

excuses. The ring ropes were loose. The referee counted too fast. The cut hurt my training. I was drugged. I should have just said the best man won, but I'd never lost before so I didn't know how to lose. I fought that fight over in my head a thousand times. Then, finally, I realised I'd lost to a great champion; probably the greatest of all time. Now I'm just proud to be part of the Ali legend. If people mention my name with his from time to time, that's enough for me. That, and I hope Muhammad likes me, because I like him. I like him a lot.'

Then I moved on to Ken Norton, who shared a poignant memory.

'When it counted most,' Norton reminisced, 'Ali was there for me. In 1986, I was in a bad car accident. I was unconscious for I don't know how long. My right side was paralysed; my skull was fractured; I had a broken leg, a broken jaw. The doctors said I might never walk again. For a while, they thought I might not ever even be able to talk. I don't remember much about my first few months in the hospital. But one thing I do remember is, after I was hurt, Ali was one of the first people to visit me. At that point, I wasn't sure whether I wanted to live or die. That's how bad I was hurt. Like I said, there's a lot I don't remember. But I remember looking up, and there was this crazy man standing by my bed. It was Ali, and he was doing magic tricks for me. He made a handkerchief disappear; he levitated. I said to myself, if he does one more awful trick, I'm gonna get well just so I can kill him. But Ali was there, and his being there helped me. So I don't want to be remembered as the man who broke Muhammad Ali's jaw. I just want to be remembered as a man who fought three close competitive fights with Ali and became his friend when the fighting was over.'

Larry Holmes held out for cash, so our conversation was short: 'I'm proud I learned my craft from Ali,' Larry said. 'I'm prouder of sparring with him when he was young than I am of beating him when he was old.'

End of conversation.

That left Joe.

Frazier wouldn't talk with me because I was 'Ali's man'. But at an evening party after the second day of taping, Joe approached me. He'd been drinking. And the bile spewed out: 'I hated Ali. God might not like me talking that way, but it's in my heart. First two fights, he tried to make me a white man. Then he tried to make me a nigger. How would you like it if your kids came home from school crying because everyone was calling their daddy a gorilla? God made us all the way we are. He made us the way we talk and look. And the way I feel, I'd like to fight Ali-Clay-whatever-his-name-is again tomorrow. Twenty years, I've been fighting Ali, and I still want to take him apart piece by piece and send him back to Jesus.'

Joe saw that I was writing down every word. This was a message he wanted the world to hear.

'I didn't ask no favours of him, and he didn't ask none of me. He shook me in Manila; he won. But I sent him home worse than he came. Look at him now. He's damaged goods. I know it; you know it. Everyone knows it; they just don't want to say. He was always making fun of me. I'm the dummy; I'm the one getting hit in the head. Tell me now: him or me, which one talks worse now? He can't talk no more, and he still tries to make noise. He still wants you to think he's the greatest, and he ain't. I don't care how the world looks at him. I see him different, and

I know him better than anyone. Manila really don't matter no more. He's finished, and I'm still here.'

Twenty-one months later, when I finished writing *Muhammad Ali: His Life and Times*, I journeyed to Ali's home in Berrian Springs, Michigan. Lonnie Ali (Muhammad's wife), Howard Bingham (Ali's long-time friend and personal photographer) and I spent a week reading every word of the manuscript aloud. By agreement, there would be no censorship. Our purpose in reading was to ensure the factual accuracy of the book.

In due course, Lonnie read Frazier's quote aloud.

There was a silent moment.

'Did you hear that, Muhammad?' Lonnie asked.

Ali nodded.

'How do you feel, knowing that hundreds of thousands of people will read that?'

'It's what he said,' Muhammad answered.

Ali's thoughts ended that chapter of the book.

'I'm sorry Joe Frazier is mad at me. I'm sorry I hurt him. Joe Frazier is a good man. I couldn't have done what I did without him, and he couldn't have done what he did without me. And if God ever calls me to a holy war, I want Joe Frazier fighting beside me.'

On the final day of our reading, Muhammad, Lonnie, Howard and I signed a pair of boxing gloves to commemorate the experience. I took one of the gloves home with me. Howard took the other.

The following spring, I was in Philadelphia for a black-tie gala celebrating the twentieth anniversary of the historic first fight between Ali and Frazier. This was Joe's night. It was a fight he'd won. But his hatred for all things Ali was palpable.

Early in the evening, Howard suggested that I pose for a photo with Muhammad and Joe. I stood between them. Joe wrapped his arm around my waist in what I thought was a gesture of friendship. Then, just as Howard snapped the photo, Joe dug his fingers into the flesh beneath my ribs.

It hurt like hell.

I tried to prise his hand away.

You try prising Joe Frazier's hand away.

When Joe was satisfied that he'd inflicted sufficient pain, he smirked at me and walked off.

Muhammad Ali: His Life and Times was published in June 1991. Joe decided that I'd treated him fairly in the book. In the years that followed, when our paths crossed, he was warm and friendly. A ritual greeting evolved between us.

Joe would smile and say, 'Hey! How's my Jewish friend?'

I'd smile and say, 'Hey! How's my Baptist friend?'

Fast-forward to 7 January 2005. Joe was in my home. We were eating ice-cream in the kitchen.

Three boxing gloves were hanging on the wall. The first two were worn by Billy Costello in his victorious championship fight against Saoul Mamby. That fight has special meaning to me. It's the subject of the climactic chapter in *The Black Lights*, my first book about boxing.

The other glove bore the legend:

Muhammad Ali
Lonnie Ali
Howard L. Bingham
Thomas Hauser
9/10 – 9/17/90

Joe asked about the gloves. I explained their provenance. Then he said something that surprised me.

'Do you remember that time I gave you the claw?'

'I remember,' I said grimly.

'I'm sorry, man. I apologise.'

That was Joe Frazier. He remembered every hurt that anyone ever inflicted upon him. With regard to Ali, he carried those hurts like broken glass in his stomach for his entire life.

But Joe also remembered the hurts he'd inflicted on other people. And if he felt he'd done wrong, given time he would try to right the situation.

There's now a fourth glove hanging on the wall of my kitchen. It bears the inscription:

Tom, to my man
Right on
Joe Frazier

'DID BARBRA STREISAND WHUP SONNY LISTON?'

(1996)

On 7 February 1996, I was in the lobby of the ANA-Westin Hotel in Washington, DC, with Muhammad Ali, Jim Brown, Ralph Boston and a handful of others. That night, HBO would present a promotional screening of *The Journey of the African-American Athlete*. In anticipation of the event, ten people had been invited to the White House to meet with President Clinton in the Oval Office. My name was on the list, along with Nancy Bronson, whom I'd been dating for six months. The minibus that would take us to the White House was pulling up to the hotel when Seth Abraham (President of Time Warner Sports) approached me with a look of consternation.

'Didn't anybody tell you?'

'Tell me what?'

'Yesterday, the White House took you and Nancy off the guest list. You've been replaced by Zina Garrison and Calvin Hill.'

Seth was apologetic.

Nancy was accepting.

And Muhammad was ... well, Muhammad was Muhammad.

'Stay by me. I'll get you into the White House.'

'Don't waste your time,' Paul Costello (Time Warner's point man in Washington) told us. 'No one just walks into the Oval Office. In fact, no one gets past the White House gate without advance security clearance. All that will happen is, you'll have to turn around and take a cab back to the hotel.'

Which seemed likely. But Nancy and I had nothing to lose, so we boarded the minibus with the others. When we arrived at the first security checkpoint by a wrought-iron gate outside the White House, a guard asked for IDs from everybody. Five minutes passed. Several limousines drove by. Then the guard returned.

'There's two people who don't have security clearance. Who are Hauser and Bronson?'

Nancy and I raised our hands.

'Come with me, please.'

Nancy and I got off the minibus and followed the guard to the security booth, where I pleaded our cause. 'I was told on Monday that we'd been approved by the White House ... No one told us our names had been taken off the list ...'

The guard was polite but unyielding. 'I'm sorry; you can't go any further.'

At which point, Muhammad joined us.

The guard repeated what he'd just said. 'Mr Ali, this man and this woman don't have security clearance. I'm sure you understand how these things work. They simply can't go any further.'

And Muhammad was understanding – 'If they don't go, I ain't going.'

Unsure as to what to do next, the guard telephoned the White House. Minutes later, an official-looking man with a moustache strode down to the gate to meet us.

'What seems to be the problem?' Obviously, he already knew what the problem was because, before I could answer, we were advised, 'Look, this is my event. Your names aren't on the list, and that's the end of it. No one without security clearance is allowed past this gate.'

'But these are my friends.'

'Mr Ali, you don't understand.'

Nancy got back on the minibus, and Paul Costello came over to monitor the proceedings. There followed an explanation about how Barbra Streisand had recently been invited to the White House. *The* Barbra Streisand, who had helped raise millions of dollars for the Democratic party and was a personal friend of the President and Mrs Clinton. Yet when Ms Streisand brought someone with her for her appointment with the President, her friend was turned away at the gate.

And Muhammad was duly impressed.

'Did Barbra Streisand whup Joe Frazier?'

'Mr Ali –'

'Did Barbra Streisand whup Sonny Liston?'

The Man with the Moustache, who I'm sure is a fine public servant and was just trying to do his job, excused himself and returned moments later. 'All right, we've got to get this show on the road, so you two [pointing to Nancy and me] can go as far as the reception area, but that's all.'

The minibus proceeded to the West Wing of the White House, where we were ushered into a reception area. There was small talk. Several minutes passed. Then The Man with the Moustache reappeared. 'Those of you with security clearance, come with me into the Roosevelt Room. You two [pointing to Nancy and me], stay here.'

The members of the group with security clearance were ushered into the Roosevelt Room, directly across the corridor from the Oval Office. Nancy and I stayed in the reception area, settling on a sofa. Inside the Roosevelt Room, various cabinet members, presidential aides and White House staffers had gathered for a 'photo op' with Muhammad.

Except Muhammad wasn't there. He was with Nancy and me in the reception area beneath a painting of 'George Washington Crossing the Delaware'.

Which is how Nancy and I got into the Roosevelt Room.

'But I'm telling you now,' The Man with the Moustache warned, 'you are not going into the Oval Office, and I mean it.'

And he did mean it.

When the time came to enter the President's office, The Man with the Moustache approached. 'You two [Nancy and me], sit over there [pointing to the far side of the conference table].'

He waited until we'd followed his command.

'Now, I'd like the rest of you to line up over here.'

At which point, I said to Nancy, 'Look, there's no way that both of us will make it into the Oval Office. When the others go in, just walk over to Muhammad and take his arm.'

'What about you?'

'I'll stay here.'

'That's not fair to you.'

'Sure, it is. I've been to the White House. I already have a photo of me with the President.'

'Not in the Oval Office.'

'It doesn't matter. You can go into the office for both of us.'

Across the corridor, the door to the Oval Office opened. We saw the President of the United States standing there.

The line started to move forward.

Nancy got up from the sofa, walked over to Muhammad, and with considerable trepidation took his arm –

The Man with the Moustache walked over to Nancy, and stood in front of her. 'Mr Ali,' he importuned. 'The President of the United States is waiting for you.'

And Muhammad walked forward, alone.

Nancy and I watched from a distance as the President greeted his guests. Then the door to the Oval Office closed, and we were left in the Roosevelt Room.

I was disappointed. I won't tell you I wasn't. For a while, we explored our surroundings, which was kind of fun. If you're ever in the Roosevelt Room, I suggest you look at the gold medallion given to Teddy Roosevelt in 1906 when he won the Nobel Peace Prize. Also, check out the bronze sculpture by Alexander Pope, and the portraits of Teddy, Franklin and Eleanor Roosevelt.

Nancy did her best to put a good face on things. 'Tom, this is really very exciting. We're having a wonderful time in Washington with Muhammad. We're in the White House. We saw the President from a few yards away. Don't feel bad for me.'

But I did feel bad, for both of us.

Muhammad and the others stayed in the Oval Office for about ten minutes. Then the door to the President's office opened and they filed out, moving down an adjacent corridor.

Jim Brown ... Ralph Boston ... Calvin Hill ... Zina Garrison. All but one.

Finally, Muhammad Ali walked out of the Oval Office ... leading the President of the United States by the arm towards the Roosevelt Room.

'These are my friends,' Muhammad told him.

Bill Clinton smiled and beckoned us forward with a wave of his arm towards the Oval Office.

'Come on in.'

The minutes that followed will remain forever etched in my mind. The President began by asking Nancy her name. Then he turned to me. We chatted briefly. The President was warm and gracious. Eventually, he even called in a photographer. But what I remember most about that afternoon, and always will, is something I've seen many times, something that has been on display for the entire world for almost four decades – the sweetness, the determination, the power and the magic of Muhammad Ali.

PART III

A LIFE IN QUOTES

Had Cassius Clay not beaten Zbigniew Pietrzykowski in a Roman boxing ring, the world might never have known him. Had he not shocked the world by defeating Sonny Liston four years later, few would have paused at his conversion to Islam. Had he not conquered Joe Frazier twice after losing in their initial encounter, he would be little more than an artefact of 'the sixties' in the minds of many. Had he not knocked out George Foreman in the heart of Africa, it's doubtful that he would have become the most recognisable man on the face of the earth. And had he never shed his shirt, put on gloves and traded blows with other half-naked men, he might not suffer from Parkinson's syndrome; a debilitation that he confronted unflinchingly while hundreds of millions of people watched him light the Olympic flame at the 1996 Atlanta Olympics.

There's no end to credible testimony about Ali's goodness. He touched people the world over with his warmth and love. Both literally and metaphorically, he has kissed without hesitation the poor and weak, the downtrodden and oppressed, the elderly and sick, and everyone else he met. New generations must rely in part on the testimony of those who lived through Ali's glory years. Then, one hopes, they will understand both Ali's legacy and the legacy of Ali's generation. Some see an inconsistency in celebrating a man as a messenger of love when he rose to fame by bludgeoning others with his fists. But history teaches that warriors often become pacifists if given enough years to live. A man who has felt the weight of violence frequently seeks to shield others from it. And because an old warrior's courage cannot be questioned, he can be an ideal spokesperson for peace.

Other fighters since Ali have graced the sweet science of boxing and been great. More great fighters will follow. Someday, as surely as autumn leaves change colour and fall to the ground, a young man will step in a boxing ring and be greater than Ali. But Muhammad Ali will always be The Greatest.

The passage above was written by Bart Barry and myself as part of a project undertaken for Barnes & Noble in 2010. The pages that follow offer a sampler of quotes and anecdotal recollections from and about Ali by others. As with the rest of this book, an effort has been made to avoid duplicating material contained in Muhammad Ali: His Life and Times. *Thus, the quotes aren't intended to be all-inclusive. Rather, they're designed to show Ali's essence, the sweep of his career and his impact on people.*

JIM BELL [a childhood classmate of Cassius Clay]: We were in elementary school together, and he was just another one of the kids. You push and you shove each other, and get into the normal fights. There were days he lost, and there were days he won. So when he beat Sonny Liston to win the championship, some of us were laughing about it, saying, 'He's not even undefeated in the neighbourhood. How can he be champion of the world?'

RONNIE O'KEEFE [Cassius Clay's opponent in his first amateur fight, which was the only fight of O'Keefe's ring career]: I weighed 89 pounds, and he weighed about the same. The fight was three rounds, a minute a round. And he hit me a whole lot more than I hit him. I had a heck of a headache that night. He won by a split decision. And right after he was announced the winner by the referee, he started shouting that he was going to be the greatest fighter ever. He was heavyweight champion of the world already, at 12 years old and 89 pounds.

JOE MARTIN [the Louisville policeman who taught 12-year-old Cassius Clay how to box]: He's been popping off before fights from the very beginning, and it's not a thing in the world but whistling past the graveyard. He's just overcoming the fear that's in him.

SISTER JAMES ELLEN HUFF [who supervised Cassius Clay's first regular after-school job]: He was a sophomore in high school. Somebody had to dust up the library. And a schoolmate, who had been doing the job and was going to leave, brought him over. He was already known. Unknown to me, but he was appearing in Golden Gloves tournaments at the time and had a whole bag of trophies that he brought out to show me later when I found out that he was a boxing champion. His friend introduced him to me as Cassius Clay. I said, 'Do they call you Cass?' And he told me, 'No, ma'am. Cassius Marcellus Clay, Junior.' So I said, 'Okay, it will be Cassius.' And he was polite; he was gentle. He always appeared on time and related to his work beautifully. Except one time. His father was a painter. And Cassius was kind of given to art too, so I gave him a paint job down in the lower area where we were working. And he resisted. He used enamel where I had asked him to use flat paint. I said, 'I thought your father was a painter.' And he told me that his father was an artist, not a barn painter. And he just lived boxing. He worked at it very hard. One evening – he'd been training pretty heavily, I think – I came back from dinner. We had some reading tables in the stacks on the second floor. I looked in, and there was Cassius on one of the tables, asleep, facing the wall. I said, 'Cassius, are you sick?' He raised himself up, kind of stunned because he'd fallen into a deep sleep, and told me, no. And after he became famous – you read about places where they say, 'Abraham Lincoln slept here.' Well, I take people into the stacks and I tell them, 'Cassius Clay slept here.'

RALPH BOSTON [gold medallist in the long jump at the 1960 Olympic Games]: I'd never heard of this guy. And at age 21, I really wasn't into other sports. I was a track-and-field man, getting ready to go to Rome. I flew into New York, took a bus to the Biltmore Hotel where the Olympic team was staying. And this young guy came up to me, put his hand on my chest and said, 'Ralph Boston! Hold on; I want to take your picture.' Then he told me, 'You don't know me now, but my name is Cassius Marcellus Clay Jr.' He had this old Brownie Hawkeye camera, where you had to look down to see what you were photograph- ing. And he proceeded to take my picture, along with pictures of just about everyone else he came in contact with during the Olympics. And there's a question I've been asking Ali all my life. 'Where is my picture?'

WILBERT 'SKEETER' MCCLURE [Cassius Clay's roommate and fellow gold medal winner at the 1960 Olympics]: When we were in Rome, we had this place where the athletes would go to dance and listen to music and relax. And Ali didn't dance. That was always interesting to me; how he could float like a butterfly in the ring, but he would not get on the dance floor. The king of moving in the ring, dancing in the ring, didn't dance. I'll bet he doesn't dance today. I'll bet he still hasn't learned how to dance.

ZBIGNIEW PIETRZYKOWSKI [Cassius Clay's opponent in the 1960 Olympic finals]: During the fight itself, I had to work at a very fast pace to avoid his punches. This was good for the first round. Clay was missing a lot of punches. But in the second round, I realised I was losing my strength and that it would be difficult for me to survive three rounds. I had to think about defence, and that hampered thoughts of victory. It left me with nothing else but to try to survive three rounds and not be knocked out. I would have done anything then to beat him. But later, I began to cherish his victories.

WILBERT 'SKEETER' MCCLURE: I was fighting an Italian in Rome for the gold medal, so I figured my chances were not too good. But I went out and beat Carmello Bosce of Italy. I beat him in the last round and I came back to the dressing-room, shouting, 'I got it! I got it! I got it!' Eddie Crook had to go out next. Eddie went out and he came back, shouting 'I got it! I got it! I got it!' Eddie was hysterical. He looked like a seven-year-old kid, he was so joyful. And Cassius, he was no nonsense. He was getting ready to go out, concentrating on his objective. Then he went out, got his gold, came back in; and we hugged each other and jumped up and down, and screamed and screamed and screamed. We just couldn't believe it.

HARTMUT SCHERZER [a German journalist who met Cassius Clay at the Rome Olympics]: He seemed like a nice young man, but we didn't pay that much attention to him. It's not like any of us knew that someday Cassius Clay would become Muhammad Ali.

DICK SCHAAP [journalist, author and television commentator]: I went down to Louisville to do a story about him for the *Saturday Evening Post* in late 1960. It was the first major magazine article that was ever done about him, and we spent a lot of time together. Louisville was a Jim Crow city in 1960; so when we went out to eat, we had to go to the black section of town. I was there for four or five days. Every night, we went to the same restaurant. It had an 8-ounce steak and a 16-ounce steak on the menu. Every night, he ordered a 32-ounce steak, and every night they gave it to him. Finally, after two or three nights, I asked him,

'How do you know they have a 32-ounce steak? It's not on the menu.' And he told me, 'When I found out you were coming, I went in and told the people here to order them for me.' But if there was a moment when I really totally fell in love with this kid, it was when we were driving down the main street in Louisville. We stopped for a traffic light, and there was a very pretty girl standing on the corner. A white girl. I turned to Cassius, which was his name then, and said, 'Boy, she's pretty.' He grabbed me and said, 'You're crazy, man. You can get electrocuted for that; a Jew looking at a white girl in Kentucky.'

DON ELBAUM [matchmaker and boxing promoter]: My first encounter with Ali was when I represented Sonny Banks. His manager was a big car dealer in Detroit; his trainer was Luther Burgess; and I was an adviser. We looked at films of Clay, and one thing we saw – like everybody else, I might add – was that he had the bad habit of leaning back from punches. So we worked for a month on the idea that, when Clay leaned back, Sonny would take an extra step forward, get on top of him, and throw the hook. Sonny could really whack. Sure enough, round one, Sonny hits him with a left hook and Clay goes down. As time goes by, it's a nice feeling to know that my guy was the first guy to put him down.

ANGELO DUNDEE: Muhammad was always susceptible to the left hook; against Sonny Banks, against Henry Cooper, against Joe Frazier, whoever. You see, no matter how great a fighter is, he always has flaws. Muhammad's problem was that left hook. He always had a problem evading it.

A.J. LIEBLING [writing in the *New Yorker* about Cassius Clay being decked by Sonny Banks]: The poet went down.

MICHAEL KATZ [sportswriter]: In the early years, you couldn't touch him. The only legitimate criticism — at least people thought it was legitimate — was that he had no chin because he went down against Henry Cooper; he went down against Sonny Banks. We didn't know how good his chin was because, except for the few times he got caught off balance, nobody was hitting him.

HAROLD CONRAD [fight publicist]: I had a gimmick worked out with Ali. It was a magic trick we did together. He'd be some-place with someone and he'd tell them about a friend of his named Mr Wizard who had mental telepathy powers. Mr Wizard was me. Ali would tell this person to pick any card out of a deck of cards, and if they telephoned Mr Wizard, he'd be able to iden-tify the card they were holding. So they'd pick a card — say, the four of clubs. Then Ali would telephone, and we had this code. As soon as I answered the phone, Ali would say, 'Could I speak to Mr Wizard?' I'd go, 'Clubs, diamonds, hearts, spades.' And when I hit the right suit, Ali would say, 'Hello, this is Muhammad.' Then I'd start counting. 'Two, three, four, five,' all the way up to ace. And when I hit the right card, Ali would say, 'Mr Wizard, I've got someone here who doesn't believe in you. I'm gonna put them on the phone, so you can show them how powerful you are.' It worked every time. No one could ever figure out how we did it.

MUHAMMAD ALI [on John F. Kennedy]: I liked him. He tried to do good, and I liked his personality. When he was killed, I felt empty. I got a chill all over. It frightened me that something like that could happen to the President of the entire country right in the centre of the country.

BOOKER JOHNSON [entourage member]: Malcolm X is the one who really inspired him to become a Muslim. Malcolm was the most eloquent speaker we had among us, and in those days he was telling us something new. He gave us courage, a feeling of independence, and this is what inspired Ali. But Ali had to be taught the religion slowly. You don't just give a baby steak because, if you do, it will choke him.

DICK SCHAAP: One night – and this goes back to when Ali was Cassius Clay – I took him and his parents on a drive around Manhattan. It was snowing and, somewhere downtown on Second Avenue, we stopped for gas. The station attendant was a huge black man; six foot six, maybe taller, real mean-looking. While he was putting gas in the tank, he was wiping snow off the windshield. Finally, I turned to Cassius and said, 'Tell him that's good enough; close the gas tank, and we'll get going.' So Clay leaned out the window and said, 'Hey, man; that's good enough.' And the guy answered, 'Who's doing this – you or me?' At that point, all Cassius said back was, 'You're the boss, man. You're the boss.' I couldn't let that pass; so as soon as he pulled his head back inside the car, I said, 'Hey, wait a minute. All night long, you've been telling me you're the greatest fighter who ever lived; you're going to be heavyweight champion of the world; you're not afraid of Sonny Liston. How can you let this guy talk to you like that?' And Cassius told me, 'That man looks meaner than Sonny Liston.'

BETTY SHABAZZ [wife of Malcolm X]: Cassius Clay asked my husband if he would bring our whole family down to Miami Beach [for the first Liston fight]. It was supposed to be our anniversary present. I was expecting, so my husband had to do some prodding to get me on a plane and to get our three little girls ready, but of course we went. Cassius was a nervous wreck. He had a great deal of apprehension about fighting Sonny Liston. But my husband talked to him like a little brother and helped him conquer his fear. And this was after Malcolm had been cautioned not to go. He was told by Elijah Muhammad that, if he went, it would be on his own as an individual, not representing the Nation of Islam; and that, if he had good sense, he would stay away because there was no way Cassius Clay could win. But Malcolm felt that, if Cassius Clay was totally focused on the fight, he could win. And one of the things he said to me was, 'If he loses, he should not be alone.'

ATTALLAH SHABAZZ [daughter of Malcolm X]: I remember going down to Florida to celebrate Muhammad's birthday in January of 1964. The fight against Liston hadn't happened yet. But there was a birthday cake. If it had been a wedding cake, there would have been a bride and groom on top. But on this cake, there was the figure of Ali [then Cassius Clay] made out of sugar with both arms raised in victory standing over Sonny Liston.

SOL SILVERMAN [the attorney appointed by the Governor of California to head a committee investigating professional boxing]: The proposed Cassius Clay versus Sonny Liston heavyweight title fight is a dangerous mismatch which could result in grave injury to the young challenger. Such mismatches not only endanger the over-matched boxer, but degrade boxing from a great sport to a sordid racket.

CUS D'AMATO: I think that Clay has the equipment with which to beat Liston, provided it's used intelligently. Clay has speed and manoeuvrability. And if he employs an unpredictable strategy in applying that speed and manoeuvrability, I think he'll be able to confuse Liston and frustrate him and, after accomplishing this, be able to hit him with the kind of punches necessary to win the fight.

DAVID HALBERSTAM: I remember being very nervous the night Cassius Clay fought Sonny Liston. Clay seemed so young and vulnerable. And I remember caring about what would happen to him, being frightened that a dark shadow would fall over him, because Liston seemed to be what he was supposed to be.

JACK MCKINNEY [sportswriter]: The problems Clay had with his vision in the first Liston fight were no accident. The two toughest opponents that Liston faced prior to Clay were Eddie Machen and Cleveland Williams. Machen lost a 12-round decision to Liston and complained afterward that he'd been bothered by an astringent in his eyes. But he'd fought so poorly that no one believed him. Everyone thought it was just an alibi. And Cleveland Williams gave Liston all kinds of trouble in the first round. I was at that fight, and after the first round there seemed to be a lot of confusion in Sonny's corner. In fact, he was late coming out for the second round because his mouthpiece wasn't in. He knocked Williams out in that round. And after the fight, Williams was obviously having trouble seeing. He kept rubbing his eyes. Later on, I kidded Sonny's cornerman, Joe Polino, who was responsible for the mouthpiece, about the confusion. Joe told me, 'Someday I'll explain it to you.' Well, I got my explanation at the first Clay–Liston fight. If you look at a film of what went on in Liston's corner between the third and fourth rounds of that fight, you'll see Polino in the ring with Willie Reddish [Liston's trainer] standing behind him, blocking everyone else's view. And Polino is at Sonny's knees, rubbing something on his gloves.

'AND THEN THERE WAS CASSIUS' [*New York Herald Tribune* editorial, published on 27 February 1964, two days after Cassius Clay dethroned Sonny Liston]: The clicking shutters; the stampeding crowd; the excited chomp chomp as sportswriters ate their words by the thousands. It was a moment of glory straight from the story-books, as the one who had seemed an impossibly outmatched underdog stood victor over the champion; a moment that might have been wrapped in red, white and blue bunting and warmed the hearts of generations to come. But then there was the voice of Cassius: 'I am the greatest! I am the king! I am the greatest' – shrilling to the world in tones that seemed to echo a thousand little Hitlers through all the ages of man, and the magic was gone. Instead of a champion, there was a boastful bully; instead of a sport, a spectacle. And it was sad. For one felt the loss, not only of what might have been a fighter's finest moment, but the loss of what might have been a hero.

MALCOLM X: Brother Cassius will never do anything that will in any way tarnish or take away from his image as the heavy-weight champion of the world. He is trying his best to live a clean life and project a clean image. But despite this, you will find that the press is constantly trying to paint him as something other than what he actually is. He doesn't smoke. He doesn't drink. He's never been involved in any trouble. His record is clean. If he was white, they'd be referring to him as the all-American boy.

BOOKER JOHNSON: Ali's father felt that he should be the administrator of his son's affairs. He and I used to argue. I'd tell him, 'This is a different situation. You're dealing with lawyers and accountants, and your son has to have the intellectual equivalent on his side in order to deal successfully with them.' After a while, he settled down and quit talking that he should be the adminis-trator. But for a long time, he felt that he was cut off from his own flesh and blood. It was a shame, because it should be a wonderful feeling for a man to know that his son is such a wonderful achiever and the most famous person in the world. What you should do under those circumstances is be proud of your son and enjoy his glory. But Mr Clay blew a lot of that feeling. He missed out on a lot of the glory that he could have enjoyed, because he didn't understand that his son was an organi-sation, his son was an institution. The job of administrator was something that he just wasn't equipped to handle.

ROBERT LIPSYTE [sportswriter]: In the 1950s and 1960s, people talked about sports as one of the few areas where black Americans could make progress. But the truth is, sports was a bastion of the old order. Black athletes could become stars, but they had to do it on the terms of an existing ruling class. They had to be grateful. They shouldn't go out with white women. They were expected to be dutiful and modest. These were men who oftentimes were egocentric, narcissistic and very vain. But they knew the drill of dealing with the press. Never talk about yourself; always talk about the team. And now, along comes Muhammad Ali, who breaks all the rules and challenges that order. He's immodest. He's not sufficiently grateful to white America. He says what he thinks. And even though he's celebrated and people are fawning over him, he knows that, as far as white America is concerned, if he were still Cassius Marcellus Clay and not the heavyweight champion of the world, he'd be parking cars.

ANGELO DUNDEE: I always let Cassius be Cassius and Muhammad be Muhammad.

ROCKY MARCIANO: It's a very bad situation now, because there's a lack of respect for the present champion and that creates a lack of respect for all past champions. Nobody questions my fights; they were all tough ones. But people just don't treat you the same way since he came along.

DICK GREGORY [political activist and human rights advocate]: A lot of people were afraid because he changed his name. You can't change your name. It's an awful thing to do to change your name. You don't believe that? Ask Coca-Cola. Tell them to change their name.

MUHAMMAD ALI: God's got me here for something. I can feel it. I was born for everything that I'm doing now.

ANGELO DUNDEE: Ali changed boxing. For a hundred years, the only thing fighters would say was, 'I do the fighting; my manager does the talking.' Then Muhammad came along, saying, 'Hey, I do the talking. I'm the star. Nobody else talks for me.'

ROBERT LIPSYTE: Ali understood television. He understood the show, whether it was the poetry, the pre-fight weigh-in or the fight itself. He was a born showman, brilliant at dramatising himself. Whether he would have been the same phenomenon without television is hard to say. But he understood what television wanted; that instead of someone coming down, smiling and shaking hands nicely for still photographers, television wanted the provocateur.

ANGELO DUNDEE: Every day is like a new toy to Muhammad.

MUHAMMAD ALI: I don't usually tell people this because they don't understand, but I don't have no fight plan. It would be the worst thing I could do to go in there with my mind all made up. I've been fighting since I was a child, and I do everything on instinct. Sometimes I wonder at myself when I see a big fist coming at my head, and my head moves without me thinking and the big fist goes by. I wonder how I did it.

ANGELO DUNDEE: Ali did things wrong in the ring and made it look like art.

MUHAMMAD ALI: The minute I'm hit; two steps backward, and I'm on the other side of the ring. Messages race out of my mind – retreat, retreat, danger, danger. I hear the messages and I'm moving away, but I'm still watching and thinking. It don't take long to clear your mind when your body is right. When you're in condition, it only takes ten seconds; then you're usually out of trouble. If he gets too close, just clinch him. Grab him, do anything. Stall for time, don't let him know you're stunned. Keep dancing with him like nothing's wrong. All this happening while the crowd is hollering.

FERDIE PACHECO [Ali's ring physician for most of his boxing career]: With the young Ali, boxing was truly 'the sweet science'.

MUHAMMAD ALI: I'm so fast, I've got moves you can't even see.

ROY JONES: People talk about Ali's defence, but I think his offence was the key to his success. When Ali was young, you didn't have time to think against him. He was always putting pressure on you because he could strike at any time. It was like, what his opponent did didn't seem to matter. And he had the safest jab I've ever seen because he didn't over-commit. He used his jab to keep you away and keep you in range until he hit you.

MUHAMMAD ALI: I don't know anything about fighting, really. Only about *me* fighting.

JOE PATERNO [football coach]: Ali would have made a great linebacker and an outstanding tight end. I don't know if he had the foot speed for any of the other skill positions, but his strength, quickness of hands and balance were awfully good. Now maybe football wouldn't have been the right game for him. Certainly, at age 18 or 19, he'd have needed guidance as to what he could and couldn't do as far as alienating his team-mates was concerned. I'm liberal politically, but I'm conserva-tive in terms of lifestyle and how I coach the team. And here at Penn State, we have a rule about players getting along with each other. You can only say you're sorry so many times. But I don't want to underestimate Ali's ability to accommodate any situation. If he'd made a commitment to it, I'm sure he would have been a team player. I know, I'd have loved the chance to coach him.

MUHAMMAD ALI: Most black people in this country are mentally dead, and we don't wake up easy. It takes something like an earthquake to wake up our people. Oh, maybe black folks will get upset about something and burn a building or two, but in a couple of days, we forget.

MUHAMMAD ALI: We were taught when we were little chil-dren that Mary had a little lamb, its fleece was white as snow. Then we heard about Snow White. White Owl cigars. White Swan soap. White Cloud tissue. White Rain hair rinse. White Tornado floor wax. White Plus toothpaste. All the good cowboys ride white horses and wear white hats. The President lives in the White House. Jesus was white. The Last Supper was white. The angels is white. Miss America is white. Even Tarzan, the King of the Jungle in Africa, is white.

MUHAMMAD ALI: Things that are solid, black people don't think about that. They just dance and sing and go to church and shout. We never thought about doing nothing for ourselves. We depend on white people to grow our food and make our clothes. Used to be a sign on Miami Beach that said, 'No dogs, Niggers and Jews allowed.' Jews got mad and united and bought the damn beach.

MUHAMMAD ALI: I got tired of watching black entertainers on TV. Diana Ross married a white man. Lena Horne married a white man. Leslie Uggams married a white man. Lou Rawls married a white woman. I said to myself, if God will just let me be big, I'll do it different. James Brown and Sidney Poitier and Diana Ross and Lena Horne and Eartha Kitt; them niggers don't talk to black people. They don't come through Alabama and talk to people. Niggers get big, and then they forget you.

TOM HOOVER [a friend]: Ali's treatment of women when he was young isn't something that should be emulated. But the things he did right were more important than the things he did wrong. He made black women feel good about being black the same way he made black men feel good about themselves. He made black women feel every bit as beautiful and desirable as white women.

MUHAMMAD ALI: Whenever black athletes want to do something, white people run to Joe Louis, and Joe Louis always talks like the boss wants him to. Joe makes himself look real ignorant when he attacks me for standing up for my people. If Joe Louis don't like what I'm doing, he should discuss it with me behind closed doors. But instead, Joe Louis is making himself an Uncle Tom for white people.

JOE LOUIS: Clay has a million dollars' worth of confidence and a dime's worth of courage. He can't punch; he can't hurt you; and I don't think he takes a good punch. I'd rate him with Johnny Paycheck, Abe Simon and Buddy Baer. A lot of guys would have beaten him if he was around when I was. I would have whipped him.

MUHAMMAD ALI: What's this about Joe Louis beating me? Slow-moving, shuffling Joe Louis beat me? He may hit hard, but that don't mean nothing if you can't find nothing to hit. What's he gonna do when I'm jumping and sticking and moving? And don't say I can only do it for a minute, because I can keep it up for 15 rounds, three minutes a round. Now how is Joe Louis gonna get to me? Would I just quit dancing that night and stand there and let him hit me? Joe Louis, you're really funny.

OSCAR BROWN JR [who later wrote the music for *Buck White*, the Broadway show that Ali starred in during his exile from boxing]: My wife Jean and I and Jesse Jackson were over at Joe Louis's house. Jean, Jesse and I were sitting with Mrs Louis in the dining-room. Joe was in the bedroom, laying in bed, looking at television. Then he came to the door, and said, 'Cassius is on TV, Cassius is on TV.' So we all got up to see Ali on TV. He was being interviewed, and he was saying, 'I'm not an Uncle Tom like Joe Louis.' He kept on ranting and calling Joe Louis an Uncle Tom, and I'm standing there with Joe Louis. I don't know how on earth it happened that I got into that position. The Lord just put me there, I guess. Joe didn't say anything. He just went on back to bed. But the next time I saw Ali, I made a point of telling him, 'I can't stand to have the hero of my adulthood talking like that about the hero of my childhood. Joe Louis meant so much to us. No matter what you think, you have no right to say those things about him. You don't know what you're talking about. You don't know what conditions Joe Louis came up under. If it hadn't been for Joe Louis, you wouldn't be here.'

JOE LOUIS BARROW JR: My father was not very happy to hear Muhammad Ali call him an Uncle Tom. He didn't appreciate that. Joe Louis was very different from Muhammad Ali. He was a quiet individual. He was a humble individual. He didn't talk a lot. My father was not into mouth. He was not into being brag-gadocious. And he had a speech impediment, so he didn't articu-late a lot. But he believed in this country, and he didn't like Muhammad Ali questioning what he felt. Joe Louis loved America. He knew that America had its problems. He was treated as an inferior citizen, and he fought against that in his way. He didn't picket; he didn't march. And he was criticised in the sixties for not being more vocal, but those who criticised him didn't have a sense of history. And frankly, I was disgusted with Muhammad Ali when he called my father an Uncle Tom, because

Ali didn't relate at that point to who Joe Louis was and what Joe Louis meant to this country.

JOSÉ TORRES [former light-heavyweight champion and Ali biographer]: Ali and Joe Louis had harsh words for each other. They had different beliefs about religion. They had different beliefs about patriotism. But I think what really bugged Ali about Joe Louis was that Louis never gave Ali credit for being a great fighter. And Joe Louis was a great fighter himself, so he had to know how truly great Ali was.

PAT PATTERSON [the Chicago policeman who served as a security aide to Ali]: There were some hard feelings early on, but Ali and Joe Louis got to be friendly later. And there was one thing I've never figured out. When Ali saw Joe Louis, he'd start dancing and boxing, throwing punches real close to Joe's face, right in his face. 'I'll eat you up; you're too slow; come on, Joe.' Every time, he'd do that. Joe would move back, like he didn't want to be bothered, and Ali would keep it up; dancing around him, throwing punches real fast. It never failed. And all of a sudden, Joe Louis would reach out and slap Ali right upside the face. Bop! A left hand, real quick. That would end it. And I never figured out whether Ali allowed it to happen that way or he couldn't stop it. Because, you see, Ali was a humanitarian and he got a kick out of making you be who you were and making you better than you were supposed to be. So I don't know if he let Joe Louis slap him or not.

MUHAMMAD ALI: I've been getting phone calls lately on my reclassification from 1-Y to 1-A. Reporters have been nagging at me. You know how they pick at you and twist things you say and make you say things you really don't know what you're talking about. They've been asking questions, and I have been with my big mouth, as usual, popping off. This time it got me in a little hot water.

FERDIE PACHECO: Ali's United States Army IQ score was 78. So what! Measuring Ali's intelligence with a standard IQ test is like trying to measure joy or love with a ruler.

MUHAMMAD ALI: I'm against all war. I said that before all this draft-card burning stuff. I made a speech at a white college in Buffalo, New York. When I got to the room where I was gonna talk, they had 34 signs stuck up on the walls and behind the platform. The signs said things like, 'LBJ – how many kids did you kill today?' So I told the man who invited me there, I wouldn't talk until they took all the signs down.

REPORTER: Why won't you fight for your country?
MUHAMMAD ALI: I'm a minister of my religion, and this country has laws for ministers. George Hamilton; why don't he fight for his country? He's making a movie. Joe Namath; why don't he fight for his country. He's playing football.
REPORTER: Joe Namath has a bad knee.
MUHAMMAD ALI: Yeah, ain't that silly. I saw Joe Namath playing football the other day – 27 passes out of 43 is all he hit. Go talk to him about fighting for his country. I'm not using them as

excuses, but you all keep jumping on me like I'm the last one; like you'll lose the war if I ain't in it.

NEW YORK TIMES EDITORIAL [published on 29 April 1967]: Citizens cannot pick and choose which wars they wish to fight any more than they can pick and choose which laws they wish to obey. However, if Cassius Clay and other draft-age objectors believe the war in Vietnam is unjust, they have the option of going to prison on behalf of their beliefs. Civil disobedience entails a penalty, but the risk is less than for those young men who willingly serve their country in Vietnam and other places of hardship and danger.

REPORTER: Are you worried about not projecting a good image?
MUHAMMAD ALI: What do you mean, project a good image? An image to who? Who don't like the image I project? That's the weakest thing I've heard yet – I'm not a good image. For my people, I'm the best image in the world.

JERRY IZENBERG [sportswriter]: Ali against Zora Folley was the last time that the crowd at an Ali fight was comprised almost totally of boxing fans. Later, we saw the capes and gold chains and beautiful people and whatever. This was like the last hurrah for an era.

HOWARD COSELL: It seems to me that you're taking Zora Folley too lightly.
MUHAMMAD ALI: Why would you say that?

HOWARD COSELL: Because every indication has been that you're confident you can beat Zora –

MUHAMMAD ALI (interrupting): I'm confident I can whup all of them. This ain't nothing new. What are you trying to make it look like something new for? I'm always confident.

HOWARD COSELL: You're being extremely truculent.

MUHAMMAD ALI: Whatever truculent means, if that's good, I'm that.

JOHN CONDON [director of publicity for Madison Square Garden]: When Muhammad was getting ready to fight Zora Folley at Madison Square Garden, there were a lot of public relations problems. But number one on the list was the fact that he'd indicated pretty clearly that, if he was drafted, he wasn't going to go into the Army. Then, about two weeks before the fight, I got a telephone call from Jack Hand of the Associated Press, who told me that Muhammad's appeal of his Selective Service classification had been unanimously rejected by the National Appeals Board. So I went over to Gallagher's Steakhouse, where Ali was having dinner. He and Angelo were leaving when I got there. I told them, 'Let's sit down; there's something I have to tell you.' So we went back into Gallagher's and I gave Ali the news. He didn't get excited; he didn't seem upset. All he did was look at Angelo and say, 'Angelo, you better tell them to sweep out that jail cell, because it looks like that's where I'm going.'

BARNEY NAGLER [sportswriter]: Muhammad Ali has claimed exemption from the draft because he is mostly concerned with preaching the words of Elijah Muhammad. The Supreme Court must decide whether it accepts Elijah's teachings as a religion and Ali as a preacher of those teachings. The boxing commissioners, being students of comparative religion, long ago cast their votes against the only authentic heavyweight champion in the world. How easy it is to espouse the popular side of an argument; how much more difficult to stand firm in behalf of a cause believed righteous in the way Muhammad Ali stands. Ali is only a prize-fighter. Perhaps too much store is put in the case of just one self-defined pacifist. But he has chosen to challenge a system that, he believes, deforms his people. And his choice is that of a man of principle.

KWAME TURÉ [formerly Stokely Carmichael]: Going to jail was my job. I'd been arrested 25 times in Mississippi and Alabama. So when they told me, 'We'll send you to jail for five years,' what I did was, I sat down and worked out a list of books that I'd finally get a chance to read. I wasn't worried. I'd get a chance to sleep, no telephones. I'm used to jail. I wasn't giving up anything. But Muhammad Ali had everything. Fame, glory, money, women, good looks, champion of the world. So when Muhammad would call me – we'd speak back and forth on the telephone – and he'd tell me, 'I ain't going,' I'd say, 'Yeah; right on!' But I always wondered, when that final moment comes and he actually has to take that step, how will it come out? Because, no question, the FBI viewed Ali as more of a threat than H. Rap Brown and myself. Muhammad Ali had a broader base than we had. The government recognised that Muhammad Ali could cause more trouble than all of us. That's why we understood that the weight of the blow would be hardest against Muhammad Ali. They were going to take his championship crown; no doubt about it. They were going to prosecute him; no doubt about it. They were going to do everything possible to bring him to his knees. Of all the people who opposed the war in Vietnam, I think that Muhammad Ali risked the most. Lots of people refused to go. Some went to jail. But no one risked as much from their decision not to go to war in Vietnam as Muhammad Ali. And his real greatness can be seen in the fact that, despite all that was done to him, he became even greater and more humane.

MUHAMMAD ALI: When a man's guilty, you don't just say, 'You're guilty.' You hold court and prove it, and then you say he's guilty. You don't tell a man he murdered somebody without giving him a chance to explain and without letting the world see why you're condemning him. I never heard of them taking nobody else's title. People such as Sonny Liston have been in jail fifteen or twenty times. There's people with scandals, people who've been caught in their cars, breaking speed limits and carrying guns. And they don't get suspended, so what's the reason for suspending me?

WALLY MATTHEWS [sportswriter]: It's very difficult to explain to young people today how important Ali was, because the society has changed so much over the past thirty years. Now black pride is taken for granted. People understand that it's possible to be a patriotic American and still believe that the war in Vietnam was wrong. And everything today is driven by money; particularly in sports, where athletes think they're making a sacrifice if they can't wear clothes with their favourite logo on them at an

Olympic awards ceremony. I mean, how do you explain to a 12-year-old that Muhammad Ali, based on an act of principle, risked going to jail and sacrificed the heavyweight championship of the world? Try explaining that to a young person today. He'll look at you like you're crazy; or maybe he'll think it was Ali who was crazy.

RON BORGES [sportswriter]: My father, who's 88 years old now, isn't the most liberal person in the world. He was a construction worker for most of his life and he never liked people who talked a lot. But when Ali was willing to go to jail for his beliefs, that got my father's attention. He told me, 'You know, I don't agree with what this guy is doing, but he's all right. You get very few chances to be a man in life, and this guy takes advantage of them.' And I'll tell you something else. My father voted for George Wallace in 1968 and for George McGovern in 1972. That's quite a change, and I have to believe that watching Muhammad Ali was part of what influenced him.

REGGIE JACKSON [Hall of Fame baseball player]: I remember how I felt when Martin Luther King was assassinated. There was no one to cling to except Ali. I don't know what I would have done if I'd had that kind of leadership burden thrust upon me. I do know that, ten years later when Ali lost to Leon Spinks, I was at my peak as a sports hero. I was Mr October. And I knew even then there was no way I could begin to carry that load.

JIM BROWN [former football great and founder of the Black Economic Union]: Ali is the only person I've ever seen who I knew was protected. Against all odds, he always came up with something because he's a spiritual person, and I don't necessarily mean religion. One thing I know for sure; you can't use logic when you talk about Muhammad Ali.

OSCAR BROWN JR: I heard the term 'exile' used in connection with Ali's inability to defend his title for a considerable amount of time, but I never thought of it as an exile. It was more just a rip-off and a robbery. Ali didn't go anyplace; he was still here. The title didn't go anyplace. The symbol of who is truly the champion of boxing is a belt that's got diamonds and stuff, and all through the whole period you're talking about, Ali had that belt in his living-room. No, boxing was in exile. Boxing went away from its own standards. Boxing went away from its own creed. Boxing went away from the championship belt. It's nonsense to talk about Ali being in exile. Ali was right here.

RAMSEY CLARK [former US Attorney General]: His independence was of a different order of independence; almost inherent, as if he was born that way. I'll bet you anything that, when he was five years old, he was like that. He just did what he thought he ought to do. He wasn't born to be forced. He's a totally independent human being. And to some people, that's very dangerous.

BILL BRADLEY [former basketball star and US Senator]: Muhammad Ali was important because he was self-possessed in the best sort of way. The fact that he was heavyweight champion added to people's awareness of him and what he believed. But what was most admirable, regardless of his title, was his willingness to take a stand. That's something everyone has to learn if we're to become whole human beings. And because Ali did it, he was a powerful influence on many lives. Because of him, people became convinced that, if they stood up for their beliefs, they could prevail.

MUHAMMAD ALI: Everyone has a right to their own opinion.

PAT PATTERSON: There was something about Muhammad that, once you were in his presence, it didn't matter what you thought about him; you revelled at being there. People who thought they hated his guts would see him, come over and shake his hand. Even racist redneck bigots would hold out their babies for him to kiss.

MUHAMMAD ALI: Life is strange. When I wasn't allowed to fight, it was the Jewish newspaper people [Jerry Izenberg, Robert Lipsyte, Stan Isaacs, Leonard Schecter] and the Jewish TV people [Howard Cosell] who supported me most.

JAMES EARL JONES: Ali visited the set at Twentieth Century Fox when we were filming *The Great White Hope*. We got in the ring together. We were both wearing boxing gloves. The photographers were busy flashing. Muhammad said, 'Go ahead, hit me as hard as you can.' Well, I'd played the Jack Johnson character since the play opened on Broadway. I'd been put through my paces by real boxing trainers. So I gave Muhammad my best left hook; he blocked the blow. And in the process, quite accidentally, he broke my thumb. You know, when a fighter like Ali blocks a punch, the block is devastating in its own power. I felt the pain immediately.

MUHAMMAD ALI [after seeing *The Great White Hope* on Broadway]: One thing is bothering me. What are they gonna do fifty years from now when they write a play about me? I wish I knew how it was gonna turn out.

MUHAMMAD ALI [on his thespian career during his exile from boxing]: I was in a play called *Buck White*. The play was a flop; it lasted six days. But I was a hit.

BARTLETT GIAMATTI [former president of Yale University and commissioner of Major League Baseball]: It is Ali who brought to the surface the actor in every athlete more success-fully and obsessively than anyone else.

DICK SCHAAP: In 1969, the year the Mets won their first World Series, I spent the last few days of the regular season with the team in Chicago. Ali was living there at the time. I was writ-ing a book with Tom Seaver, and the three of us went out to dinner together. We met at a restaurant called The Red Carpet. I made the introductions. And of course, this was the year that Tom Seaver was Mr Baseball, maybe even Mr America. Ali and Tom got along fine. They really hit it off together. And after about half an hour, Ali in all seriousness turned to Seaver and said, 'You know, you're a nice fellow. Which paper do you write for?'

COED: Would you say you're the greatest?

MUHAMMAD ALI: I don't say that no more. Would you say, I'm pretty? Let me hear you.

COED: I'm pretty.

MUHAMMAD ALI: But you're not just asking me to say I'm great. You're asking me to say I'm the greatest. You say, I'm the prettiest.

COED: I'm the prettiest.

MUHAMMAD ALI: You're lying! [The audience dissolves into laughter] No, darling; I was just playing. Don't pay no attention. You're as pretty as you believe and as pretty as you think you are.

HOWARD BINGHAM [Ali's personal photographer and friend]: Ali had one of those faces that you could not get enough of. All you had to do was aim, and every photo was an excellent photo. You could not miss with Ali.

KAREEM ABDUL JABBAR: Ali would kid me all the time. He'd say I was almost as good-looking as he was. That's the best compliment I ever got; someone saying I was almost as good-looking as Ali.

MUHAMMAD ALI: Talking is a whole lot easier than fighting.

HOSEA WILLIAMS [civil rights activist]: When Ali gave up the championship, he became America's number one role model in the black community. And when he came back, he truly convinced us all that, if you stand up and speak out for what is right, you will win in the end; that as tough as it is, even though you're black and poor, you can make it if you really try.

BRYANT GUMBEL: Joe Frazier was an available symbol behind whom people who hated Ali could unite. Was it Joe's fault? Of course not. In fact, one of the sad stories to be written about that era is that Joe Frazier never got his due as a man. In some ways, he symbolised what the black man's struggle was about far more than Ali did. But it was Joe's misfortune to be cast as the opponent of a man who was the champion of all good things.

JOHN CONDON: Joe never liked Ali. He doesn't like him, didn't like him and never will like him. But except for that one incident before their second fight when he went at Muhammad in a TV studio, Joe kept his feelings inside. He bottled them up, stored his hatred and let everything out in the ring.

BUTCH LOUIS [boxing promoter and former 'road buddy' of Joe Frazier]: Ali and Joe were like peanut butter and jelly. They needed each other to make things happen.

JOHN CONDON: You've seen the press-guide photo for the first Ali–Frazier fight; the one with Ali and Joe standing nose to nose, forehead to forehead. That was taken at Joe's gym in Philadelphia. I wanted something different, so I told both guys,

'Put your foreheads together.' And they did. Then I said, 'Get closer. Touch noses.' But they wouldn't do it. So I went over, put their heads closer together with one hand behind Ali's head and the other behind Joe's, jumped out of the way, and told the photographer, 'Get it!' And he got it. It was a great photo. The problem was, it was so great that no one believed it was for real. Everyone thought it was superimposed. I had to show people the negative to prove it was real.

DAVE ANDERSON [sportswriter, on Ali–Frazier I]: I've never forgotten the noise that I heard, the thunderclap of Ali crashing on the canvas about three feet in front of me. But as powerful as Frazier's punch had been, as flattened as Ali was, he was up at referee Arthur Mercante's count of three; up as fast as any human could be.

BERT WATSON [business manager for Joe Frazier in the 1980s and 90s]: The first trip that Joe and I took together, we were driving in Florida and stopped for gas. We'd been talking about Ali. Right before I got out of the car to go to the bathroom, I said, 'One thing you've got to admit: the man was a great fighter.' Anyway, I go to the bathroom, come back, and Joe is gone. I had to hitchhike to the motel where we were staying. Finally, I got there. Joe was in his room. I went in and said, 'What happened? Why'd you leave me like that?' And Joe told me, 'When you work for me, you don't say nothing good about Ali.'

LEROY NEIMAN: One interesting thing about Ali's appearance is that he spanned an era when people wore big bushy Afros and lots of facial hair, but he never gave in to that trend except for a few weeks when he had a moustache. I personally took it upon myself to tell him to get rid of it. Maybe, given my own moustache, I shouldn't criticise someone else's, but he looked ridiculous. When a prominent person has a certain look, he doesn't change it. Dwight Eisenhower didn't start wearing a hairpiece. George Bush isn't going to grow a beard. Except for the Army, Elvis Presley never got a crewcut. In fact, most people, whether they're famous or not, tend to keep their look. Maybe they make a few changes in deference to the style of the times, but Ali didn't even do that. And he was so extraordinarily good-looking that I thought the moustache was a real detriment.

PAT PATTERSON: Ali could walk up to a piano and entertain you, like you'd swear he could play the piano. He memorised how to play a few songs, and he'd sit there and play just enough to impress you. Little Richard was his favourite – 'Bop-bop-a-lu-bop-a-wop-bam-boom!' He'd play and he'd sing; and by the time he got through, you'd say, 'Wow; this guy is really talented.' But once he did that, he couldn't play nothing else; not at gunpoint if his life depended on it.

CATHAL O'SHANNON [Irish television host]: With Ali, there was no way you could go wrong from an interviewer's point of view. He was such a bloody showman.

JERRY IZENBERG: I've never gone through the formality of playing Russian roulette. About as close as I ever came to it was getting on a bus with Ali. You don't want to be on a bus with Ali for more than an hour. Because after an hour, Ali wants to drive and then you're in trouble. He loves to drive and he loves to drive fast. One time, we were in London. We were standing on line with everybody else to get on a bus. By everybody else, I mean the unsuspecting people of London, who were waiting to go home at the end of the day. Ali put his money in like everybody else and asked the bus driver, 'Can I drive?' And the bus driver, of course, said, 'Muhammad Ali! Why certainly, you can drive.' And the people on the bus were yelling, 'Great! Great! Great! Muhammad Ali is going to drive us.' And Angelo Dundee was saying, 'No! No! No! Don't let him drive. You don't understand.' But the will of the people could not be ignored, so Ali got behind the wheel. There was a terrific grinding of gears. The bus took off at a terrific rate of speed. And Ali had it pretty much under control, except for the fact that this was London, so while he was driving on the right-hand side of the road, the traffic was coming straight at him.

HUGH MCILVANNEY [sportswriter, in response to Angelo Dundee's claim prior to the 'Rumble in the Jungle' that Muhammad Ali knew how to beat George Foreman]: I, too, know a way to beat George Foreman. But it involves shelling him for three days and then sending in the infantry.

HAROLD CONRAD: You know, it used to be the Belgian Congo. Then they had a revolution, kicked the Belgians out and renamed everything. The name of the country was changed to Zaïre. The Congo River became the Zaïre River. Congo became a dirty name. But it was still a police state and Mobuto had censors who read everything that went out on the wire. Anyway, the night before the fight, they had a big jazz concert in the same stadium where the fight was going to be. One of the writers reviewed it and wrote about how great this guy was on the conga drums. And a censor changed it to the Zaïre drums. I'll never forget that: the Zaïre drums.

MUHAMMAD ALI [to Stokely Carmichael – considered by many to be the originator of the slogan 'Burn, baby, burn' – as Carmichael entered Ali's compound in Zaïre]: 'Stokely Carmichael, don't you burn nothing over here, or Mobuto's people will put you in a pot and cook you.'

FERDIE PACHECO: Norman Mailer decided one night in Zaïre that he was going to do roadwork with Ali. Ali told him, 'If you want to run with me, you can. But I run five miles in the jungle; and if you get tired, there are no cabs to take you back. If you get tired, you'll have to run down the trail by yourself. I'm not going to stop for you and I'm not going to send anybody back with you.' Well, Norman was pretty potted by then; and he's afflicted by the need to always be part of the scene and assert his macho image. So about four o'clock in the morning, he went out to run with Ali. He ran for maybe a quarter of a mile and then he fell behind, totally out of gas. In a jet black jungle. There wasn't even a firefly. Just total darkness. And then Norman heard this colossal roar. And if there's one distinctive sound in this world, it's the sound of a lion roaring in the jungle. That sound is distinct. You cannot mistake it for anything else. It's big and it's hungry and it rattles your bones. So Norman thought that his end had come. He didn't know whether to try to outrun it – he certainly couldn't outrun a lion – or ease on down the road, or just stand still and hope the lion went by. So he stood still for a while. And then he decided that, since he hadn't been eaten yet, he might as well try to get back to the compound, which he did. Ali had come back by this time. The sun was rising. Norman told him that the literary world had come close to losing one of its great geniuses, because he'd almost been eaten by a lion. He's telling Ali, 'There's a lion out there; you shouldn't be running.' And Ali says, 'Yeah, I know. There's a whole family of lions out there. They won't bother you.' So Norman asks if Ali is crazy. And Ali takes him by the arm and walks him down the road about a quarter of a mile to where the lions were caged in President Mobuto's zoo.

MUHAMMAD ALI [acknowledging a dashiki-clad visitor in Zaïre]: Welcome, brother. Do you speak English?
VISITOR: Yeah; I'm Tom Johnson from the *New York Times*.

GIL CLANCY [boxing commentator and trainer]: George Foreman might have appeared strong to the rest of the world, but he had almost no confidence in himself. That was his nature. He wouldn't play you at anything, not even throwing coins against the wall, unless there was a stacked deck on his side. And that fight against Ali destroyed what little confidence George had.

Without that fight, George would have annihilated Jimmy Young. He'd have walked right through him; but instead, Young beat him on points. Psychologically, that fight with Ali took away everything George had.

JIM BROWN: After the fight, I went to Ali's dressing-room to congratulate him, and then I went to Foreman's. Archie Moore was the only other person there. There was Foreman, Archie, me and Foreman's dog. George kept looking in the mirror at the lumps on his face, as though he couldn't believe what he saw. Then we went back to the hotel and George got a telephone call from Jim Marshall, who had been in three or four Super Bowls with the Vikings and never won one. Marshall did his best to console him. Foreman said, 'Don't worry, I'll be all right.' But you could see, he was totally bewildered by it all.

JERRY IZENBERG: If you wanted to make an allegory about good and evil and patience and virtue, after that fight in Zaïre you really could. It was like God waited until it was over. Then there was a tremendous clap of thunder, and we were caught in the worst kind of African cloudburst. It was the most intense rainstorm I've ever seen. If it had happened two hours earlier, the fight would have been wiped out. There were terrible winds, flash-flooding. And then, as suddenly as it had come, the storm was over. Dawn arrived; the sun came up. And it was like the whole history of 'I ain't got no quarrel with them Vietcong' and the hatred and the ugliness had been washed away. I remember that morning, standing with Ali by the Zaïre River. There were just a couple of us. The air was sticky sweet with that aroma of

African flowers and the ground was damp from that tremendous storm. Ali was looking out over the river and he said to us, 'You'll never know how long I waited for this. You'll never know what this means to me.'

JOHN CONDON: The 'rope-a-dope' didn't get its name until 1975. Ali, [publicist] Patti Dreifus and I were in an ice-cream shop at the Tropicana Hotel in Las Vegas right before Ali fought Ron Lyle. We're talking about a point in time six months after he won the title from George Foreman. I kept telling Ali, 'You know, this stuff you're doing on the ropes; you've got to give it a name. You've done it against Foreman; you've done it against Wepner; you're gonna keep doing it. Give it a name. So we're sitting there, and we come up with 'on the ropes … if someone tries to hit you when you're on the ropes, he's a dope'. And then we came up with 'rope-a-dope'. Ali's eyes lit up, and he said, 'That's good.'

IRVING RUDD [boxing publicist]: You can talk about George Washington; you can talk about the Kennedys. But as far as I'm concerned, the closest thing to a king that this country has ever had is Muhammad Ali. And it's worldwide; not just here. If Ali went into a hut in Africa, a village in Asia, the outback in Australia or a marketplace in South America, the people would look at him, smile and say, 'Muhammad Ali.'

MUHAMMAD ALI: I have no power. I've got a cold right now that I can't get rid of. The biggest man in the world, struck down by a germ. I'm nothing, same as everyone else.

MUHAMMAD ALI: Oxford University, that's a big university, wants me to be a professor of poetry and some kind of social something. They say I won't have to go there but once or twice a year for a lecture. The salary they pay won't pay my telephone bills, but I said I'd come over for the prestige. Very few boxers can be professors at Oxford University.

BUTCH LEWIS: Ali could convince you that his ice cube was colder. I mean, if he had an ice cube and you had one, his ice cube was colder than your ice cube.

MUHAMMAD ALI: It's not the same any more. Used to be, all I thought about was fight, fight, fight. Be the greatest. Be the champion. Now it's like I go to work, put in eight hours a day, do my job. I got other things on my mind.

MUHAMMAD ALI: My intention is never to hurt an opponent. I didn't actually carry fights in a way that's crooked. But I will admit that I've seen opponents in physical unconsciousness on their feet and saw chances to really hurt them to the extent where it was possible to have a brain concussion, and I knew I was winning and the fight was just about over, so I backed off. I lost all my fighting instinct and hoped the referee would stop it. I don't like really hurting someone for the pleasure of a blood-thirsty audience. I'm a classy boxer. I don't want to kill nobody. I'm out there to box.

FRED GRAHAM [host of the CBS interview show *Face the Nation*]: You have a reputation as a man who has a sharp eye for the ladies. What about this image as a womaniser? How is that going to be consistent with your role as a religious leader in the years ahead?

MUHAMMAD ALI: As far as my personal problems with family are concerned, these are things I don't discuss in public; especially on high-class shows like I was told yours would be.

LANA SHABAZZ [Ali's cook in training camp]: When Ali's children were growing up, he never wanted them in the newspapers or on TV. Partly, that's because he was afraid that, if someone crazy knew who they were, they might be kidnapped. But more so, it was because he didn't want any of them going around with a swelled head, saying, 'Look at me, I'm important.' That's what happens to children when they're in the papers or on TV. And Ali wanted very much for his children just to be normal kids.

MARYUM ALI [the oldest of Ali's children]: When I was a little girl, the training camp was packed every day with all sorts of people. Sparring partners, newspaper men, celebrities, television reporters. People would come by the busload from New York. And I wasn't allowed in the gym. I had to stay in the house with a babysitter because my parents were afraid that, if I went outside, someone would snatch me. I hated that. I wanted to be where the action was, and I couldn't be.

LEON GAST [producer of the Academy Award winning film *When We Were Kings*]: One time, we went down to Deer Lake to record Ali. This was between Zaïre and Manila. Belinda was there; Ali's four kids were there. Ali's son was maybe three years old, and Ali was shouting at him, 'Your daddy is the baddest nigger.' The kid was trying to emulate Ali, but for whatever reason, he couldn't say 'nigger'. He'd say, 'My daddy is the baddest nigo.' Ali would say, 'No! Nigger! Nigger!' And the kid would say 'Nigo, nigo.' It drove Ali crazy. No matter how hard he tried, he just couldn't get his son to say 'nigger'. Then, later on, he was playing with the twins. He had identical twin daughters, Rasheda and Jamillah. One of them was on his lap. He was kissing her, saying, 'Rasheda, you know I love you. You're the sweetest girl in the world.' Belinda came out and said, 'Ali, which daughter do you have there?' Ali told her, 'Well, this is, ah, um, Rasheda.' Belinda asked, 'Are you sure?' And Ali answered, 'I think so.' He was right, but he wasn't sure. And to tell you the truth, those girls looked an awful lot alike. I couldn't tell them apart.

JERRY IZENBERG: Ali's grasp of geopolitics is limited. One time, he was in London to cut the ribbon at the opening of a supermarket. And of course, everyone there loved him. There were hugs and kisses and cheers, the usual adulation. Muhammad was quite moved by it all and said to me, 'These people in England are so nice. I'll bet, in their whole history, they never had a war.'

DICK SCHAAP: I learned a lot from him. I learned about laughing and enjoying and having fun with your work. I learned that life doesn't have to be solemn to be serious. He never believed all the myths and legends. He understood that a lot of it was show, and he would wink and let you know. He taught me that you can do so much with a wink. The athletes, the politicians, the people who don't wink; they're the ones who should frighten you.

JOHN SCHULIAN [sportswriter]: Ali never gave anyone the same ride two days in a row.

MUHAMMAD ALI: I was the Elvis Presley of boxing.

GEORGE FOREMAN: Muhammad Ali was the greatest showman in the history of sports.

DAVE WOLF: It was fascinating how tight the security in Manila was [prior to Ali–Frazier III]. There was a curfew. And when Joe and Ali went out to do their roadwork in the early morning, it took place before the curfew was lifted. Somebody had a list of everybody who was authorised to run or follow in the cars. If your name wasn't on that list, forget it. There were military people lining the roads where they ran. The troops could literally shoot anybody who turned up without proper authorisation on the street. And it was typical of both camps that no one was curious about the politics of this. It was just taken for granted that there was some trouble going on. Whether or not the 'troublemakers' were deserving of sympathy was irrelevant.

BUTCH LEWIS: Joe was very self-conscious about his speech and his education. He came from the south; he grew up on a plantation. At one time, Joe was very hesitant to speak, because he took a lot of abuse about how he sounded and people maybe didn't understand him. And verbally, Ali would eat Joe alive. Joe was very upset about it. He longed to win some of those verbal sparring matches, but he knew he couldn't. The only way he could get even was in the ring.

MUHAMMAD ALI: Joe Frazier is so ugly. His mother told me that, when Joe was a little boy, every time he cried the tears would stop, turn around, and go down the back of his head.

JOE FRAZIER: I don't want to knock him out. I want to hurt him. If I knock him down, I'll stand back, give him a chance to breathe. It's his heart I want.

MUHAMMAD ALI: I got something new for Joe Frazier. I got a balloon punch and a needle punch. The balloon punch is a left jab, which swells him up, blows him up, puffs him up. And the needle's gonna bust him. That's the right hand. Whop!

JERRY IZENBERG: Inside the ring, Muhammad Ali and Joe Frazier brought out the best in each other. Outside the ring, they brought out the worst.

DAVE WOLF: It's possible that, by the time Ali and Joe reached Manila, neither one of them was the best heavyweight in the world any more. Joe was nowhere near the fighter he'd once been, and neither was Ali. But as occasionally happens in boxing, their declining curves crossed at exactly the same spot. They were so evenly matched and put so much of themselves into the fight that it was historic.

MUHAMMAD ALI [in an Ali–Frazier III post-fight interview conducted while sitting on a stool in mid-ring]: I was surprised Joe had so much stamina. There was too much pressure. He's the greatest fighter of all times next to me. This is too painful. It's too much work. I might have a heart attack or something. I want to get out while I'm on top. And one more thing. I want everybody to know that I'm the greatest fighter of all times, and the greatest city of all times is Louisville, Kentucky.

BOBBY GOODMAN [a publicist for Ali-Frazier III]: After the Thrilla in Manila ended, Ali went to his dressing-room and collapsed on a couch. He was completely exhausted. I told him the media was waiting for the post-fight press conference. And he said, 'Tell 'em I'm too tired. I can't move.' I'd never seen him like that before, where he couldn't do anything but lie there. But I had to do my thing as a publicist and get someone to the press conference, so I ran across to Joe Frazier's dressing-room. Joe and Eddie Futch were there, very down, very depressed. I said, 'Joe, I know it's tough, but we need you for a post-fight interview. Muhammad is finding it hard to get there. Can you help me out?' They said they'd do it. That gave me the opportunity to run back to Muhammad's dressing-room and say, 'Champ, Joe Frazier's down at the press conference.' Ali found that hard to believe. But finally, he said, 'All right. Get me my robe. If Joe Frazier's there, I'm gonna be there too.'

JOE FRAZIER: Ali was the one who spoke about being nearly dead in Manila; not me.

MUHAMMAD ALI: I got tired of seeing Joe Frazier in the ring. And I guess he got tired of seeing me too, because I whupped him two out of three times that we fought.

LARRY MERCHANT: Ali was a warrior. He was in a hurting business, a hard business, the toughest game there is. And no matter what his style was, underneath it all he was one tough son-of-a-bitch. Most people never thought of him that way. If you looked at how people saw Muhammad Ali, that wouldn't be high on the list. But I'm telling you, in the ring he was as tough a son-of-a-bitch as anyone who ever lived.

DICK GREGORY: We live in a society where we claim we don't want our children to drink. Even drinkers say they don't want their children to drink. But when the World Series, the basketball championships, any great athletic competition is over, there's always champagne. Little kids see their heroes pumping champagne, guzzling champagne, pouring champagne on each other's heads. And until Ali, you never heard praise to God. He was the first great athlete to show the world the importance of prayer. After his fights, right in the ring, the whole world got to see the spiritual Ali. When they put that television microphone in front of him, the first thing Ali always did was give thanks to God, and then the interview could begin.

LEROY NEIMAN: I did a life-size painting of Ali once. It was eight feet tall. John Condon presented it to Ali at some big Madison Square Garden boxing dinner. When the dinner was over, Ali's not going to walk out with an eight-foot painting. So Don King said to him, 'Don't worry, Ali. I'll take care of it for you and see that you get it.' And of course, the next thing you know, the painting is in King's office at Rockefeller Center behind King's desk. Ali asked him about it at one point, but all he got was a lot of double-talk. And Ali acted like he didn't care, because that's the way he is. Then, about a year later, I went to Don's office and the painting wasn't there. I asked what happened to it and he told me Herbert had it. Herbert had taken a shine to the painting and put the screws to Don to get it. And a little while after that, I got a phone call from Ali. Ali actually called me up and said, 'Veronica [his wife at the time] really wants that painting.' I told him Herbert had it, and he said, 'Well, if Herbert has it, I can't get it from him. But if you call Herbert and tell him it's my painting, maybe you can get it.' He gave me Herbert's home telephone number. So I called Herbert and said, 'Ali really wants that painting. He must want it pretty bad, because he asked me to call you. And it's Ali's painting.' Herbert didn't want to give it up. He said, 'How do you know it's Ali's painting? I got it from Don King.' I told him, 'Herbert, I know it's Ali's painting because I gave it to him. I didn't give it to Don King. I gave it to Ali.' Herbert said, 'Well, Ali doesn't really want it. It's Veronica who wants it.' And I told him, 'Herbert, it doesn't matter. I gave that painting to Ali.' Finally, after much pushing and prodding, Herbert sent the painting to Ali. Then, after the divorce, Veronica sold it to Joe Weider.

HAROLD CONRAD: Ali's old man was completely nuts. He always fancied himself a singer; always wanted to sing 'The Star-Spangled Banner' before Ali's fights. We never let him, but I got him a gig once. We were in Puerto Rico for the Coopman fight. They had a half-assed lounge in the hotel, and I asked the manager, 'Do you want to have Muhammad Ali's father singing here?' The manager said all right. So we put him in the lounge and he sang 'My Way' every night.

JERRY IZENBERG: Jean-Pierre Coopman, who was known as 'The Lion of Flanders', was probably the worst fighter that Ali ever fought. Someone involved in the promotion said to me, 'Listen, don't be deceived. This kid can fight. He could hurt you.' And I pointed out, 'Coopman ain't fighting me. He's fighting Muhammad Ali.'

MICHAEL KATZ: Ali looked awful against Jimmy Young, but I go crazy every time somebody tells me they think Young won that fight. You can't win a round by sticking your head out of the ring, which is what Young did all night. Each time a fighter sticks his head out of the ring, that should be a two-point round. It's like seeking shelter during the middle of a fight. You're not allowed to do that in boxing.

RANDY NEUMANN: I was a fringe contender in the mid-1970s. The name of the game was, play your cards right and maybe you could make a couple of hundred thousand dollars by signing to fight Ali. Probably he would have beaten me, because basically I was a jabber and he had the best jab in the business.

But if I'd gotten outpointed, so what? That happened in the gym all the time. And Ali wasn't an intimidating fighter like Foreman or Frazier, who'd beat the crap out of you. In fact, at the end of his career, he was going 15 rounds with guys like Alfredo Evangelista and Jimmy Young, and I was better than they were. In fact, I beat Jimmy Young, and Young almost beat Ali. So Ali was the brass ring that kept me and a lot of guys like me going. I'm sorry I didn't have the chance to fight him. I'd have made a fortune and had a ball.

IRVING RUDD: Madison Square Garden wanted to match Ali with Duane Bobick in 1977. They even had a verbal commitment from Herbert to do the fight for $2,500,000. But then Bundini got to Ali and said, 'The Garden is trying to get you knocked off by a white guy. They want a white guy to win the title.' So Ali told Teddy Brenner that he wanted Earnie Shavers instead. Teddy told him, 'Shavers is a much tougher fight.' But Ali was insistent, so they made Ali–Shavers. And while we were waiting for that fight to happen, Ken Norton destroyed Bobick in 52 seconds. I watched Norton–Bobick with Ali and some of the other entourage members. As soon as it ended, Ali got up, walked over to Bundini and said, 'You dumb nigger, you told me that white boy could fight.' Slap. Slap. 'You dumb nigger. What's wrong with you? I could have fought that white boy for $2,500,000.'

EARNIE SHAVERS: The Acorn. Yeah, I remember. You see, Ali nicknamed a lot of the fighters he fought, and he called me The Acorn because of my shaved head. Well, Ali found out that night that The Acorn is a hard nut to crack.

WILT CHAMBERLAIN: I always felt that the worst chink in Muhammad's armour was that he had no close friends who he trusted, who cared enough about him to give him good advice and help him in the right direction. If he'd had friends like that, they'd have told him, 'The time has come for you to do something besides boxing. Use everything you've got going for you outside the ring, because right now whenever you fight you're getting your head beaten in.' I know for myself, I've been fortunate to have friends with the balls to tell me when it's time to give something up or not do something else, and I've listened to what they had to say. Ali had nobody like that advising him in the right direction. He fought long after he should have retired. And from what I've heard, he was used and continues to be used in ways that aren't very nice.

AL BERNSTEIN: Boxing is like everything else. Nobody quits when they're on top. Frank Sinatra is still singing long past the time when he could sing. There are dozens of ageing sportscasters running around, doing mediocre play-by-play. The only reason Steve Carlton and Tommy John aren't playing baseball any more is that no team would let them. Unlike other sports, boxing has no cuts to make and it doesn't have to put its best players on the field. Promoters are happy to put anyone in the ring if they can make money off them, and most boxing commissions let them. So it's sad, really. Ali should have been one of the guys who got out okay, but he didn't. In the end, even though it was his own fault, there's plenty of blame to go around.

SYLVESTER STALLONE: The people around him were bad people. They used him as a payday and badgered him to go on and on long after he should have quit. They all saw him coming apart. It didn't happen in one night.

BILL RUSSELL: I never saw him fight. I would never go to a fight. I just wouldn't. I went to one a long time ago and I told myself I'd never go back. They're much cleaner on television.

JOHN SCHULIAN: Laughter was constant when you were in Ali's presence. Yet as I think of the pieces I wrote during the last five years of his career, I cannot ignore the capacity he also had for turning a smile upside down.

HUGH MCILVANNEY: No one has been able to explain to Ali that fooling around with dreams of immortality can shorten your life.

JERRY IZENBERG: Ali has a huge head. That made for wonderful photographs. But once his legs began to fail him, it also made a pretty good target.

GIL ROGIN [former Editorial Director for Time, Inc.]: I was lucky. I never had a bad moment with Ali. I wasn't there at the end.

REX LARDNER: It is one of the illusions of Muhammad Ali that, no matter how bloody the carnage in an endless series of battles fought, he will be the last to leave the field.

HUGH MCILVANNEY: The ring activities of Muhammad Ali now have all the grace and sporting appeal of Russian roulette played with a pump-action shotgun. The unquestionable lesson is that it is no longer his time. Muhammad Ali can still preach and philosophise, boast and charm. What he can't do is fight. The genie is gone from the bottle forever.

JERRY IZENBERG: As far as Ali–Holmes is concerned, Ali had come to the right town. If you want to be deluded, go to Las Vegas. That's the place where, whatever you want, they'll pander to it. Whatever dream you have, they'll let you pursue it; but with the clear understanding that, when it's all over, the house wins. So if you wanted to dream that Ali could be heavyweight champion of the world again; that's okay, suckers. Pick a year and we'll freeze the calendar for you – until the bell rings.

JOHN SCHULIAN: What awaits us [in Ali–Holmes] may be a mismatch on the order of cockroach versus heel.

ALEX WALLAU: I'll never forget walking with Howard Cosell two or three days before the Holmes fight. There was an atmosphere in Las Vegas that gave Ali a chance. His physical skills had diminished; his reflexes were shot; his motor skills weren't the same. But there were intelligent ringwise boxing people who thought he might win. I can take you to the exact spot in the parking lot at Caesars Palace where Cosell said to me, 'You know, Holmes is vulnerable to the right hand, and Ali has always been able to land the straight right. I think the old master is going to do it one more time.' And I told him, 'Howard, not only is Ali not going to win the fight; not only is he not going to win a round; he's not going to win ten seconds of any round.'

MICHAEL KATZ: When Ali fought Larry Holmes, he wasn't in condition to shadow box for 15 rounds.

DR DONALD ROMEO [who examined Ali for the Nevada State Athletic Commission before Ali–Holmes and okay'd the fight]: So he takes some blows to the region of the kidneys and there's blood in his urine. Big deal. It clears up in a day or two; end of story. They talk of brain damage. That's a bunch of bunk.

BOB ARUM: Greed is the essence of boxing. And it wasn't only the promoter's greed; it was the regulators' greed. The State of Nevada allowed that fight to happen.

LLOYD PRICE: I was in Vegas for Ali–Holmes and it sickened me. I couldn't handle it. And what I thought about all through that fight was a day I'd spent in New York with Ali and Joe Louis maybe ten years earlier. Joe had been with me because there was a little bird singing in my band who he liked a lot, and Ali and I had been friends for years. Somehow or other, we got together and they were talking, mostly about boxing. I was listening. They got along well that day; no tension of any kind between them. Ali asked, 'Joe, tell me something. What happens in the ring when you get old?' He was asking about Joe's fight against Rocky Marciano, when Joe was 37 years old with that bald spot in the middle of his head; when he got knocked through the ropes and was counted out. Joe said, 'Ali, let me tell you something. When

I was young and wanted to throw a punch, I could throw it as fast as I wanted. But when I got old, my brain would tell me to do something and my arms just wouldn't do it.' Ali was listening, but I don't think he understood what Joe was saying; not until he fought Larry Holmes.

LARRY HOLMES: Don't think that I went to bed those nights and had a good sleep, because I didn't. I was fighting Muhammad Ali. I knew I could beat this guy, but I never knew what trick he had up his sleeve. It was mind-boggling. Everywhere I went, there was Muhammad Ali. I got on the airplane – and who do I see on the airplane? Ali. I get to Las Vegas, and all these newspaper people, camera people, critics – who do they run to? Ali. We went through the casino, and all I heard was, 'Ali! Ali!' And Ali could put a lot of things on your mind if you listened to him. He'd shadow box and show you how quick he was. He'd pull his shirt up and show you how thin he'd gotten. He was always saying, 'Hey, I told you with Sonny Liston. I told you with George Foreman.' And if you listened, you'd believe him. You'd say, 'What the hell am I fighting this guy for?' So it was rough for me to sleep at night. I was fighting Muhammad Ali.

SYLVESTER STALLONE: Ali against Larry Holmes. Oh God, that was painful; like seeing your child playing on the railroad tracks with a train coming and you can't get him out of the way. I just sat there and watched. It was like an autopsy on a man who's still alive. And I also felt for Larry Holmes because he had a terrible job to do and he knew it. He had to go out and dismember a monument.

RED SMITH: If it had been any fighter except Muhammad Ali, he would have been thrown out of the ring and his purse withheld. Only a deity or a myth could get away with the performance Ali gave against Larry Holmes. Sluggish on feet of low-grade clay, unable to throw a respectable punch or ward off Holmes's circumspect attack, Ali struggled through the unappetising charade long enough to fulfil the contract worth six million dollars to him and then quit. When they speak of someone going out with a whimper, it's impossible to recall a champion or former champion who came up so empty at the end. There has always been a certain amount of con man in Ali along with his skills. Now only the con was left.

LOU DIBELLA [boxing promoter and former television executive]: Ali wasn't tarnished by his fight against Larry Holmes. By that point, Ali was above and beyond being tarnished by anything that happened in a boxing ring. But that fight tarnished boxing terribly, and it troubles me enormously that it was allowed to happen. Still, I have to say, it infuriates me whenever people use Ali as an example of why boxing should be banned. What would Cassius Clay have become without boxing?

BILL CAYTON [manager and fight film collector]: They didn't have 'punch stats' when Ali was fighting. But I've reviewed all the films of his fights, and they tell a story that's quite remarkable. When Muhammad was young, he was virtually untouchable. The two hardest punchers he faced in that period were Sonny Liston and Cleveland Williams. There was no clowning around in those fights. The last thing Ali wanted was to get hit. In the first Liston fight, if you throw out the round when Ali was temporarily blinded, Liston hit him with less than a dozen punches per round; most of them jabs. In the second Liston fight, Liston landed only two punches. When Ali fought Cleveland Williams, Williams hit him a grand total of three times the entire night. But if you look at the end of Ali's career; in Manila, Joe Frazier landed 440 times, and a high percentage of those punches were bombs. In the first Spinks fight, Spinks connected 482 times, mostly with power punches. Larry Holmes scored 320 times against Ali, and 125 of those punches landed in the ninth and tenth rounds when Ali was most vulnerable and Holmes was throwing everything he had. Those numbers alone tell you that Ali fought on long after he should have retired from boxing.

JIMMY ELLIS [Ali's childhood friend and, later, WBA heavyweight champion]: We can all look back and say, 'Well, Ali might have fought too long or he might have got hit too many times.' But it's hard to give boxing up when you've been doing it for a long time, and you know you were good, and you know you can still whup some of the guys that's out there, but you just can't beat guys that's on a certain level. It was his decision, you know. He knew what boxing was all about and he knew what he wanted to do. He made his life what it was. And I got to give the man credit. He showed the world he could come back. He won the title three times.

ALEX WALLAU: I'd pick Ali over every other heavyweight in history and that includes Joe Louis. Louis was a more complete fighter and certainly he had a better punch than Ali. But Ali had one extraordinary skill that distorted the equation, and that was his speed. He had the speed to make opponents miss throughout a fight; and the few times they connected, he had the chin and heart to see him through. Also, Louis avoided a lot of tough fighters, particularly the other black heavyweights. And Ali really fought everybody.

FERDIE PACHECO: If you add it all up, Muhammad Ali reigned officially as heavyweight champion for less than seven years. There were three years in the mid-sixties before they took away his title; three years in the mid-seventies after he beat George Foreman; and a few months in 1978–79 after he regained the championship from Leon Spinks. But he dominated boxing for twenty years, and boxing isn't the same without him.

ALI'S NICKNAMES FOR OPPONENTS:
Sonny Liston – The Big Ugly Bear ('Because he's ugly and smells like a bear.')
Archie Moore – The Old Man ('He's old enough to be my grandfather.')
Floyd Patterson – The Rabbit ('In the ring, he's frightened like a rabbit.')
George Chuvalo – The Washerwoman ('He punches like a woman who's washing clothes.')
Ernie Terrell – The Octopus ('He grabs and holds a lot when he fights.')
Joe Frazier – The Gorilla ('He's ugly and looks like a gorilla.')
George Foreman – The Mummy ('George is slow. Clomp! Clomp! He moves like a mummy.')

Earnie Shavers – The Acorn ('He's got a shaved head that looks
   like an acorn.')
Leon Spinks – Dracula ('The man is missing his front teeth.')
Larry Holmes – The Peanut ('His head is shaped like a peanut.')

MUHAMMAD ALI RATES HIS OPPONENTS:
The most skilled as a boxer – Floyd Patterson
The scariest – Sonny Liston
The most powerful – George Foreman
The roughest and toughest – Joe Frazier

MUHAMMAD ALI RATES HIS FIGHTS:
When I was at my best – against Cleveland Williams
The best fight for fans – against Joe Frazier in Manila
The fight that meant the most to me – beating George
   Foreman to win the championship of the world again

MUHAMMAD ALI RATES THE GREATEST HEAVYWEIGHTS OF ALL TIME:
(1) Me
(2) Jack Johnson
(3) Joe Louis

MUHAMMAD ALI'S LIST OF 'THE TEN BEST-LOOKING HEAVYWEIGHT CHAMPIONS EVER':
I'm number one. After me, it don't matter.

DAVE KINDRED: There's no cruelty left in him. As a fighter, it was necessary. As a fighter, you're supposed to be cruel. In the ring, if you're a nice guy, you get knocked out in a hurry. But that cruelty is no longer a part of him.

JOSÉ TORRES: The only bad thing that Ali left behind was his boxing style. His style – hands down, chin up in the air – is detrimental to fighters who try to imitate him because they don't have the timing, the genius and the magic that Ali had. So they try to imitate him and they get knocked out.

EARNIE SHAVERS: Ali did things that nobody did before in life. Never did them after, neither.

TEDDY ATLAS: People talk about Ali being a hero. But a lot of people lose sight of the fact that one of the most heroic things about Ali was his almost complete unselfishness. I'll give you an example. In the 1988 Olympics, Greg Louganis cut his head on the diving board. At the time, Louganis knew he was HIV-positive. Now Greg Louganis is a magnificent athlete. I give him all the credit in the world for his athletic skills and the fact that he continued to live a full life after learning that he was carrying the AIDS virus. But Louganis took the easy, selfish way out. Instead of telling the doctor who treated him, 'Look, you'd better get some gloves,' he put his own personal interest ahead of the safety of the doctor. Now 99.99 per cent of the people in the world would have handled that situation the same way as Louganis. They wouldn't have jeopardised their public image or their chance to win an Olympic gold medal. But by acting the way he did, Greg Louganis knowingly put another man's life at risk. And I don't think Ali would have done that. Muhammad Ali always put other people first. I believe that, if it had been Ali on that diving board, regardless of what it cost him, he would have told the doctor to put on a pair of gloves before he allowed the doctor to suture him up.

HAROLD CONRAD: Ali is a decent man, a kind man; and it doesn't do you any harm to be around one of those. You've got to pick up some of it. Sometimes I wish I could be more like him.

LARRY HOLMES: If you treated Ali right, he'd treat you right. And if you didn't treat him right, he'd still treat you right. That's just one reason why people love Ali.

DICK GREGORY: If people from outer space came to Earth and we had to give them one representative of our species to show them our physical prowess, our spirituality, our decency, our warmth, our kindness, our humour, and most of all, our capacity to love – it would be Ali.

LARRY HOLMES: Ali opens his arms right up to people. They don't have to approach him. He approaches them and makes them feel comfortable.

EARNIE SHAVERS: Ali's got a heart as big as all outdoors and a love that encompasses all people. He's as pretty on the inside as he is on the outside. Always has been; always will be.

DICK GREGORY: If I wanted to teach a little grandchild of mine about the universe, I'd go and get Muhammad Ali's story and say, 'Here is what happened to the universe. One day, something went from nothing to BOOMMMM. The big bang. And it keeps getting bigger.'

LOU DIBELLA: Ali's style has been taken to extremes in ways that I'm sure he never intended it to be. Now you have boastfulness and bragging, but with no sense of irony and no principles behind it. These guys – Deion Sanders, Barry Bonds, all of them – they just don't get it. Ali was the best 'sound bite' in history. Ali was 'prime time' before Deion Sanders was born. Ali did that schtick better than anyone. But with Ali, there was social relevance and substance behind it.

MUHAMMAD ALI: I used to daydream all the time about being successful in boxing and being famous. One time I remember, Floyd Patterson was heavyweight champion of the world. I was at the Olympics in Rome and I went to sleep in my room, pretending I was heavyweight champion. This was even before I won the gold medal. But I lay in bed, pretending I was famous, pretending everyone liked me and looked up to me the way I looked up to Floyd Patterson. And God blessed me. My dream came true. But I got different dreams now. Now I dream about doing something to stop all the hating in the world. I dream about feeding people who are hungry. I dream about children learning how to read and write. And sometimes, when I'm really dreaming, I dream about being a rock star like Elvis or Little Richard.

JOHN THOMPSON [former Georgetown University basketball coach]: In 1989 before the start of the NCAA tournament, I played a tape of Ali for the team. It was a tremendous piece, a documentary that I wanted them to see as an inspirational thing. Then, in the locker room right before the first game, I talked with them about motivation and confidence. And just before they went out on the floor, the kids put their hands together and shouted, 'Float like a butterfly, sting like a bee. Rumble, young man, rumble. Ahhh!' Then the game started, and we came within a basket of losing to Princeton.

KWAME TURÉ: Muhammad Ali has a responsibility, and he knows what that responsibility is. His image must be used for positive reasons. His image must be used to advance humanity; his image must be used in the struggle against injustice; and his image must be used to harness souls towards a belief in God.

JEFFREY SAMMONS [professor of African-American studies]: One of the things that troubles me about Ali is his association with conservative Republicans. And finally, I came to the conclusion that Ali likes power: real power. In fact, I don't have any question about it. He likes the spotlight, the attention, the stage; that's part of it. But there has always been something more. I think Ali has always wanted power. When he was boxing, he had a legitimate power base outside of the political system because of his affinity for people and skill at media manipulation. Because of the political and racial climate, he was an important figure. But that political and racial climate has passed him by, and boxers rarely have much influence after they leave the game. Yet, in his mind, Ali still seeks power. And I believe he feels the only way he can have that power now is by associating with powerful people. But it's no longer on his own terms. It has to be on theirs.

JULIAN BOND: Watching Ali with Ronald Reagan and Orrin Hatch was worse than watching him against Larry Holmes.

JERRY IZENBERG: During the [1991] Persian Gulf War, there was virtually no resistance from the Iraqi military. And as speculation about Saddam Hussein's strategy continued to mount, you began to hear that maybe he was conducting some form of 'rope-a-dope' defence. Now the use of that phrase tended to obscure the fact that tens of thousands of people were dying. But it also said something about the way in which Muhammad Ali has transcended sports and entered the world's consciousness.

DAVID HALBERSTAM: One of the great things about this country is that you can invent yourself and reinvent yourself many times. And Ali was a true American original in every aspect of his life. I mean, really; what other country in the world could have created Muhammad Ali? If you look at his childhood, his rise, his complexity and contradictions, he's unmistakably American. He might be a Muslim, but he's a hell of an American too. And it speaks well for this country, not only that we created him, but also that we came to understand what he was about in time to admire him; that he's not a prophet without honour in his own land.

WILLIAM NACK [sportswriter]: Even though he's still with us, I miss him. I miss his voice. I miss his sense of the absurd. Ali had a sense of the unpredictability and craziness and hypocrisy of life. I wish he was still running around, making speeches and doing all the other things he used to do. You know, in addition to being the quintessential civil disobedient and a walking lesson in decency and independence, Ali was one of the few people I know of who could make almost anyone laugh out loud.

ROBERT LIPSYTE: Athletes die young. And ultimately, all athletes make a Faustian bargain that they have to pay off on in the end. So for the people who hated Ali, everything is fine now. He's a ruin; he's a wreck. And in retrospect, weren't they confident all the time that it would end this way as they moved on with their own civil-service kind of lives towards picket fences, retirement and whatever else they think of as security.

TIM WITHERSPOON: One thing bothers me about me and Ali. [In 1986] I was getting ready to fight Tony Tubbs in Atlanta. And to sell tickets for the fight, Don King brought Ali in to spar with me. That's when people were starting to talk a lot about how Ali took too many punches and he's not co-ordinated and he's not talking right. Ali wanted to slow the talk down, so he sparred with me for a week. Every day, he had on a sweatsuit, headgear, mouthpiece. And in the ring, he's telling me to hit him in the head. 'You can punch me; hit me hard. Come on, sucker; give me your best shot. Go to the head.' In my mind, I didn't want to do it. But I was training for a world championship fight, so I went to his body pretty hard. I only went to his head a little bit. But I went to his body hard.

RALPH BOSTON: I'm not sure I'm good enough with words to express what I feel when I see Ali today. Maybe what I should say is, I remember all the chance meetings he and I had, passing each other in airports, heading in different directions. I'd see him through the crowd and wave, and he'd wave back, and maybe we'd talk for ten seconds. At the beginning, he was always so incredibly vocal and alive. But then I began to see that he was getting a step slower and talking a little softer. And seeing him now – he's still alive, he's still sharp mentally – but it bothers me.

DICK SCHAAP: As the years have gone by, I think it's become harder and harder to be Muhammad Ali. It's probably the toughest role that anybody has had to play in the twentieth century. And to play that role 24 hours a day, day after day, year after year; I think that's taken as much of a toll on him as the punches.

LOU DIBELLA: I hear people talking about how they feel sorry for Ali, and isn't what happened to him terrible. But to be honest with you, I don't have that reaction. Sure; it makes me sad that his health isn't what it used to be. But he's still the same person. He still enjoys life. The sense of decency and principles that drove him in the 1960s still drive him. What does bother me, though, is the way some people react to Ali: like he's infirm or mentally deficient or in need of care. Watching people react to Ali like that depresses me. Seeing Ali himself is still very much uplifting to me.'

LONNIE ALI: There are times when Muhammad allows his physical condition to take things away from him unnecessarily. He doesn't speak as often as he should; partly because he doesn't like the way he sounds, and partly because he can accomplish most of what he wants to accomplish by communicating non-verbally. Still, I have to say that Muhammad isn't as self-confident as he used to be, and still should be. Sometimes, I think back to how in love he was with the camera, and how in love the camera was with him. And it makes me sad to see the way Muhammad sometimes shies away from cameras today.

BETTY SHABAZZ: Muhammad Ali has been a giver and not a taker. He lived life as he saw it. I look at his physical condition and I cannot bear it. I know he could have done differently; but he didn't, so we accept what he is. I hope that people will speak kindly of him, always.

RALPH WILEY [sportswriter]: People look at Ali's condition today and say, 'That's sad.' But they forget that, over the years, Ali punched a lot of people. He did damage to other people's brains too.

JOE FRAZIER: God has shut him down. He can't talk no more because he was saying the wrong things.

MUHAMMAD ALI: I'd rather be punished here in this life than in the hereafter.

JULIAN BOND: Ali doesn't say as much now as he did before, but he doesn't have to. He said it all, and said it when almost no one else would.

TIM WITHERSPOON: When I see Ali today, the way he is now, I wish it wouldn't be.

ROY JONES [after a 1997 mock sparring session with Ali in which no blows were struck but a lot of strategising went on]: When I'm fighting, the first thing I do is, I want to see my opponent's jab to find out if there are any flaws in it. The first time my opponent makes a mistake, I pick up on it. The moment Ali and I started sparring, I could see he was searching for the hole, looking for a flaw in my jab. Right away, he picked up on something I do that I can get away with because of my speed. He thought there was a flaw and he found it. I've never seen anyone who could go out and search for the flaws that quickly. I said to myself, this guy fights like I do. I run fights against guys like Sugar Ray Robinson and Marvin Hagler through my head from time to time. I have a strategy for beating all of them. So after sparring with Ali, I asked myself, 'If I was fighting the young Muhammad Ali and we were both the same size, what would I do?' I don't know the answer. If I was fighting the young Ali, I'd try to get inside his head, jab with him, go to the body. There'd be no sense in trying to knock him out. But then again, it would be very hard to outpoint him. In a lot of ways, it would be a tactical fight. But to be honest, against Ali when he was young, I don't see much that anyone could do with him. And I'll tell you something else. Sparring with Ali has made me feel better about where he's at today. Physically, he's still strong and a lot quicker than I thought he'd be. The man could get in a boxing ring tomorrow and beat the average person walking down the street easily.

REGGIE JACKSON: Muhammad likes me. I can feel him like me. I don't think he knows or understands or cares what I've accomplished in baseball. I've told him that I was called Mr October, but that doesn't mean anything to him. He has no idea that I hit five hundred home runs or what that means. Still, I have to say, it's a nice feeling, to be liked by Muhammad Ali.

RON BORGES: I was in Miami for the Super Bowl a couple of years ago. It was a Friday night, and I was on a bus full of sports-writers who were about to leave for one of those big Super Bowl parties. Anyway, I looked up and there was Ali getting on the bus. The first thing Ali did when he got on was reach out and shake hands with the bus driver. And of course, not a single one of us on the bus except for Ali had in any way acknowledged the driver. Then we got to the party. We walked in and the first thing Ali did was shake hands with two waiters who were at the door. Don Shula saw Ali and came running over, but Ali stood there talking with the waiters and Shula had to wait his turn. That's the way Ali was the entire night. All the little people – the wait-ers, the busboys, the people that most of us never bother to think about – Ali stopped for every one of them.

FERDIE PACHECO: Ali has an awareness that he's somebody gigantic in this world. But the truth is, he's remarkably humble and it's not an artificial humility. As far as using ego in the sense of a Hollywood actor or some superstar athlete who's puffed up by his fame and self-importance, there's none of that. 'I'm the great Ali, give me a hotel room.' Never. 'I'm Ali, get me on this airplane even if you have to throw someone else off.' Not a chance. He's just not like that.

CRAIG HAMILTON [boxing collectibles expert]: I remember going to a sports memorabilia show at Hofstra University. Ali was there and I had some photographs I wanted him to sign. He was sitting at a table. I handed him the photos. He looked at each one very carefully. And one came up; it was that famous photo you've seen of Cassius Clay sitting on a mountain of money. Anyway, Ali stared at the photo for a long time and then he asked how much money I wanted for it. I said what I hope anyone would say under those circumstances: 'Champ, it's yours.' And I'll never forget: Ali stood up, put his arms around me and hugged me like I'd just given him, not the photo, but the whole mountain of money. That's the way Ali is. He appreciates every little thing that anyone does for him and doesn't think twice about giving away the world.

LOU DIBELLA: One night, several years ago, I took my wife to dinner in Manhattan. As we were walking to the restaurant, I saw something close to a mob on the sidewalk. It was a crowd of people around Muhammad Ali, who was signing autographs. Anyway, my wife and I had dinner. And when we came out of the restaurant, Ali was still there, playing with kids, posing for pictures, signing for everyone who came up to him. I think about that now, when I look at today's athletes, who in the larger scheme of things mean absolutely nothing, who make millions of dollars, who won't take five seconds to give a kid an auto-graph. And I compare today's so-called 'superstars' with Ali; a man in his fifties with Parkinson's syndrome, standing on the street that night, embracing every person he met.

MUHAMMAD ALI: Every time I give an autograph, the person I give it to goes off happy and smiling and keeps my autograph for ever. And to me, it's just a little thing, no more than a couple of seconds.

DR DENNIS COPE [one of Ali's personal physicians]: In the end, what impresses me most about Muhammad is his extraordinarily charitable spirit. He's an incredibly giving man and always seems able to marshal the resources to help whoever might be around him. I remember one time when he was at the UCLA Medical Center. There was a patient in the hospital, an elderly man who was near death, who was a big fan of his. I asked Muhammad if he would go down to see him, and Muhammad said yes. We went down to this other patient's room, but he was off the floor for a procedure. I said to Muhammad, 'Well, that's too bad; we weren't able to see him.' And Muhammad said, 'No, let's wait for him.' We waited for half an hour, and the man still hadn't come back, so Muhammad said, 'Let's go look for him.' Finally, we found him. Muhammad talked with him for a while and then went back to the room with him and they talked some more. This man's spirits were so lifted by meeting Muhammad. I can't tell you how happy it made him. He talked about it constantly until he died. I've been astounded so many times like that by

Muhammad's capacity to give. I've never seen him disappoint anybody who wanted a moment of his time.

LONNIE ALI: It's gratifying for Muhammad to see the way people respond to him. And what's even more gratifying is the way young people who weren't even born when Muhammad was fighting are drawn to him. These are five- and six-year-old children, who come up to Muhammad and hug him. It's truly a blessing from God that the love Muhammad has for people and the love people have for him keep growing from generation to generation, and that every new generation of children seems to know who Muhammad is.

BETTY SHABAZZ: One of the things that has been constant through Muhammad Ali's life is that he loves children. His children, other people's children. I don't think that Muhammad Ali could have too many children.

MARYUM ALI: Everybody knows what my father was like when he was young; the boxing, the controversies, I am the greatest. But they don't understand what he's doing now and how deeply he believes in Islam. As soon as he changed his name to Muhammad Ali, he began making plans to propagate Islam when he retired. No one took him seriously then. People said, 'Well, he won't really do anything like that.' But he has. He meant it then and he's doing it now.

MUHAMMAD ALI: If I could go back in time, I'd like to be there the day Muhammad received the first revelation from God and went home to tell his wife about it. And I'd like to be there with Moses the day he opened up the Red Sea; and with Jesus on the day of the crucifixion to see if it was really him on the cross, because Muslims believe it was someone else.

ROGER WILKINS: I was the co-ordinator of Nelson Mandela's trip through the United States in 1990, and I was extraordinarily moved by the sustained love and joy that greeted him from one end of the country to the other. But after a while, it began to wear him down. Every big-shot politician and celebrity wanted a piece of him. They were all grabbing and grasping. Mandela went through it with incredible grace, but I will tell you, he was unimpressed by the behaviour of many of the politicians and so-called superstars that he came in contact with. Then we got to Los Angeles, which is star-studded to begin with, and they turned out every star you can imagine. Mandela was more than tired by then; he was exhausted. We were walking together at yet another fund-raising event. Mandela was leaning on me. And all of a sudden, I saw his face light up as I'd never seen it light up before. He looked past me with a radiant smile. I felt his entire body straighten up and come to life. Almost reverentially he whispered, 'Champ.' And, of course, walking towards us was Muhammad Ali.

ALEX HALEY [author of *Roots* and Malcolm X's collaborator on *The Autobiography of Malcolm X*]: I see Muhammad Ali today very much as a spiritual leader. You know, here's a man who can go into the Islamic world, which is huge beyond our imagination, and you need troops to clear the way for him. I don't know if there's anybody on earth who could go to those countries and draw the crowds that Muhammad Ali can draw. To tell you the truth, and I don't mean to be irreverent, I doubt the Pope could draw crowds as large as Muhammad Ali. I think he's probably the single most powerful religious figure in this country, and maybe in the world, today.

MUHAMMAD ALI: If you love God, you can't separate out and love only some of His children. To be against people because they're Muslim is wrong. To be against people because they're Christian or Jewish is wrong. To be against people because they're black or white or yellow or brown is wrong. Anyone who believes in One God should also believe that all people are part of one family. People are people. God created us all.

RAMSEY CLARK: To me, Muhammad Ali is a totally spiritual person. It doesn't have to do with the Christian faith in which he was raised, and it doesn't have to do with the Islamic faith to which he converted; both great religions. It has to do with his love for life, his faith in the human spirit and his belief in the equality of all people. I see Ali as a human being whose sense of purpose in life is to help others. He must lay awake at night, wondering what he can do to help people, because wherever people are in need, his priorities are there. He sees children who are right next to him, but children who are starving in Africa and threatened by bombing in Iraq are also within the scope of his imagination. He wants to help everyone and he travels at great personal burden and financial expense to be wherever he's needed. I say, God bless him. He makes an enormous difference.

MUHAMMAD ALI: Life is short; we get old so fast. It doesn't make sense to waste time on hating.

FERDIE PACHECO: I'm sure that God looks down on Ali from time to time, shakes his head in wonderment, and smiles.

EARNIE SHAVERS: And on the eighth day, God created Ali.

BILL CLINTON: Muhammad Ali taught us all that, whatever colour you are, whatever religion you are, you can be proud of who you are.

JERRY IZENBERG: This is a man who spent his whole life telling the world, 'I am the Greatest!' And whenever you got exasperated with him and said, 'Shut up, because you're not,' he'd do something to prove that he was.

RALPH BOSTON: There are lots of good athletes and a few great athletes. But there's only one Ali.

DAVE KINDRED: Rainbows are born of thunderstorms. Muhammad Ali is both.

JERRY IZENBERG: People don't really think of Ali as being black any more. He's one of a kind; he's Muhammad Ali. That's the wonderful ultimate irony: that this man who was once viewed as a dangerous militant black nationalist revolutionary should turn out to be without colour in the eyes of America.

RALPH BOSTON: If a young boy were to ask me today, 'Why should I care about Muhammad Ali?' I'd tell him, 'Because Ali cares about you.' That might be hard for some people to understand, but that's the way Ali is. He cares about every single person on this planet.

JOHN CARLOS: Muhammad Ali is love.

PART IV

LEGACY

THE LOST LEGACY OF MUHAMMAD ALI

(2004)

In 1960, shortly after the Rome Olympics, a Soviet journalist asked Cassius Marcellus Clay Jr how it felt to win a gold medal for his country when there were restaurants in the United States that he was forbidden to eat in. Clay's response was short and sweet: 'Tell your readers we got qualified people working on that problem. To me, the USA is the best country in the world, including yours.'

Seven years later, that same young man was one of the most vilified personages in America.

People today understand that Muhammad Ali defied the United States government and alienated mainstream America because he stood up for his principles. But they don't know what those principles were. Generally, they are aware that, after beating Sonny Liston to capture the heavyweight championship in 1964, Clay announced that he had accepted the teachings of a religion known as the Nation of Islam and changed his name to Muhammad Ali. Thereafter, he refused induction into the US

Army during the height of the war in Vietnam. But to younger generations, Ali today is famous primarily for being famous. There has been a deliberate distortion of what he once believed, said and stood for. History is being rewritten to serve political, social and economic ends.

Thus, it's important to revisit the Muhammad Ali who, in the words of author Dave Kindred, was 'as near to living flame as a man can get'.

In the early 1960s when Ali first entered the public consciousness, sport was considered one of the few areas where black Americans could compete on equal footing with whites. But in reality, sport reflected the old order. Black athletes could become stars, but only within guidelines dictated by the establishment. And away from the playing fields, as Ali himself once noted, 'Many coloured people thought it was better to be white.' Black Americans were scorned, demeaned and denied even self-love.

In 1961, while in Florida training for a fight, Cassius Clay met a man named Sam Saxon. Saxon was one of a small group of adherents (known to the media as 'Black Muslims') who attended Nation of Islam meetings at a Miami temple and followed the black separatist teachings of a self-proclaimed 'messenger' named Elijah Muhammad. Clay accepted Saxon's invitation to attend a Nation of Islam service, and thereafter was indoctrinated with the tenets of the religion.

The Nation of Islam taught that white people were devils who had been genetically created by an evil scientist with a big head named Mr Yacub. It maintained that there was a wheel-shaped Mother of Planes half a mile wide in the sky, manned by black men and that, on Allah's chosen day of retribution, fifteen hundred planes from the Mother of Planes would drop deadly explosives, destroying all but the righteous on earth. Neither of these views are part of traditional Islamic thought or find justification in the Qur'an. Moreover, while the concepts of Heaven and Hell are central to traditional Islamic doctrine, the Nation of Islam rejected both.

Herbert Muhammad, one of Elijah Muhammad's sons, later explained and sought to defend his father's teachings as follows:

> Black people knew their life was bad. They wanted something to make it better. And my father's message was to gain dignity and self-respect and make black people the master of their own needs. As long as other people controlled what we needed, then these people would be able to control us. So my father sought to make black people self-reliant and take them away from gambling, alcohol, prostitution and drugs. He taught us that the answer to what black people need is in God and in ourselves. And you have to ask what it was that enabled my father to get a man or woman off drugs when right now the whole government can't do it. You have to ask what it was that could bring a man out of prison, and the next month have that man be clean-shaven, wearing clean clothes, completely clean. You see, my father saw that black people had a deep inferiority complex. He saw that white people had a great superiority complex. And by the whites being in an upper-hand position, blacks would never come up

unless someone gave them a philosophy that they were better than whites.

From 1964 until his conversion to orthodox Islam in 1975, Muhammad Ali was the Nation of Islam's most visible and vocal spokesman in America. Nation of Islam teachings were at the core of who he was at that time in his life. Among the positions Ali preached were:

On integration: 'We who follow the teachings of Elijah Muhammad don't want to forced integrate. Integration is wrong. We don't want to live with the white man; that's all.'

On intermarriage: 'No intelligent black man or black woman in his or her right black mind wants white boys and white girls coming to their homes to marry their black sons and daughters.'

On the need for a separate black homeland: 'Why don't we get out and build our own nation? White people just don't want their slaves to be free. That's the whole thing. Why not let us go and build ourselves a nation? We want a country. We're forty million people, but we'll never be free until we own our own land.'

On brotherhood: 'We're not all brothers. You can say we're brothers, but we're not.'

Ali was black and proud of it at a time when many black Americans were running from their colour. 'He lived a lot of lives for a lot of people,' said social activist Dick Gregory. 'And he was able to tell white folks for us to go to hell.'

For more than a decade, Ali was the gloved fist of John Carlos and Tommie Smith every day of the year. The establishment media, and sportswriters in particular, came down hard on him. Jim Murray of the *Los Angeles Times* labelled Ali the 'white man's burden'. Jimmy Cannon of the *New York Journal American* called his ties to the Nation of Islam 'the dirtiest in American sports since the Nazis were shilling for Max Schmeling as representative of their vile theories of blood'.

A lot of white liberals and black Americans also took issue with Ali. 'I never went along with the pronouncements of Elijah Muhammad that the white man was the devil and that blacks should be striving for separate development; a sort of American apartheid,' said Arthur Ashe. 'That never made sense to me. It was a racist ideology, and I didn't like it.'

Joe Louis added his voice to those opposing Ali and opined, 'I'm against Black Muslims. I've always believed that every man is my brother. Clay will earn the public's hatred because of his connections with the Black Muslims. The things they preach are just the opposite of what we believe.'

Former heavyweight champion Floyd Patterson concurred with Louis, declaring, 'I've been told that Clay has every right to follow any religion he chooses, and I agree. But by the same token, I have every right to call the Black Muslims a menace to the United States and a menace to the Negro race. I do not believe God put us here to hate one another. I believe the preaching of segregation, hatred, rebellion and violence is wrong. Cassius Clay is disgracing himself and the Negro race.'

Still, whether or not one liked what Ali represented, it was clear that his demand for full entitlement for all black people was on the cutting edge of an era. And to many, he was the ultimate symbol of black pride and black resistance to an unjust social order. In that vein, Jeremiah Shabazz, who was one of Ali's first teachers within the Nation of Islam, recalled, 'When Elijah Muhammad spoke, his words were confined to whatever city he had spoken in. But Ali was a sports hero and people wanted to hear what he had to say, so his visibility and prominence were of great benefit. His voice carried throughout the world.'

Outside the ring, Ali was never violent. His threat to the status quo was one of ideas, which is ironic because he himself was never a 'thinker'. But beneath it all, there was fear within the establishment that the ideas Ali preached could be converted to rebellion in the streets. Indeed, one can make the case that Ali and the Nation of Islam frightened the powers that be in America into embracing the agenda of moderate civil rights leaders as a way of muting the cries of those who wanted more.

Arthur Ashe later recalled, 'I can tell you that Ali was very definitely, sometimes unspokenly, admired by a lot of the leaders of the civil rights movement, who were sometimes even a little bit jealous of the following he had and the efficacy of what he did. There were a lot of people in the movement who wished that they held that sort of sway over African-Americans but did not.'

'Muhammad was probably the first black man in America to successfully break with the white establishment and survive,' posited civil rights pioneer Andrew Young.

And before Cassius Clay ever changed his name, Malcolm X maintained, 'Clay will mean more to his people than Jackie Robinson, because Robinson is the white man's hero but Cassius is the black man's hero.'

'It's very difficult to imagine being young and black in the sixties and not gravitating towards Ali,' Bryant Gumbel later recalled. 'He was a guy who was supremely talented, enormously confident, and seemed to think less of what the establishment thought of him than about the image he saw when he looked in the mirror. And to people who were young and black and interested in tweaking the establishment, and in some cases shoving it up the tail of the establishment, you had to identify with somebody like that. The fact that he won all the time made it even better. You know, for all our passions of those years, we didn't have a lot of victories. More often than not, we were on the losing side, so the fact that Ali won was gravy. He was a heroic figure, plain and simple. In every sense of the word, he was heroic.'

The civil rights movement and Ali as a fighter both peaked in the mid-1960s. Then the war in Vietnam intervened.

In 1964, Ali had been classified 1-Y (not qualified for military service) as a result of scoring poorly on a Selective Service mental aptitude examination. Then, in early 1966, with the war expanding and manpower needs growing, the test score required for induction into the armed forces was lowered, leaving him eligible for the draft. Ali requested a deferment, but on 17 February 1966, his request was denied and he was reclassified 1-A (available for the draft). Several hours later, a frustrated Ali blurted out to reporters, 'I ain't got no quarrel with them Vietcong.'

The following day, Ali's outburst was front-page news across the country, and the sporting press raged against him. Red Smith of the *New York Times* proclaimed, 'Squealing over the possibility that the military may call him up, Cassius makes himself as sorry a spectacle as those unwashed punks who picket and demonstrate against the war.' Jimmy Cannon continued the assault: 'Clay is part of the Beatle movement. He fits in with the famous singers no one can hear and the punks riding motorcycles with iron crosses pinned to their leather jackets and the boys with their long dirty hair and the girls with the unwashed look and the college kids dancing naked at secret proms held in apartments and the revolt of students who get a check from dad every first of the month and the painters who copy the labels off soup cans and the surf bums who refuse to work and the whole pampered style-making cult of the bored young.'

Ali wasn't a political thinker. His initial concern over being drafted wasn't religious or political. It was that of a 24-year-old who thought he had put the draft behind him and then learned that he was in danger of having his life turned upside down.

'Muhammad never studied day-to-day current events like the thousands of white kids who opposed the war,' Jeremiah Shabazz later acknowledged. 'But even though he was unso-phisticated in his thinking, he knew it was a senseless, unjust war. And of course, in addition to that, Muslims following the Honorable Elijah Muhammad decided long ago that we weren't going to fight the white man's wars. If he starts them, he can fight them.'

On 28 April 1967, citing his religious beliefs, Ali refused induction into the US Army. 'Clay seems to have gone past the borders of faith,' Milton Gross wrote in the *New York Post*. 'He has reached the boundaries of fanaticism.'

Less than eight weeks later, on 20 June, Ali was convicted of refusing induction into the armed forces and sentenced to five years in prison. He was stripped of his title and precluded from fighting by state athletic commissions throughout the country. His 'exile' from boxing lasted for more than three years.

Ali's refusal to accept induction was part and parcel of a schism within the civil rights movement.

'The more conservative black leadership was troubled by his opposition to the war,' Julian Bond later recalled. 'The civil rights movement at that time was split. There was one group of people who said, "Let's not have any opinion about the war because this will alienate us from the powers that be, from President Johnson and successor presidents." And there was another group that said, "Listen, this war is wrong. It's killing black people disproportionately; it's draining resources that could be applied to the war on poverty; it's wrong in every respect." So people in the first group were horrified by Ali. They thought he was a dunce manipulated by the Nation of Islam. And those in the second group felt entirely differently about him. Still,' Bond continued, 'it's hard to imagine that a sports figure could have so much political influence on so many people. When a figure as heroic and beloved as Muhammad Ali stood up and said, "No, I won't go," it reverberated through the whole society. People who had never thought about the war before began to think it through because of Ali. The ripples were enormous.'

Andrew Young had similar memories in recalling the reaction of his own mentor, Martin Luther King Jr, to Ali's decision.

'Martin made his most publicised speech against the war in Vietnam at Riverside Church [in New York] on 4 April 1967; exactly one year to the day before he was assassinated,' Young remembered. 'It was soon after that speech that Muhammad refused to take the step forward, and I know Martin was very proud of him.'

However, others within the black community took a less favourable view of Ali's conduct. 'He's hurting the morale of a lot of young Negro soldiers over in Vietnam,' said Jackie Robinson. 'And the tragedy to me is, Cassius has made millions of dollars off of the American public, and now he's not willing to show his appreciation to a country that's giving him a fantastic opportunity.' Joe Louis was in accord with his baseball counterpart, saying, 'Anybody in America who don't want to fight for this country; I think it's very bad, especially a guy who has made a lot of money in this country. I was champion at the time World War Two started; and when my time came up, I had to go. I think that he should fight for his country.'

More significantly, though, Vietnam deflected attention from Ali's racial views and put him in a context where many whites and white opinion-makers could identify with him. There had been an ugly mood around Ali, starting with the assassination of Malcolm X in February 1965. Thereafter, Ali seemed to take on a bit of the persona, not just the ideology, of the Nation of Islam. But when the spotlight turned from Ali's acceptance of an ideology that sanctioned hate to his refusal to accept induction into the US Army, he began to bond with the white liberal community, which at the time was quite strong.

Thus it was that Ali was martyred and lived to talk about it. Ultimately, he returned to boxing. After wins against Jerry Quarry and Oscar Bonavena, he lost a historic 15-round decision to Joe Frazier at Madison Square Garden. Then his conviction for refusing induction into the US Army was reversed by the United States Supreme Court on a procedural technicality. After that, Ali reeled off ten more victories but suffered a broken jaw in a 12-round loss to Ken Norton. That made him an 'underdog' in the eyes of America. People who had once bristled at his words and conduct began to feel sorry for him.

Ali earned a measure of revenge against Frazier and Norton with victories in hard-fought rematches. Then, on 30 October 1974, he dethroned George Foreman to recapture the heavy-weight championship of the world. But more importantly, by that time, America had turned against the war in Vietnam. It was clear that Ali had sacrificed enormously for his beliefs. And whether or not people liked the racial component of Ali's views, there was respect for the fact that he had stood by them.

On 10 December 1974, Ali was invited to the White House by President Gerald Ford. It was an occasion that would have been unthinkable several years earlier and marked a turning point in the country's embrace of Ali.

Then, on 25 February 1975, Elijah Muhammad died.

'After Elijah died,' Ali said later, 'his son Wallace took over as leader. That didn't surprise us, because we'd been told Wallace would come after his father. But what surprised some people was, Wallace changed the direction of the Nation. He'd learned from his studies that his father wasn't teaching true Islam, and Wallace taught us the true meaning of the Qur'an.'

Elijah Muhammad's death marked a seismic shift for the Nation of Islam and foreshadowed a significant change in Ali's public pronouncements on race. In the past, the public and private Ali had seemed almost at war with one another over whether white people were truly evil. Now Ali was able to say openly, 'I don't hate whites. That was history, but it's coming to an end.'

Some of Elijah Muhammad's adherents refused to accept the teachings of his son Wallace. Ministers like Jeremiah Shabazz and Louis Farrakhan maintained that Elijah had been a prophet and continued to preach what he had taught them. Meanwhile, Ali's religious views were evolving and he later acknowledged, 'When I was young, I followed a teaching that disrespected other people and said that white people were devils. I was wrong. Colour doesn't make a man a devil. It's the heart and soul and mind that count. What's on the outside is only decoration. Hating someone because of his colour is wrong. It's wrong both ways; it don't matter which colour does the hating. All people, all colours, got to work to get along.'

Ali is now a living embodiment of Martin Luther King Jr's message that all people are deserving of love. As Jerry Izenberg, one of America's foremost sports journalists, observed, 'Ironically, after all he went through, the affection for Ali is largely colour-blind. Late in his career, he developed a quality that only a few people have. He reached a point where, when people looked at him, they didn't see black or white. They saw Ali. For a long time, that mystified him. He expected black people to love him and crowd around him, but then he realised white people loved him too; and that made him very happy.'

Ali's love affair with America and the world reached its zenith in 1996. Fifteen years earlier, his public profile had dropped after his retirement from boxing. Thereafter, if Ali appeared at an event, those in attendance were excited but he wasn't on the national radar screen.

Then Ali was chosen to light the Olympic flame in Atlanta. It was a glorious moment. Three billion people around the world watched on television and were united by love and caring for one man. But there's a school of thought that the 1996 Olympics carried negatives as well, for it was in Atlanta that corporate America 'rediscovered' Ali. Since then, there has been a determined effort to rewrite history. In order to take advantage of Ali's economic potential, it has been deemed desirable to 'sanitise' him. And as a result, all of the 'rough edges' are being filed away from Ali's life story.

'Commercialisation is a natural process in this country,' says Jerry Izenberg. 'But the Ali I fell in love with wasn't for sale. He fought the good fight in and out of the ring, and that was payment enough for him. He wasn't looking to get paid in dollars, and the true worth of the stands he made wasn't commercial. Then corporate America latched onto Ali at the Olympics,' Izenberg continues, 'and he became a gravy train for everyone who wants to make a movie or sell something to the public. But the public gains nothing when Ali is commercialised and marketed the way he is today.'

No event crystallised the commercialisation of Ali more clearly than his appearance at the New York Stock Exchange on 31 December 1999. That was an important day. By most reckonings, it marked the end of a millennium. The Ali who won hearts in the 1960s could have been expected to celebrate the occasion at a soup kitchen or homeless shelter to draw attention to the plight of the disadvantaged. Many hoped to see Ali spend 31 December 1999 in a spiritual setting. Instead, the man who decades earlier was a beacon of hope for oppressed people around the globe and who refused to become a symbol for the US Army became a symbol for the New York Stock Exchange.

'If it [the stock market] goes up, then you will have been blessed by my presence,' Ali told the assembled financial elite. 'If it goes down, I had nothing to do with it.' As the clock struck midnight, Ali was in Washington, DC, dining on beluga caviar, lobster and foie gras. That saddened a lot of people. Ali makes his own decisions, but those decisions are made based on how information is presented to him. One can be forgiven for thinking that, had the options been explained differently to him, he would have chosen to serve as a different symbol that day.

The commercialisation of Ali is also typified by the 2001 feature film that bears his name. The movie *Ali* represented a unique opportunity to depict its subject for generations, now and in the future, that didn't experience his magic. It cost the staggering sum of $105,000,000 to make and was backed by a multinational promotional campaign that cost tens of millions of dollars. But instead of being faithful to its subject, *Ali* rewrote history.

Ali featured countless factual inaccuracies for 'dramatic purposes', as though Ali's life to date hasn't been dramatic enough. The screenplay was disjointed, and the film suffered from the hard reality that no one but Ali can play Ali. But the biggest problem with the movie was that it sanitised Ali and turned him into a virtual Disney character.

'I hated that film,' says director Spike Lee. 'It wasn't Ali.'

'The movie was appalling,' adds Robert Lipsyte, who for years covered Ali as a *New York Times* reporter. 'They got the plastic covering on Elijah Muhammad's living-room furniture right, but that's about all.'

'Will Smith playing Ali was an impersonation,' adds Jerry Izenberg, 'not a performance.'

Also, in an effort to remove all of the warts from Ali's character, *Ali* the movie painted a portrait of its subject – and in the process, of America – that was flat-out wrong. Some of this sanitisation, such as reducing Ali's profligate womanising to a single meaningful relationship, is understandable. Ali's penchant for the opposite sex, while at odds with his public religious pronouncements, was not at the core of his public persona. But other omissions were far more damaging to the historical record and integrity of the film.

For example, Ali's cruelty towards Joe Frazier was completely ignored. In real life, Ali played the race card against Frazier in a particularly mean-spirited way. For the entertainment of white America, he labelled Joe as ugly and dumb. And at the same time, speaking to black America, he branded Frazier an Uncle Tom, turning him into an object of derision and scorn within the black community. The latter insult was particularly galling. Joe Frazier is a lot of things, not all of them good. But he's not an Uncle Tom. Yet to this day, there are people who think of him as a less-than-proud black man because of Ali's diatribes more than three decades ago.

'One of the many paradoxes about Ali,' says historian Randy Roberts, 'is that he embraced an ideology that disparaged white people; yet he was never cruel to white people, only blacks. Except for occasional humorous barbs, Ali's white opponents were treated with dignity and respect. But things got ugly with Floyd Patterson, Ernie Terrell and Joe Frazier. And sure, Patterson and Terrell might have asked for it because of things they said. But Joe was innocent. And to deny the cruelty of what Ali did to Joe Frazier is to continue to be cruel to Joe.'

In truth, it takes a certain amount of cruelty to be a great fighter. Let's not forget: Ali beat people up and inflicted brain damage on them as his livelihood and way of life for years. And the time when he was at his peak as a fighter coincided with the time when he was most openly angry at the circumstances he found.

Thus, the biggest problem with the film was not its portrayal of Ali's conduct but its misrepresentation of his thoughts. In an effort to create a simple conflict between good and evil (with Ali being good), the movie ignored the true nature of the Nation of Islam. Watching the film, the audience was left with the impression that Nation of Islam doctrine is Islam as practised by more than one billion people around the world today. *Ali* depicted only that portion of Nation of Islam teachings that highlighted black pride, black self-awareness and self-love.

Moreover, in promoting the view that America turned against Ali in the 1960s because he was a 'Muslim' – as opposed to a member of the Nation of Islam – the makers of *Ali* fed into the dangerous view that America is 'anti-Islam'. The truth is, there were people who assailed Ali because they thought he was unpatriotic. There were people who assailed Ali because he was spouting a racist ideology or because they thought he was an 'uppity' black man who didn't know his place. But Americans did not assail Ali because he was a Muslim. Other public figures such as Lew Alcindor, who converted to orthodox Islam and changed his name to Kareem Abdul-Jabbar, were not vilified for their religious beliefs.

In sum, Ali is now being retroactively turned into a forerunner of Michael Jordan and Tiger Woods. 'A bargain has been struck,' says Robert Lipsyte. 'Ali and the people around him get their money. And I'm glad Ali is making money. He's showing great gallantry in the face of his physical condition, and he never made what he should have made before. But the trade-off is, Ali is no longer threatening. He's safe; he's comfortable. He's another dangerous black man who white America has found a way to emasculate. You know, white America still hasn't figured out how to deal with powerful black male figures who don't play football or basketball other than to find ways to tame them and take away any real power and influence they might have. So the bottom line is, if we can control Muhammad Ali, it makes us more powerful. And at long last, we've brought Muhammad Ali under control.'

Mike Marqusee, author of *Redemption Song: Muhammad Ali and the Spirit of the Sixties*, is in accord with Lipsyte and observes, 'Ali's power in the Third World grew precisely because he was a symbol of defiance against racism and the use of United States military power abroad. And those issues are very much alive today; so it means a lot to the powers that be if Ali can be used to suggest to the rest of the world that they aren't problems anymore. Governments and corporations have this incredible power to incorporate imagery and attach whatever meanings they choose to that imagery in pursuit of their goals. Nothing can take away Ali's past. It happened; it's part of history. But that history is now being plundered and deliberately obscured to sell commercial products and, more significantly, ideas. Ali is being reduced to serving as a mouthpiece for whatever ideas and products those with influence and power want to sell. And the people guiding him are letting it happen for narrow financial reasons.'

'Most great athletes can sell Wheaties,' notes Ramsey Clark. 'But they can't impact upon social and political issues. It's very hard, if not impossible, to do both.'

Clark's voice is significant. As Attorney General of the United States, he oversaw as a matter of duty the 1967 criminal prosecution of Ali for refusing induction into the US Army. However, he has long been aligned with liberal causes and has worked closely with Ali on a number of occasions.

'There's a common tactic among the dominant opinion-makers,' says Clark. 'They want to influence the population they're communicating with, so they transmit information selectively and create an image that's unreal but very powerful. On the one hand, they'll demonise their subject. Or in the other direction, they'll overlook the sins of someone they want to popularise and focus on the aspects of that person's life which reflect values they want to promote. It's a question of what those in power want to impose and consider safe. And what we have now in many of the depictions of Ali is the portrait of a man who is heroic, well-intentioned and good – all of which he was and still is – but who is presented to us in an unreal, artificial manner.'

Ron Borges of the *Boston Globe* has followed Ali and the American scene for decades. 'It's not uncommon for historical figures to slip out of focus when removed from their time by several generations,' says Borges. 'But this is something more. There's a deliberate distortion of what Ali's life has been like and what his impact on America really was. Maybe someone thinks that this sort of revisionism makes Ali more acceptable. But acceptable to whom and for what purpose other than selling products and making money? They're cutting out all the things that made him Ali. Frankly, I wonder sometimes what Ali is about these days other than making money. I know that, underneath the facade, Ali is still there. But to a lot of people, it's like he's a ghost. Twenty-year-olds today have no idea what Ali was about. As far as they're concerned, he's just another celebrity. That's what it has come to, and it steals Ali's true legacy.'

Dave Kindred authored a number of ground-breaking stories about Ali for the *Atlanta Constitution* and *Washington Post.* 'In the past,' says Kindred, 'there were reasons, a lot of them, for admiring and respecting Ali. Now you're asked to admire and respect him because he's a living saint. And I never thought of Ali as a saint. He was a rogue and a rebel, a guy with good qualities and flaws who stood for something. But now, it seems as though he stands for everything and nothing. All of the barbed edges have been filed down. His past is being rewritten. They're trying to remove any vestige of Ali that might make it harder to use him to sell automobiles or expensive watches or whatever other product he's endorsing at the moment. That, to me, is the heart of it. Ali today seems to be blatantly for sale. He's trotted around to high-profile events and events where he's paid large sums of money for being there, and often I find myself asking, "What's he doing there?" I assume he enjoys it. I'm sure he likes the attention. His need for the crowd has always been there and he's entitled to the money. But the loss of Ali's voice is very sad. And I'm not talking about his physical voice, because the people around Ali have figured out a way to deal with his infirmities and still keep him centre stage. I'm talking about content and hard edge and the challenge that attached to some of the things Ali said in the past. There was a time when Ali forced us to think about race and religion and many of the other fundamental forces that affect our lives. He was right on some things and wrong on others, but the challenge was always there. And that Ali is gone now, with the result that there's a whole new generation – two generations, actually – who know only the sanitised Ali, and that's very sad.'

Jeffrey Sammons, a professor of African-American studies at NYU and author of *Beyond the Ring: The Role of Boxing in American Society*, is in accord. 'What's happening to Ali now,' says Sammons, 'is typical of what has happened to so many black figures. It's a commodification and a trivialisation. Maybe the idea is that, by embracing Ali as a society, we can feel good about having become more tolerant. We can tell ourselves that we're not like those bad people in the 1960s who took away Ali's title and his right to fight. But by not showing what Ali was, we're also not showing what American society was at that time. And if the rough edges on Ali are filed down, you have the revision of history in a very dangerous way. By distorting America's past, you make it impossible to understand the past. And if you can't understand the past, then you won't be able to understand the present or the future.'

None of the above comments is intended to take away from Ali's greatness. Each of the speakers is a long-time admirer of Ali. Each of them would no doubt agree with the assessment of boxing maven Lou DiBella, who says, 'In many respects, the way Ali is portrayed today is simply a reflection of how well-loved he is and the fact that he's a great person. All of us are open to adoration and, in Ali's case, he deserves it. He's older, wiser and mellower now than he was decades ago. He enjoys being who he is. And whatever good things he gets, he deserves them.'

Still, Ali's legacy today is in danger of being protected in the same manner as the estate of Elvis Presley is protecting Elvis's image. New generations are born; and to them, Ali is more legend than reality, part of America's distant past.

Meanwhile, 2004 has brought more of the same. The year began with IBM, Gillette and Adidas featuring Ali in multinational commercial campaigns. Taschen Books published an Ali coffee-table tome bound in silk and Louis Vuitton leather that retails for $3,000 a copy with a 'special edition' that sells for $7,500. The book is entitled *GOAT*, which is an acronym for 'Greatest of All Time' and also the name of Ali's personal company.

'I think it's significant,' says Jerry Izenberg, 'that the book is named after Ali's corporation and not Ali.' Then Izenberg adds, 'For those who didn't live through the 1960s, it takes some work to understand the true importance of Ali. And people are lazy; the media is lazy. No one wants to read and study. So they take the product that's given to them by IMG, Columbia Pictures and others, and accept it whole cloth. The result is that, the further removed in time we become, the more Ali is distorted. And I get very angry about that because the distortion of history breeds ignorance. If Ali isn't remembered as the person he truly was, we'll all be poorer. It will wipe out some very important lessons that America learned. Let's face it; most people today don't have a clue about Ali. They have no idea what Ali and the country went through in the 1960s. Ali isn't the same person now that he was then. Like most of us, he changed as he grew older. But I don't worry about the changes in Ali. I worry about the misperception of what Ali stood for. Ali can be all things to all people but, unless there's truth, it's worthless.'

Ali in the 1960s stood for the proposition that principles matter; that equality among people is just and proper; that the war in Vietnam was wrong. Every time he looked in the mirror and preened, 'I'm so pretty,' he was saying 'Black is beautiful' before it became fashionable to do so. Indeed, as early as March 1963, *Ebony* magazine declared, 'Cassius Marcellus Clay – and this fact has evaded the sportswriting fraternity – is a blast furnace of racial pride. His is a pride that would never mask itself with skin lighteners and processed hair, a pride scorched with memories of a million little burns.'

And Ali's role in spreading that pride has been testified to by others:

> Arthur Ashe: 'This man helped give an entire people a belief in themselves and the will to make themselves better.'

> Reggie Jackson: 'Muhammad Ali gave me the gift of self-respect.'

> Hosea Williams: 'Ali made you feel good about yourself. He made you feel so glad you are who you are; that God had made you black.'

In sum, the experience of being black changed for millions of men and women because of Ali. But one of the reasons Ali had the impact he did was because there was an ugly edge to what he said.

By focusing on Ali's ring exploits and his refusal to serve in Vietnam, while at the same time covering up the true nature of Nation of Islam doctrine, the current keepers of Ali's legacy are losing sight of why he so enthralled and enraged segments of American society. And equally important, by rewriting history and making Ali out to be in the mainstream of the black civil rights movement, the revisionists demean Ali's personal struggle because they gloss over the extent to which he was cut off from mainstream support.

Thus, Ramsey Clark warns, 'Legacies are important but they have to be true. The distortion of a legacy is a distortion of public truth and a disservice to history, as are all distortions of values and character.'

Ali himself once recalled, 'For three years, up until I fought Sonny Liston, I'd sneak into Nation of Islam meetings through the back door. I didn't want people to know I was there. I was afraid, if they knew, I wouldn't be allowed to fight for the title. Later on, I learned to stand up for my beliefs.'

Ali's views have changed since then, but he is unrepentant regarding what he once believed. 'Elijah Muhammad was a good man,' Ali has said, 'even if he wasn't the Messenger of God we thought he was. Not everything he said was right, but everyone in the Nation of Islam loved him because he carried what was best for us in his heart. Elijah taught us to be independent, to clean ourselves up, to be proud and healthy. He stressed the bad things the white man did to us so we could get free and strong. If you look at what our people were like then, a lot of us didn't have self-respect. We didn't have anything after being in America for hundreds of years. Elijah Muhammad was trying to lift us up and get our people out of the gutter. I think he was wrong when he talked about white devils, but part of what he did was make people feel it was good to be black. So I'm not apologising for what I believed.'

It's the ultimate irony then, that so many of the people shaping Ali's legacy today are 'spin-doctoring' with regard to his beliefs. Ali stood up for his convictions and sacrificed a great deal for them. Indeed, in a recent commercial for IBM's Linux system, Ali speaks the words, 'Speak your mind; don't back down.' So why hide the true nature of what Ali's principles were?

Also, it should be said that, in 2004, there's a particularly compelling reason to mourn the lost legacy of Muhammad Ali.

We live in an age marked by horrific divisions among the world's cultures and religions. If we are to avoid increasingly violent assaults and possibly a nuclear holocaust, the people of the world must learn to understand others with alien beliefs, find the humanity in their enemies and embrace that which is good in those they abhor.

Muhammad Ali is the ideal messenger for this cause. He is a man who once preached an ideology that was anathema to most Americans; an ideology that he himself now rejects in significant measure. Yet America has found the humanity in Ali, embraced the good in him, and taken him into its collective heart. And vice versa.

Also, it should be noted that, were he so inclined, Ali is still capable of influencing public debate. All he would need to say is two words regarding the current war in Iraq: '*It's wrong!*' That wouldn't dictate what people think, but it would have a significant impact on what a lot of people thought about. However, instead, Ali has held to the theme advised by those around him and advanced when he was asked about al-Qaeda in June 2002.

'I dodge those questions,' Ali told David Frost on HBO's *Real Sports*. 'I've opened up businesses across the country, selling products, and I don't want to say nothing and, not knowing what I'm doing, not [being] qualified, say the wrong thing and hurt my businesses and things I'm doing.'

It's hard to imagine Muhammad Ali in the 1960s declining to comment on war and racism for fear that it would hurt his business ventures.

Great men are considered great, not only because of what they achieve, but also because of the road they travel to reach their final destination. Sanitising Muhammad Ali and rounding off the rough edges of his journey is a disservice both to history and to Ali himself. Rather than cultivate historical amnesia, we should cherish the memory of Ali as a warrior and as a gleaming symbol of defiance against an unjust social order when he was young.

THE LONG SAD GOODBYE

Muhammad Ali told me in 1997 that he planned on living until age 90. We were on a bus in Boston en route to an elementary school for an assembly devoted to teaching students about tolerance and understanding. Muhammad's speech was noticeably affected by then as a consequence of Parkinson's syndrome. But he was still physically strong and his thought processes were clear.

As we approached the school, Ali was reminiscing about some of the departed souls who had played a significant role in his life. His father, Elijah Muhammad, Sonny Liston, a few others. 'Ninety would be good,' he told me. 'I think I'll live to be 90. But if I'm feeling good when I'm 89, I might change my mind and ask God to let me live longer.'

Ali, unfortunately, didn't feel good as he got older. Not physically. And his decline was on display for the whole world to see.

★ ★ ★

In September 1984, Muhammad Ali checked into the Columbia-Presbyterian Medical Center in New York for an eight-day series of diagnostic tests.

'I'm not suffering,' Ali told reporters. 'I'm in no pain. It's really nothing I can't live with. But I go to bed and sleep eight, ten hours. And two hours after I get up, I'm tired and drowsy again. Sometimes I have trembling in my hands. My speech is slurred. People say to me, "What did you say? I can't understand you." I'm not scared, but my family and friends are scared to death.'

Ali, in 1984, was suffering from a series of symptoms – slurred speech, difficulty in maintaining balance, a facial mask and a tremor in his hands – known as Parkinson's syndrome.

Dr Stanley Fahn is Director of the Center for Parkinson's Disease and Other Movement Disorders at Columbia University. In 1984, he was the supervising physician for Ali's evaluation at Columbia-Presbyterian. Fahn spoke openly with me regarding Ali's medical condition pursuant to a waiver that Muhammad had signed to facilitate my research when I was writing *Muhammad Ali: His Life and Times.*

Ali did not have Parkinson's disease in 1984. His condition, Dr Fahn concluded, had been caused by physical trauma that destroyed cells in his brain stem.

'He has asked that I speak freely and completely,' Dr Fahn told me. 'So I'll tell you my diagnosis that it was a post-traumatic Parkinsonism due to injuries from fighting. It's highly unlikely that it all came from one fight. My assumption is that his physical condition resulted from repeated blows to the head over time.'

In the three decades that followed, the world witnessed something unprecedented for its transparency and duration: the long slow sad physical decline of one of the most beloved icons of all time.

We watched Ali slowly and inexorably lose one physical characteristic after another; his movement, his voice, his good looks. Once, his face had sparkled with happiness. In his later years, there were times when it seemed as though all the suffering and cares of the world were etched on that face. Instead of being drawn to images of Ali with anticipation and joy, we expected the worst. It prepared us for the end.

Boxing takes a heavy toll on those who practise the trade. No fighter knows with certainty that the sweet science will lead him to a dark place. Few fighters believe that what happened to Joe Louis, Sugar Ray Robinson and countless others will happen to them.

But all of the heavyweight champions who reigned before Ali claimed the throne died before he did. Muhammad had 61 professional fights against 50 different opponents. Twenty-eight of those men are known to have predeceased him. And Ali inflicted brain damage on his opponents too. The punishment wasn't all one way.

People talk about the lineage of heavyweight champions. Jack Dempsey beat Jess Willard who beat Jack Johnson, and so on back to James Corbett who beat John L. Sullivan. But there's another kind of lineage.

Like Ali, Joe Louis was a larger-than-life symbol as a fighter. Boxing fans of a certain age remember Louis in a wheelchair being brought to ringside on 2 October 1980, as Muhammad Ali was about to be brutalised by Larry Holmes. Once, Joe Louis had embodied America. He was the symbol of a nation's strength as it readied for the inevitable confrontation with Adolf Hitler's evil empire.

Budd Shulberg's notes of Louis at ringside for Ali–Holmes read as follows: 'Joe Louis wheeled in – mouth hangs open – eyes staring. He holds his head in his hands. An attendant wipes spittle from his mouth. His head sags. He sees nothing. The crowd cheers as Ali comes down the aisle. Louis doesn't see him.'

Later that night, Schulberg wrote, 'Our Joe Louis, the greatest before "The Greatest", destroyer of Max Schmeling, slumped beside me in his wheelchair. After the early rounds of the fight, in which Larry Holmes established immediate dominance and exposed Muhammad Ali as an old man, we found ourselves calling on the Lord of this cruel sport to spare us the sight of a wheelchair for Ali.'

In the ring, Ali always got up. In and out of the ring, he was willing to pay the price to accomplish what he wanted to achieve. At the end of his life, we saw the price.

We wanted Ali to become a hale, hardy old man like Jack Dempsey and Gene Tunney, who grew old gracefully together. It wasn't to be.

In the new millennium, Ali's physical condition crossed over a line. He went into shock from a kidney problem. There was surgery to fuse a disc in his neck. He was taken to the hospital on several occasions after falling unconscious.

Ronald Reagan and Margaret Thatcher each suffered a long, slow physical and mental decline at the end of their respective lives. But the image of a weak, impaired Ronald Reagan or Margaret Thatcher was never disseminated to the world. Ronald Reagan could have been brought to a fund-raising event, had his hand raised and smiled for the camera. It would have generated millions of dollars. But he was protected and shielded from public view.

Ali and the people charged with his wellbeing chose a different path. The decision to keep Muhammad in the public eye was an inspiration to many. It was a reminder that all people, no matter how debilitated in mind and body they might be, are deserving of respect, care and love.

But the consequence of this decision was that the entire world was aware of Ali's decline. We saw it happening before our eyes.

In December 2014, George Foreman told me, 'I look at a man's insides. And Muhammad Ali is about the only human being I know of who has had no sign of deterioration inside. He was so special, and it's still there inside him. Muhammad is as beautiful on the inside today as he ever was.'

That said, the young Ali – strong, vibrant, rebellious – was a glowing representation of youth. He was arguably the most handsome, most charismatic, most physically gifted person on earth. To see this man, who once floated like a butterfly and stung like a bee, confined to a wheelchair, unable to lift his head, was heartbreaking.

We live in a world with sunsets and roses, Mozart's music and the Sistine Chapel, happiness and love. But concomitant with these glories is the knowledge that we will all die. If we live long enough, each of us will become physically and mentally impaired to some degree.

Some endings are sadder than others. There are good 'golden years' and golden years that are not so good. Ali's good years were great. His final years were not so kind. His very public physical decline spanned three decades.

We could tell ourselves that this wasn't our decline; that it was happening to someone else; that we didn't take the blows to the head that Ali took. But for those who lived through Muhammad's glory years, following the arc of his extraordinary life to its inevitable end was a reminder of our own mortality.

That's the dark side of reality.

Twenty-five years ago, Ali told me, 'I don't want anyone to feel sorry for me, because I had a good life before and I'm having a good life now. It would be bad if I had a disease that was contagious. Then I couldn't play with children and hug people. But my problem with speaking bothers other people more than it bothers me. It doesn't stop me from doing what I want to do and being what I want to be.'

Lonnie Ali built on that theme, saying at the time, 'It's scary for anybody to experience a physical decline. But when the whole world is watching and so much of your life has been defined by your physical skills, to lose that is very difficult. And what happened was, for the first time in Muhammad's life, he became intimidated. He stopped speaking as freely as before because he was afraid that, as soon as he opened his mouth, people would say, "Listen to Muhammad; he can't even talk." Then other people tried in good faith to explain away the situation by saying, "Muhammad is bored; Muhammad is tired; Muhammad is fine; he's just a little depressed." And those people might have been trying to help, but the truth is, Muhammad does have a physical problem. And that problem shouldn't be treated in hushed tones as an embarrassment any more than cancer or a stroke. Muhammad faces up to his condition, and so should everybody else.'

Ali's physical condition worsened markedly after that. His symptoms became more pronounced. In his final years, when he tried to speak, the words didn't come out. He found it increasingly difficult to communicate, not just with the public, but with those he loved. It was sad for everyone who cared about Ali. And it was sad for Muhammad. But one had the sense that he was at peace with himself.

In early 2015, Rasheda Ali (one of Muhammad's daughters) told me, 'When my dad was first diagnosed, he was devastated. That would be true of anyone. But he doesn't put a lot of meaning on what's happening now. It's the afterlife that matters to him. And how he feels about it transforms how we feel about it. The good days as far as his communicating effectively are fewer and further in between. But he can talk if you catch him at the right time. It depends on which day and what time of day you're with him. The disease has its own mind.

'He's my dad,' Rasheda continued, 'so I look at it differently from the rest of the world. I want to be able to talk with him whenever I want. "Hey, Dad, what's going on?" Ask him for advice, and do all the things that a father and daughter do together. But for most of my life my dad has had difficulty talking, so I experience it differently from the way other people who knew him way back when might experience what's happening now. Every day presents new challenges. But he has a lot of love and support, which many people in his condition don't have. And he never complains. It hasn't destroyed his spirit.'

Ali's faith ameliorated his suffering. He comforted himself with the belief that his final years were a transition period as he waited to enter heaven.

'I accept it as God's will,' he said. 'I know that God never gives anyone a burden that's too heavy to carry. What I'm going through now is short in time compared to eternity.'

Rasheda Ali put matters in further perspective, saying, 'I never ask, "Why him?" because he never asks, "Why me?"'

Ali spent very little time in his life looking back with regret. One moment that I remember well from our experiences together came when Lonnie read a quotation from television boxing analyst Alex Wallau to Muhammad. Wallau had expressed the view that, even if Ali had foreknowledge of how boxing would affect his physical condition, 'If he had it to do all over, he'd live his life the same way. He'd still choose to be a fighter.'

When Lonnie read those words, Ali responded immediately, 'You bet I would.'

In that vein, Kareem Abdul-Jabbar long ago observed, 'When I see Ali, part of me feels sad, but I know what it's all about. It's the result of his having had every bit of fun that he wanted to have.'

George Foreman holds to a similar view. In December 2014, George told me, 'We're all born with our own personal journey. To me, what's sad is if a person never had a gleam in his eye. Ali has had a wonderful life. And he has lived his life with a gleam in his eye. He's a beautiful man. I'm still jealous of him.'

But certain realities are hard to ignore.

Jerry Izenberg knew Ali as well as any writer. 'We had a pretty good idea of what Ali once was,' Izenberg observed as 2014 drew to a close. 'We don't know what he is now. There's a person inside. I know that. And he carries his personal history in him. But I don't care what anyone says; he's not Muhammad Ali any more. I'm fighting to block what I see now from entering my mind any more than it has to. This isn't the way I want to remember him.'

Ali's second wife also struggled with what she saw.

Khalilah Ali Camacho grew up in the Nation of Islam. She married 25-year-old Muhammad Ali on 17 August 1967, when she was 17 years old. They had four children together: three girls (Maryum, Rasheda, Jamillah) and a son (Muhammad Jr). Ali was a womaniser at that time in his life and was unfaithful throughout the marriage. There were public liaisons with other women and several children out of wedlock. Ten years later, they were divorced.

I spoke at length with Khalilah on 19 December 2014.

'The way it started for me in terms of seeing Ali's illness,' Khalilah recalled, 'was I hadn't seen him for a while. Then I saw him at Maryum's wedding [in the mid-1990s]. He was shaking and he was talking funny. I couldn't understand what he was saying. It scared me. I said to him, "Something is wrong. You shouldn't be like this." And he told me, "Sometimes I don't talk clear. But I ain't fighting no more. It will be okay."'

It wasn't okay.

'He didn't deserve this,' Khalilah said during our interview. 'In his heart, Ali is a good man. It hurts so much to see him like this. If he hadn't gotten old so fast, who knows what else he might have done. People make choices. Sometimes the choices are good, and sometimes they're not. Ali did so many crazy things. Good crazy, bad crazy. Some of the best choices he made were when he was young. He made bad choices as a family man, but most of the other choices he made when he was young were good. The struggles he went through and conquered were an inspiration. He lost his way for a while, but I believe that, spiritually, he's in a good place now. His faith has gotten stronger. He prays that he goes to Heaven, that he'll spend eternity in a happier place.'

Then I asked Khalilah when the last time was that she'd seen Ali.

'I think it was at Joe Frazier's funeral [on 15 November 2011]. Lonnie and her sister, Marilyn, were trying to walk Ali in. I'm thinking, "Don't try to walk him. Get a wheelchair. That's what wheelchairs are for. He was suffering, trying to walk. I worked in a hospital. I know what it is to be a caretaker. Don't make him struggle to walk. Get him a wheelchair." Finally, they got him in his seat, and I went over to say hello. Whenever I see him, I try to say something happy. He kept looking at me. He was trying so hard to be nice, but he couldn't talk. It brought tears to my eyes, seeing him struggling to communicate. And you know what's really sad to me? Ali doesn't laugh or even smile any more. He used to laugh a lot, and he had the prettiest smile ever.'

Larry Holmes was also at Joe Frazier's funeral. Like Frazier, Holmes hit Ali hard in the head. Although, as Larry is quick to point out, Muhammad hit him too.

'Joe's funeral was the last time I saw Ali,' Holmes told me in December 2014. 'I went over and shook his hand. I've seen him on TV a few times since then. Each time, he looks worse than he did before.'

'It's a shame,' Holmes continued. 'But it was all up to him. Ali should have stopped fighting when he couldn't get away from punches any more. But he did what he wanted to do. I thought I'd be 25 for the rest of my life too.'

Then Holmes's thoughts turned to Ali's relationship with Joe Frazier.

'You have to separate out Ali the man and Ali the symbol,' Holmes said. 'People put Ali on a pedestal, but he had flaws just like everyone else. Look at the way Ali treated Joe. Joe was my man. I liked Joe. Joe and I used to hang out. The last time I saw Joe was a few weeks before he died. I was in Philly and saw him before he went into the hospital. It was two buddies, just hanging out, talking about people, music, everything. And you know what happened to Joe. He was broke, living in a room above his gym. And they were selling the gym. I feel sadder about the way Joe ended than I do about Ali. None of us is promised tomorrow. What happened to Ali can happen to anyone. But it's more likely to happen if you do what a fighter does.'

Lennox Lewis is well aware of that.

Lewis retired from boxing in 2004 while still heavyweight champion of the world. In the years that followed, as was the case with Ali, he was offered tens of millions of dollars to fight again. Unlike Ali, Lennox stayed retired.

'It's a bad feeling to see Ali the way he is today,' Lewis told me shortly before Christmas 2014. 'I grew up watching Ali. He was my hero. When I was boxing, people would say to me, "Look at the condition Ali is in." It saddened me, but it also made me look ahead and understand that it was important that I leave boxing with all of my faculties.'

'We're not just boxers,' Lennox continued. 'We're fathers; we're husbands. We're sons and brothers and friends. I have a different life now, and I enjoy my new life just as much as I enjoyed my old one. I'm getting old, but I'm getting old in a good way. To see Ali, my hero, my icon, the way that he is now saddens me. But I learned some very important lessons from him. One of those lessons is that time is always going forward. That has special meaning for boxers because boxing is such a dangerous sport and we're dependent to such a great degree on our physical skills.'

As Ali became increasingly disabled, more and more people tended to think of him as a symbol and forget that there was a person inside. But unlike many infirm ageing people, he wasn't avoided or ignored.

The 1960s were the foundation of Ali's importance. The 1970s were a victory lap and vindication for what he represented. By the time he defeated George Foreman in 1974, his most important work in and out of the ring was complete.

Lighting the cauldron at the 1996 Olympics in Atlanta was the last building block for the Ali legend. It gave people from all over the world the opportunity to celebrate his life on a grand stage and tell him how much they loved him.

The cauldron was slow to light. The flames from the torch licked at Ali's hands and arms. His body was shaking. But he wouldn't submit. He refused to let go of the torch until the job was done.

That was two decades ago. There were celebratory moments after that, but most of them were bittersweet.

In his final years, Ali made numerous public appearances, many of them in conjunction with fund-raising events to benefit the Ali Center in Louisville and other charitable organisations.

On 19 February 2012, he attended a 70th birthday party in his honour at the MGM Grand Hotel and Casino in Las Vegas. Six weeks later, Ali was at the opening of the new Florida Marlins baseball stadium in Miami. That was followed by an appearance at the London Olympics in July 2012 and an unannounced visit to a Baltimore Ravens practice in September. 2013 saw a fund-raiser in Phoenix to benefit research dedicated to finding ways to better treat Parkinsonism. On 30 October 2014, Ali attended a Louisville versus Florida State college football game.

All of these appearances were marked by people showing their adoration for Ali. They wanted to be in his presence to pay homage to him. He was old. He was mute. But he was still Muhammad Ali.

Each time that Ali appeared in public, the images were transmitted within minutes around the world. The fact that he couldn't talk publicly in a way that was understood underlined his problems. The silence was deafening.

As Ali's voice was stilled, the world was subjected to a stream of public statements and tweets in his name. The words were attributed to Ali, but they were written in ways he never spoke and didn't come close to matching his spirituality or what had once been his fire and trademark wit.

'They might speak in Ali's name,' Khalilah Ali observed. 'But I know how Ali thinks. I've known him for more than 50 years, and that's not Ali.'

'One of the saddest things to me,' Khalilah continued, 'is that Ali lost the control of his own life. Even when he was healthy, he let people control him if they knew how to play the religion. They manipulated him. They controlled what he did and they controlled the money. Now, because of the illness, people control him in a different way. He can't talk any more, not at all. So they can say he said whatever it is they want him to say.'

In February 2013, Rahman Ali (Muhammad's brother) told *The Sun*, 'My brother can't speak. He doesn't recognise me. He's in a bad way. He's very sick. It could be months, it could be days. I don't know if he'll last the summer. He's in God's hands. We hope he gently passes away. It's best he goes now. The longer he goes on, so does his suffering and misery.'

In January 2014, Muhammad Ali Jr stated publicly that there was 'no chance' his father would survive the year and said, 'I just want, hope and pray to God that this awful disease takes my dad sooner rather than later.'

On 20 December 2014, Ali was hospitalised with pneumonia. He was living a long-drawn-out end-game as a prelude to the time when he would be forever young. Yet through it all, his incredible heart kept beating.

Did what the world saw in Ali's final years impact upon how he'll be viewed by future generations? This wasn't how he wanted to be remembered. What will the lasting image of Ali be?

Ali has special meaning for those who lived through the 1960s. 'You have no idea how much he meant to us' is a refrain that's often heard. He was an important part of the fabric of so many lives.

Jim Lampley recounted for this author being at an American Broadcasting Company function the night that Ali fought Larry Holmes.

'It was one of those luxurious happenings where they showed the fight on closed-circuit television in a big room with exquisite food and as many A-list celebrities as possible,' Lampley recalled. 'The fight had reached a point where it was hard to watch. Ali was getting brutalised. Sometime around the eighth round, Mick

Jagger, who was there, tapped me on the shoulder and said to me, "You know what we're watching, don't you? It's the end of our youth."'

Younger generations have no first-hand memories of Ali in his prime. People under age thirty today might have respected Ali. But they didn't love him the way preceding generations loved him because they didn't live through his time. The images from recent years of a physically debilitated Ali will always exist as part of the world's consciousness. These images are how two generations experienced Ali 'in real time'. Anything more is history to them and the shared memories of people who are older than they are.

It will take time for the image of the ageing Ali to fade away and for the image of the young Ali to be restored. But endless video of Ali in his prime is available for the watching. As time passes, the healthier, more vibrant, electrifying man he once was will return to focus through the lens of history. Future generations may well see Ali more clearly than young people do now.

For many years, I've been asked what I thought Ali's legacy would be apart from his greatness as a boxer. Each time, I pointed to his being an exemplar of black pride and his refusal to accept induction into the US Army.

'He stood as a beacon of hope for oppressed people all over the world,' I'd say. 'The experience of being black changed for tens of millions of people because of Ali. Every time he looked in the mirror and said, "I'm so pretty," he was saying "Black is beautiful" before it became fashionable. And when he refused induction into the US Army, he stood up to armies all over the world in support of the proposition that, unless you have a very good reason for killing people, war is wrong.'

But in recent years, I've come to believe that there's an equally important component of Ali's legacy. He was the embodiment of love.

Ali doesn't need eulogies. The way he lived his life is tribute enough. In the ring, he epitomised the romance of boxing and also the horror of it. As a fighter, there was something almost spiritual within him that allowed him to go beyond the physical limitations that most fighters have. He evoked the words of Lord Byron: 'There is that within me which shall tire torture and time and breathe when I expire.'

Boxing brought glory to Ali, and Ali brought glory to boxing. But his reach extended far beyond the sweet science. Most fighters are remembered by history for what they did in a boxing ring. Ali will be remembered just as vividly for what he did outside the ropes. He elevated his sport into a metaphor for American society. Over time, the entire planet became his stage. May his life be fairly remembered. He was a hero to the heroes of our time.

Mark Twain once observed, 'It is curious that physical courage should be so common in the world and moral courage so rare.' Ali had both. He didn't change the world as much as he wanted to, but the world is better today because he was here. He brought joy to virtually everyone he encountered and was a warm presence in our lives. If he thought that he could do something to help someone, he did it. He was in love with life and had more love in him than anyone I've ever known. He didn't have to meet people to touch them.

One of the things that people fear most about death is the thought of being forgotten. Ali enjoyed a status that has been conferred upon only a handful of men and women in history. He will be remembered for as long as there are people on Earth. He became immortal in his own lifetime.

Don't cry because he's gone. Smile because we had him. He did what he was meant to do. His dreams inspired the world.

MUHAMMAD ALI'S RING RECORD

Professional record: 56 wins, 37 by KO; 5 losses, 1 by KO

OLYMPIC RECORD

Yan Becaus (Belgium)	KO 2
Genadiy Schatkov (USSR)	W 3
Tony Madigan (Australia)	W 3
Zbigniew Pietrzykowski (Poland)	W 3

(Won Olympic Light-Heavyweight Gold Medal)

PROFESSIONAL FIGHTS

1960

29 Oct	Tunney Hunsaker	Louisville, KY	W 6
27 Dec	Herb Siler	Miami Beach, FL	KO 4

1961

17 Jan	Tony Esperti	Miami Beach, FL	KO 3
7 Feb	Jim Robinson	Miami Beach, FL	KO 1
21 Feb	Donnie Fleeman	Miami Beach, FL	KO 7
19 Apr	Lamar Clark	Louisville, KY	KO 2
26 Jun	Duke Sabedong	Las Vegas, NV	W 10
22 Jul	Alonzo Johnson	Louisville, KY	W 10
7 Oct	Alex Miteff	Louisville, KY	KO 6
28 Nov	Willi Besmanoff	Louisville, KY	KO 7

1962

19 Feb	Sonny Banks	New York, NY	KO 4
28 Mar	Don Warner	Miami Beach, FL	KO 4
23 Apr	George Logan	Los Angeles, CA	KO 6
19 May	Billy Daniels	New York, NY	KO 7
20 Jul	Alejandro Lavorante	Los Angeles, CA	KO 5
15 Nov	Archie Moore	Los Angeles, CA	KO 4

1963

24 Jan	Charlie Powell	Pittsburgh, PA	KO 3
13 Mar	Doug Jones	New York, NY	W 10
18 Jun	Henry Cooper	London, England	KO 5

1964

25 Feb	Sonny Liston	Miami Beach, FL	KO 7

(Won World Heavyweight Championship)

1965

| 25 May | Sonny Liston | Lewiston, ME | KO 1 |

(Retained World Heavyweight Championship)

| 22 Nov | Floyd Patterson | Las Vegas, NV | KO 12 |

(Retained World Heavyweight Championship)

1966

| 29 Mar | George Chuvalo | Toronto, Canada | W 15 |

(Retained World Heavyweight Championship)

| 21 May | Henry Cooper | London, England | KO 6 |

(Retained World Heavyweight Championship)

| 6 Aug | Brian London | London, England | KO 3 |

(Retained World Heavyweight Championship)

| 10 Sept | Karl Mildenberger | Frankfurt, W. Germany | KO 12 |

(Retained World Heavyweight Championship)

| 14 Nov | Cleveland Williams | Houston, TX | KO 3 |

(Retained World Heavyweight Championship)

1967

| 6 Feb | Ernie Terrell | Houston, TX | W 15 |

(Retained World Heavyweight Championship)

| 22 Mar | Zora Folley | New York, NY | KO 7 |

(Retained World Heavyweight Championship)

1970

| 26 Oct | Jerry Quarry | Atlanta, GA | KO 3 |
| 7 Dec | Oscar Bonavena | New York, NY | KO 15 |

1971

8 Mar	Joe Frazier	New York, NY	L 15
	(Challenged for World Heavyweight Championship)		
26 Jul	Jimmy Ellis	Houston, TX	KO 12
17 Nov	Buster Mathis	Houston, TX	W 12
26 Dec	Jürgen Blin	Zurich, Switzerland	KO 7

1972

1 Apr	Mac Foster	Tokyo, Japan	W 15
1 May	George Chuvalo	Vancouver, Canada	W 12
27 Jun	Jerry Quarry	Las Vegas, NV	KO 7
19 Jul	Al Lewis	Dublin, Ireland	KO 11
20 Sept	Floyd Patterson	New York, NY	KO 7
21 Nov	Bob Foster	Stateline, NV	KO 8

1973

14 Feb	Joe Bugner	Las Vegas, NV	W 12
31 Mar	Ken Norton	San Diego, CA	L 12
10 Sept	Ken Norton	Los Angeles, CA	W 12
21 Oct	Rudi Lubbers	Jakarta, Indonesia	W 12

1974

28 Jan	Joe Frazier	New York, NY	W 12
30 Oct	George Foreman	Kinshasa, Zaïre	KO 8
	(Won World Heavyweight Championship)		

1975

24 Mar	Chuck Wepner	Cleveland, OH	KO 15
(Retained World Heavyweight Championship)			
16 May	Ron Lyle	Las Vegas, NV	KO 11
(Retained World Heavyweight Championship)			
30 Jun	Joe Bugner	Kuala Lumpur, Malaysia	W 15
(Retained World Heavyweight Championship)			
1 Oct	Joe Frazier	Quezon City, Philippines	KO 14
(Retained World Heavyweight Championship)			

1976

20 Feb	Jean-Pierre Coopman	San Juan, PR	KO 5
(Retained World Heavyweight Championship)			
30 Apr	Jimmy Young	Landover, MD	W 15
(Retained World Heavyweight Championship)			
24 May	Richard Dunn	Munich, W. Germany	KO 5
(Retained World Heavyweight Championship)			
28 Sept	Ken Norton	New York, NY	W 15
(Retained World Heavyweight Championship)			

1977

16 May	Alfredo Evangelista	Landover, MD	W 15
(Retained World Heavyweight Championship)			
29 Sept	Earnie Shavers	New York, NY	W 15
(Retained World Heavyweight Championship)			

1978

15 Feb	Leon Spinks	Las Vegas, NV	L 15
	(Lost World Heavyweight Championship)		
15 Sept	Leon Spinks	New Orleans, LA	W15
	(Won World Heavyweight Championship)		

1980

| 2 Oct | Larry Holmes | Las Vegas, NV | L by KO 11 |
| | *(Challenged for World Heavyweight Championship)* | | |

1981

| 11 Dec | Trevor Berbick | Nassau, Bahamas | L 10 |